'*ACTivate Your Life* with this fantastic new self-help book. Based on the revolutionary new therapy – Acceptance and Commitment Therapy (ACT) – this comprehensive workbook will help you to effortlessly navigate your way through the challenges in your life and transform it for the better. Whether you simply feel a little stuck or are chronically depressed, the three simple steps (Open, Aware and Active), case studies and worksheets will support you on your journey to enjoying life again '

Dr Guy Meadows, author of *The Sleep Book*

'All the latest research and a wealth of clinical experience have gone into this book. Clear, friendly language, fun illustrations and easy to use worksheets cut through the tangle of difficult thoughts and feelings so many people struggle with and allow themselves to be held back by. A state of the art, logical and supportive book that reassures you that you are not a freak for struggling in the first place, helps you identify the unhelpful strategies that drive and maintain your difficulties, builds your resilience and unlocks your potential.'

Suzy Dittmar, ACT therapist, London

'ACT helps me when I'm struggling or having a tough day, and it helps clients I work with too. This book uses new metaphors, reframes 'classic' ACT images and presents realistic examples to explain the concepts in a way that makes them understandable and worth tr~~~ ~ ~~~ this to clients and friends.'

Dr Ben Sec

'Psychological suffering is inevitably interwoven into human life and this book addresses that simple truth. Although it is only natural to not want to suffer, desperate attempts to blow out the flame of emotional suffering often make it even bigger. *ACTivate Your Life* proposes how to deal with our vulnerabilities, weaknesses and imperfections without struggle, and teaches us how to meet them with gentleness and self-compassion. The book can be used by everyone as a guide to navigating a wide range of common psychological problems and challenges, such as depression, anxiety, anger and low self-esteem.'

**Stanislaw Malicki, Senior Licensed Clinical Psychologist
and peer-reviewed ACT trainer,
Akershus University Hospital, Norway**

'This outstanding new book allows you to use the ACT approach to bring a greater sense of meaning, purpose, and vitality into your own life *right now.* This is an excellent resource for anyone struggling with anxiety, worry, depression, lack of self-esteem, loss of life direction, or anger issues. However, I want to be bold here and suggest that *everyone* should read this book. Why? Because it shows how modern psychology views the human condition, and illustrates how to relate skilfully to the strange internal world of thought and emotion that we all experience.'

**Dr Paul Flaxman, Senior Lecturer in Psychology,
City University London and author of
*The Mindful and Effective Employee***

'Destined to become an ACT self-help classic, *ACTivate Your Life* provides a witty and charming delivery of ACT concepts that brings the reader along in a compassionate and gentle style. The examples are easy to identify with and the exercises well-timed. A great way to be introduced to the ACT model and an excellent contribution from creative and influential authors in the ACT field.'

Dr Louise McHugh, Lecturer in the School of Psychology, University College Dublin and author of *The Self and Perspective Taking*

'This book is not a magic wand that will effortlessly free you from all of your problems: it invites you to actively participate in what could be hard personal work. Written with great wisdom and expertise, but also from a place of compassion and full of our common humanity, Oliver, Hill and Morris have placed in your hands a supremely practical resource for changing how you approach your life, and building a more meaningful and fully-lived existence.'

Dr David Gillanders, Academic Director, Doctoral Programme in Clinical Psychology, University of Edinburgh

ACTivate Your Life

ACTivate Your Life

Joe Oliver, Jon Hill and
Eric Morris

ROBINSON
London

ROBINSON

First published in Great Britain in 2015 by Robinson

Text copyright © Joe Oliver, Jon Hill and Eric Morris, 2015

Illustrations copyright © Bernard Yan, 2015

The moral right of the authors has been asserted.

All rights reserved.
No part of this publication may be reproduced, stored in a retrieval
system, or transmitted, in any form, or by any means, without
the prior permission in writing of the publisher, nor be otherwise
circulated in any form of binding or cover other than that in which it
is published and without a similar condition including this condition
being imposed on the subsequent purchaser.

A CIP catalogue record for this book
is available from the British Library.

ISBN 978-1-47211-191-3 (paperback)
ISBN: 978-1-47211-396-2 (ebook)

Typeset in Palatino by Initial Typesetting Services, Edinburgh
Printed and bound in Great Britain by Clays Ltd., St Ives plc

Robinson
is an imprint of
Constable & Robinson Ltd
100 Victoria Embankment
London EC4Y 0DY

An Hachette UK Company
www.hachette.co.uk

Contents

1. Introduction: Getting Unstuck and
   Enjoying Your Life   1

2. **Open**: The Skill of Opening Up to
   Thoughts and Feelings   30

3. **Aware**: Noticing What's Going on Inside and
   Connecting with the World Around You   76

4. **Active**: Knowing What's Important and
   Moving in That Direction   133

5. Getting Unstuck from Depression and Activating   196

6. From Vigilance to Values: Living More Effectively
   with Anxiety and Worry   259

7. Cooling the Anger Process   330

8. Moving from Self-Esteem to Self-Acceptance   389

9. Keeping It Going   436

   Index   461

1 Introduction: Getting Unstuck and Enjoying Your Life

If you've picked up this book then two things are likely to be true:

> There is something in your life that you would like to change.

> You are not sure what to do to change it.

Perhaps you find yourself spending more time than you'd like in your head – worrying about the future, dwelling on the past – so that it seems as if life is passing you by. Maybe you notice yourself feeling hopeless and unhappy and yet you feel unsure of how to move forward. Perhaps you notice yourself feeling angry and irritable, as if you are being controlled by your fluctuating moods. Possibly you just feel stuck – as if everyone else is living their lives and you are on the sidelines looking in. This is an uncomfortable, unpleasant, and often painful place to be, and the temptation in this kind of situation can be to look outside of ourselves in the hope that someone somewhere has the elusive magic formula, the set of rules that will make life feel effortless. Maybe you have even found a set of rules that has worked for you in the past, which has allowed you to make changes and get more of what you want out of life for a while. But now here you are again, reading these words and still wishing for something to change.

Life Is Messy

The truth is that life is messy. It's chaotic, unpredictable and change is just about the only thing that remains constant. Just when you think you've got it all figured out, life changes and you need a new set of rules! Even the most robust and well-intentioned set of 'rules for life' will come up short at some point.

So, what if there was no magic answer, no set of rules? What if the messiness and chaos of life wasn't actually the problem? What if it were possible to live a rich, meaningful and rewarding life despite all the storms and uncertainty, the fears and the setbacks?

You Have the Skills!

As humans, we are pre-programmed with the skills necessary to negotiate even the most challenging of life situations, and we use these skills every day without even noticing. Have you ever been in a situation where you took action even when every thought in your head and every atom in your being was telling you to hide? Think hard – try to think of an example, just one. Maybe you had an important job interview and your mind started showing you lots of scary images of yourself getting tongue-tied and not knowing what to say, but you went ahead and did the interview anyway? Maybe you arranged a dinner date with someone you really liked and felt your stomach tying itself up in knots as you approached the restaurant, but you were able to go inside, sit down and enjoy the evening anyway? Maybe you just woke up one morning and felt like staying in bed, but you got up, had a shower and went to work all the same?

We're willing to bet that, as soon as you thought of one example of a time when you did what was necessary (regardless of how you felt), your mind would have offered up three examples of times when you **weren't** able to do that! When uncomfortable thoughts, feelings, memories, urges or sensations actually **did** get in the way of your doing what you wanted to, and living the kind of life that you wanted to live. But that's OK: we're not going to try to convince you that it's always easy. We just want to invite you to notice that it **is** possible to take action that enriches your life, even when all you internal stuff is urging you not to – in fact, you do it all the time! And sometimes you don't do it. The aim of this book is not to set out a lot of complex rules about how to manage your internal world and live your life. The aim is simply to encourage you to learn from your past experience – to do more of the stuff that works for you and less of the stuff that doesn't work, and to practise these useful habits until they become second nature.

Life Is for Living

This book is based on Acceptance and Commitment Therapy (which is usually shortened to ACT and pronounced 'act') and is **not** a set of rules – **it is a way of life**. ACT has been proven to be one of the most effective ways of helping people to 'un-stick' themselves: to escape from the quicksand of uncomfortable internal experiences, not by fighting, suppressing or trying to change them, but by developing a sense of willingness to do the things that bring them fulfilment, even when that means coming into contact with painful thoughts and feelings. When we talk about 'acceptance' we do not mean simply resigning oneself to a life of pain and unhappiness. We mean acknowledging that certain things in life are outside of our control. We are going to propose that we have a lot less control over our thoughts and feelings than we have been taught to believe, but that we can still take full responsibility for what is within our control – what we do and say, how we live our lives every day.

But ACT is also about more than that. Life is for living and many of us are so busy attending to the **business** of living our lives – jobs, bills, responsibilities, routine – that we don't stop to think about what is really important to us. ACT involves pressing the pause button and asking the questions that most of us rarely spend much time considering. What kind of a person do I want to be? What do I want to stand for in life? How do I really want to use the limited amount of time and energy available to me every day? We use these questions to help us to set goals that will take us closer to the lives that we want, and to motivate us to take actions – even tiny ones – that are true to our values.

Open, Aware, Active

ACT is simple. It doesn't require that you delve deep into your past to find hidden answers or to spend your days identifying and challenging 'wrong' thoughts. Using ACT, anyone can transform their lives for the better by being three things – *Open, Aware* and *Active*.

Open

Being *Open* means learning to respond more effectively to the painful and unpleasant thoughts and feelings that are an inevitable part of the human experience, so that they no longer act as a barrier between you and the things that you value.

Aware

Being *Aware* means easing out of automatic pilot mode and beginning to connect with what is going on around us and inside us **right here and now**. It means using the skill of *mindfulness* to notice the small details and beauty around us that we can miss when we're wrapped up in our busy minds, problem-solving, comparing, judging, criticising and doing all the things that minds are great at! That awareness can also help us to notice the opportunities that may have slipped under our radar – opportunities to know ourselves better, opportunities to do more of the things that make life worth living.

Active

Being *Active* simply means becoming clear on what matters to us most in life, and then pursuing those things vigorously – living life on purpose, rather than drifting through unconsciously. It's about knowing the kind of person that you want to be, the kind of life you want to live, and then intentionally taking steps in that direction. More than that, it's about doing so even when you know that it might be uncomfortable or challenging, and being fully open to and aware of the experience as you go.

Helen Keller, the American author, political activist and lecturer who experienced and overcame considerable adversity in her life, said that 'Life is either a daring adventure or nothing at all.'[1] ACT gives you the tools to set sail on that adventure, and to keep your ship moving forward, whether the seas are calm or stormy – to get out of your head and start living your life again. Each of us has years of experience in applying these principles at work and in our own lives. We are really excited to introduce you to the world of ACT – to help you get unstuck and ACTivate your life.

[1]   'The Open Door' (Doubleday, 1957)

Meet Tim, Marcia, Samantha and Dave

In this book, we are going to introduce you to four characters: Tim, Marcia, Samantha and Dave. They represent real people with real problems with whom we have each worked over the years, and their stories will give you a full sense of how the skills of being *Open*, *Aware* and *Active* can be successfully applied.

Tim's Story – 'Why can't I stop worrying?'

Tim, a thirty-year-old man working in human resources, came to therapy after struggling for two years with increasing worry and anxiety. In the first session Tim described his worrying as 'out of control' and said that he did not know how to switch off his mind. He found that he was spending all of his energy and time trying to avoid making mistakes or letting 'bad' things happen. Tim said that because of this constant worry, life was passing him by.

Tim had moved from his home city for his current job several years ago, and lived with flatmates near his workplace. Tim's parents still lived in his home city, and were retired. He described having a good relationship with them: he phoned them regularly and visited them for holidays. Tim said that he got along with his flatmates (friends from university), although he spent only a small amount of time with them, due to the long hours that he worked. Tim was single, having come out of a long-term relationship a couple of years ago. He described that while he had friends, he didn't socialise often due to work demands. Tim said that, while he would like a relationship, he had felt 'too busy' for this lately. He admitted that he frequently felt lonely.

Tim said that he felt that his main issue was that he frequently worried about potential problems and catastrophes, both at work and home. His most common worries were about making big mistakes at work, which would cost the company a substantial amount of money and lead to him losing his job. To make sure this didn't happen, Tim was extra cautious – always double-checking (sometimes triple-checking) his work and constantly thinking about potential future problems. He found that he took much longer to complete tasks than others in his team, which meant that he often worked late.

He also found worries intruding in other areas of his life: he worried about being single, and ending up alone for the rest of his life; that an accident would happen to his parents; or that he would make a poor financial decision and end up living with crippling debt. He also worried about his health: he felt tired a lot and so he was concerned he may have a serious health problem, such as cancer. He'd had several check-ups with his doctor and he'd been told his physical health was fine. The doctor suggested that the worrying may be a sign of a mental-health issue. This led Tim to worry more!

Tim described how difficult it was to live with such a high level of worry. He was frequently anxious and unhappy, and the worries affected his enjoyment of many things. He also shared that he experienced trouble sleeping, with a key time for worrying thoughts being when he was trying to get off to sleep at night. During the day, Tim was frequently tired and fatigued, and reported being quite fidgety and agitated and having trouble concentrating. He described other symptoms of anxiety, such as a nauseous feeling in his stomach and breathlessness. On one occasion when he was so worried about making a mistake at work he had had a full-blown panic attack.

As part of his motivation to try therapy, Tim described the various ways he had attempted to stop worrying so much, without ever really getting on top of the problem. He said that he'd tried telling himself not to worry, that he was being silly, and blocking out the worrying thoughts, but these strategies didn't seem to stop them. Tim said that he occasionally wrote down his worries and tried to problem-solve, but found that this actually increased the amount that he worried, rather than reducing it. He said that he sometimes called his parents to discuss his worries. They would usually try to reassure him that things would work out OK, but that it only helped him feel less anxious for a short period of time. He had found that his father had been less patient with him more recently.

Tim said that he occasionally coped with his worrying by drinking alcohol, although this led him to be concerned about becoming an alcoholic. He did not drink regularly, but described that when his worrying became overwhelming and he didn't have to go to work the next day, then he would drink up to half a bottle of wine 'to bring down the tension'. This did seem to work, at least in the short term, although it would tend to make him feel hung-over and lethargic the next day.

Tim said that he felt pretty stuck – like the worrying had taken over his life.

How *Open, Aware* and *Active* Is Tim?

The therapist agreed with Tim that the worrying certainly did seem to be having a big influence on his life now. Tim accepted that living as though the worst was going to happen was costing him a lot. It was as though the task of living was to avoid all possible errors, mistakes and calamities, rather than about, well, *living*.

Let's now think about to what extent Tim was being *Open*, *Aware* and *Active*: at what stage do you think Tim is?

Open

A key observation that Tim made is that he found it hard to tolerate uncertainty or risk and the feelings that accompanied such situations. While in certain situations it can be useful to be cautious, it looked as if he was being overly cautious in many areas of his life.

Tim was also responding to his thoughts about the future almost as if the catastrophic events he worried about had actually already happened. It was as if he was taking these thoughts literally, and they deserved his full attention and needed an immediate response. It was hard for him to see that **these thoughts are part of the process of living**; it was as though to him they represented what life was all about.

Aware

Rather than being aware of the present moment, Tim was in fact spending most of his time living in the future: a worrying fantasy of the future from which he found it hard to escape. It is no wonder that he was experiencing physical symptoms of stress. Tim had noticed that he was frequently caught up in these worries and the thought that life may be passing him by: currently, he finds his worries so consuming that he spends much of the time totally disconnected from the present moment.

Tim's sense of his identity – who he is – appeared to be threatened by his worrying thoughts. It was as if he was being held hostage by the worries and that whatever he tried it would be a big risk.

Active

Tim had a clear idea about how he would like to live: to have an intimate relationship, to connect with someone, to act like a caring and reliable friend, and to be a dedicated and thoughtful worker. However, his actions were more influenced by trying to handle his worries at the expense of other important aspects of his life. This was most apparent when he reflected on the amount of time he spent working in order to avoid some catastrophic event from happening. Instead of pursuing and developing other areas of his life, Tim was driven by his worries, staying in the office until 9 p.m. in the hope that this would help him to feel better. In fact, Tim's suffering was two-fold: the pain of the anxiety that came with the worrying thoughts and images that filled his head, and the pain of living a life that was shrinking around him. His experience told him that this was no way to live.

> **Marcia's Story** – 'I want to feel happy like every-one else'
>
> Marcia was thirty-eight years old and, for the past six months, she had often found herself inexplica-bly tearful and feeling a deep sense of loneliness. This was not normally like her but she'd started to notice that other people around her seemed to

be much happier, more confident and more able to enjoy their lives. In comparison, she thought that she didn't feel as good as other people, which she found hard to understand as she felt as if she did everything right in her life. She was always helpful, she never got angry with others and she worked hard. She couldn't make sense of where these feelings were coming from.

She worked in the fundraising department of a local charity and had been in the same position for the past ten years. She enjoyed her job and felt she was good at it, although she occasionally wondered what it would be like to be in a more challenging senior role. However, when she thought this, she would typically tell herself, 'you'd never be good enough, just stick to what you know.'

Marcia also worried what would happen to her mother if she changed jobs and had less time to devote to her. Her mother, with whom she lived and was very close, needed a lot of support as she had a number of complex mental and physical health issues. Her father had died in a car accident when she was in her late teens. Since then, her mother had experienced bouts of severe depression, and Marcia had often needed to look after her. Although she had a good relationship with her mother, Marcia occasionally felt her mother could be demanding and needy.

Marcia tended to keep herself very busy and spent most evenings and weekends out with friends or helping her mother. While she enjoyed this, she did her best to avoid time on her own because that was when she felt most lonely, a feeling she really struggled with. On the rare occasion she spent an evening alone, she found herself comfort eating and drinking wine to dull these feelings. She tended to be very critical of herself when she did this – 'you're fat and lazy – such a loser'.

She had an active social life and enjoyed spending time with her friends and being involved in her local church. All her friends saw her as a bright, bubbly, cheerful person who was always busy and willing to help out. In her friendships, she often found herself giving a lot but receiving little in return. She felt a certain sense of pride that she was always there for other people, however she intermittently found herself wishing she had someone to look after her.

One thing Marcia did for herself was running. She would run most days in the morning and loved the sense of energy and freedom. She occasionally felt guilty about doing this as she felt she was being selfish but she allowed herself this one 'guilty pleasure'.

Recently, a close friend, Theresa, had noticed that she seemed down and asked whether there was something wrong. Initially, Marcia was reluctant to say anything: 'You don't want to hear me moaning on about my problems!' But Theresa insisted, and Marcia opened up about all the things that seemed to be wrong with her and her life. Theresa asked her what she wanted out of life. Marcia was surprised to find herself becoming tearful: 'I just want to be happy, like everyone else!'

How *Open*, *Aware* and *Active* Is Marcia?

With Theresa's support, Marcia decided that she wanted to do something to change things. She bought a self-help book and started to reflect a little on her thoughts and feelings, and how they seemed to keep getting in the way of the life she really wanted for herself. Slowly she came to see that the life she was living was not *Open*, *Aware*, or *Active*.

Open

Marcia noticed that there were certain thoughts, feelings, memories and sensations that she would just rather not have, so she ended up avoiding situations that might trigger them. In particular, feelings of anxiety and loneliness felt almost unbearable for her. There also seemed to be lots of rules – shoulds, oughts and musts – that Marcia was following in order to decide what she should think, feel and say. On reflection she could see how much these were restricting her choices in life.

Aware

Marcia noticed that she often tended to be 'wrapped up' in her thoughts – dwelling on the past or worrying about the future — and therefore not so aware of what was going on around her. She told Theresa that she struggled to really enjoy anything in life as she always had a sense that she was missing out and that other people were doing better than her. In particular, she could see that she was not so good at recognising her own feelings, desires and wishes.

Active

Listening to her talk, her friend Theresa heard several things that sounded as if they were important to Marcia. It was clear that her relationships with other people were important, in particular, being there for others. At the same time, Theresa wondered about Marcia's values related to **herself** – when she wasn't looking after others what were the things that were important to her? It seemed that sometimes these weren't very clear for Marcia.

> **Samantha's Story** – 'I'm just so angry all the time!'
>
> Samantha is a forty-six-year-old woman who referred herself for therapy after being reprimanded at work by her manager, following a heated argument with a co-worker in a meeting. Samantha described struggling with her temper over the past year.

Samantha said that she wanted therapy 'in order to handle stress better' and 'act like the person I was before'. Samantha said that her problems with anger had not just been in the workplace, but also in her personal life. Her husband had confronted her about her anger, stating that her behaviour was making him unhappy. Samantha also had a falling out with a close friend, and described saying things in anger that she wished she could take back.

Samantha lived with her husband, Colin, and had two young children, Charlie (seven years old) and Emma (five years old). Samantha described that she and Colin had argued more since there had been changes in his work, and his employer had asked him to work longer hours. This had resulted in Colin helping less with childcare, and coming home late in the evening. Samantha felt guilty about arguing with him in front of the children. She also struggled with her sense of shame about 'losing it' when the children misbehaved, being quicker to raise her voice and harsher in how she reprimanded them. Both Emma and Charlie told Samantha that they had 'felt scared of mum' when she became angry like this. Samantha worked part-time as a receptionist in a busy medical practice. Her job had become more stressful lately and involved interacting with patients in a GP surgery, which at times meant dealing with people who were demanding or were unhappy when appointments ran late. She said that she had found herself becoming more easily irritated by patients in these situations. While Samantha reported that she had never criticised or lost her temper at work, she had recently experienced occasions when she had felt strong urges to shout at people. She said that she worried about losing control in this way. In addition, she had been impatient with and critical of her colleagues, becoming annoyed by situations that she found unfair or by management decisions that she saw as errors. Samantha frequently found herself thinking that she shouldn't have to put up with other people doing a poor job. On one occasion she expressed this view to a co-worker in a meeting, leading to an argument where they both started shouting at each other. On several occasions she expressed her critical views to her manager, who responded defensively. Samantha reported feeling exasperated and trapped by her work situation: at times she felt like 'making a statement' by quitting her job, but she also knew that she would not do this because of family financial commitments.

Samantha reported that many times she feels her anger is justified ('I had to say something, I shouldn't have to put up with it'), that there were unfair and silly situations that she had to deal with, and that others do not take the care and attention required to do things properly. On other occasions, however, she described feeling regretful for becoming annoyed, reflecting that she 'made a mountain out of a molehill' and that expressing her anger inflamed the situation rather than changing it for the better.

Samantha said that she had tried to cope with her temper by telling herself to calm down, and to lower her standards. She found that this didn't really work: instead she ended up getting frustrated and focused on how outrageous it was that she had to put up with a bad situation. Samantha described feeling her anger like a 'red ball' inside her chest, and while there were a number of occasions when she noticed this feeling and didn't act on it, it felt as though things 'build up like a pressure cooker that is just going to explode'. At times Samantha tried to avoid confrontations by telling people she didn't want to discuss things while she was angry; she found that this just seemed to make people avoid discussing things with her.

How *Open, Aware* and *Active* Is Samantha?

In the session the therapist explored with Samantha about how her problems could be thought of in terms of the skills of *Open, Aware* and *Active*:

Open

Samantha said that she often felt controlled by her anger, which meant that she ended up acting in a way that didn't reflect who she was and what was important to her. She also described sometimes making conscious efforts to avoid or reduce the thoughts and feelings she had when something triggered her anger. Other times she would just allow herself to 'go with' her thoughts and feelings, usually finding herself getting further caught up with a sense of injustice and a need to be right. Neither approach seemed to be working for her.

Aware

Samantha was often strongly influenced by the thoughts, feelings and memories that showed up when she experienced provocations. She described having thoughts that had a very 'right and wrong' feel, and getting caught up with her judgements about the unfairness and pointlessness of situations. She also had quite critical thoughts about others and herself that she responded to as though they were the truth. At the time there was little room for Samantha to take a flexible view of her experiences, to take the perspective of others, or to treat herself with a sense of compassion.

Active

Samantha was not acting like the person she would like to be at home, in her friendships, or at work. Samantha described doing things that sabotaged her efforts to repair or improve situations. From the position of needing to be right and defending what she felt was unfair, there was little room for her to do things that give her a sense of vitality and meaning.

Tearfully, Samantha said that she didn't want to act like someone that other people would rather avoid. Instead, she would like to be nurturing and warm to others, and to think creatively about how to improve the situation at work and home.

Dave's Story – 'Why am I always sad and low? I want to be free of this black hole.'

Dave sat in his chair and glared at the counsellor. He clearly didn't want to be in the meeting and said as much. 'Talking is a waste of time and will only make things worse for me.' He admitted that the only reason he was in the meeting was because his sister had pushed him into coming along. 'She thinks if I don't change soon, I might end up doing something silly. I suppose she might be right . . .' Dave reluctantly admitted that he was feeling depressed and very stuck, and that he didn't know how to get himself out of his situation. In spite of himself, Dave started to tell his story.

Dave was a forty-two-year-old marketing executive. Things had started to go downhill for Dave after he had recently been made redundant from his job. Up until six months ago, he had worked in a large sporting goods company. He had started in the company in his early twenties and had steadily worked his way up within the organisation through regular promotions. With each successive promotion, he found the responsibility and time commitment increased, which he enjoyed. The money gave him a greater sense of financial security and he liked the sense of respect from his colleagues. However, as Dave continued to progress in his career, he'd noticed the rest of life starting to fade into the background as work took up more and more time. He'd had a series of short, unfulfilling relationships that had often ended as he'd been unwilling to make a more serious commitment. He'd given up on the prospect of ever having children. Dave had a reasonably large circle of friends, who he knew mostly from work. Social activities were largely based around drinking after work. At times he'd noticed a sense of loneliness and isolation, however, he didn't have too much time to think about this.

It was a major restructuring that had led to Dave being made redundant. Dave couldn't believe it had happened and had not seen the redundancy coming. Although the company had clearly struggled recently, he'd assumed his position would be safe. He felt like his whole life had been completely turned upside down and his identity had been stripped from him. He was devastated and described feeling 'completely at sea'.

In the weeks afterwards he experienced strong feelings of resentment about the fact he'd been made redundant. He often found himself spending long periods of time angrily ruminating about how his employer had let him go. The redundancy package he'd been given meant he didn't have to look for work immediately, for which he was grateful. He felt he needed time to collect himself before thinking about going back to work. Eventually, he started to send out his CV but received several early knock-backs that shook his confidence. He started to notice himself becoming increasingly pessimistic about the future, saying to himself, 'What's the point, no one is going to want to employ a washed-up has-been' or 'I'm just not as good as everyone else on the job market these days'. Often at these times he would end up drinking to relieve some of these feelings but found that this would spiral him into deep feelings of self-loathing because he would beat himself up for being 'soft'. He remembered his father telling him that men who couldn't handle tough times were weak.

Dave found himself withdrawing from his friends and family and spending increasing amounts of time watching television. Eventually, he'd noticed the feelings eased up and he felt more numb. Initially he'd enjoyed this respite, but he sometimes worried that he didn't have any drive or motivation.

He didn't feel he could open up to anyone about what he was going through as he worried what they would think of him. The longer he left contacting friends the harder it was to think about reaching out. After some time his sister contacted him to see how he was doing. He'd never been particularly close to her but he ended up telling her everything that had been going on. She had pushed him to seek out some help and had set up the initial assessment appointment with the counsellor for him.

How *Open, Aware* and *Active* Is Dave?

Open

Although Dave was experiencing, to some degree, a normal and natural response to a big life change, he had some fairly inflexible rules about how he should feel that made it hard for him to make space for his emotions. This meant he tended to do things that would temporarily distract him from feelings of sadness and hopelessness (like watching TV or drinking) and avoid situations that he anticipated might be difficult or uncomfortable (like seeing friends, talking about his problems or looking for work).

Alongside this, his therapist noticed that Dave had a tendency to respond to his negative, self-critical thoughts in one of two unhelpful ways. He either gave in to them and went along with them or he ended up fighting and struggling with them. His therapist wondered about the impact these response styles had on Dave's ability to stick with doing the things that were important to him.

Aware

Dave was often very wrapped up in his thoughts, dwelling on the past and worrying about the future. This meant he was often not very mindful of how he was actually feeling. While this could provide short-term respite, it meant that he limited his ability to finding out what works best for him.

Also, this reduced his ability to step outside of his experiences, and take a different perspective on what he was going through.

Active

Dave had clear values related to work and invested a lot in his job over the years. In some ways, this heavy investment had prevented him from thinking more broadly about how he wanted his life to be. As such, when faced with a significant change in his working life, he didn't have other resources to draw on to sustain him.

Dave's behaviour also appeared to be largely driven by a desire to think and feel better before he took action. He believed that only once he was thinking more positively and feeling more optimistic would he be able to do what he needed to do. This approach meant he severely limited his opportunities to take effective action in the present moment. Waiting until he was thinking and feeling better could mean he would be waiting for a long time!

How *Open, Aware* and *Active* Are You?

In this next section, we'd like to invite you to think about how *Open, Aware* and *Active* you are. We'd like you to fill in the worksheet below, answering the prompt questions, to help you get a sense of both where your skills lie and also the areas in which you need to improve.

OPEN, AWARE and *ACTIVE* WORKSHEET

Briefly describe here the main problem(s) that you had in mind when you picked up this book. Keep this problem in mind as you answer the following questions:

Open

Generally, how open are you to internal experiences such as thoughts, feelings, emotions, memories and physical sensations?

- *Which of these internal experiences do you struggle with particularly?*

- *Are there times when you're able to be open to uncomfortable internal experiences?*

Aware

How aware are you of your thoughts and feelings as they occur? How good are you at recognising and labelling them? How mindful are you of what is going on around you?

- *Do you find yourself often running on autopilot, wrapped up in your own thoughts?*

- *How easy do you find it to step out of yourself to take someone else's perspective?*

- *Do you find it difficult to go easy on yourself and be self-compassionate?*

Active

Do you have a clear direction forward in life? Do you know what is important to you? Or do you feel lost and confused about how you want your life to be going?

- *What are the moments when you feel most alive, vital and engaged?*

- *How good are you at setting a course in life, making goals and sticking with them – even when things get rough?*

Open, Aware and *Active* **Chart**

Once you've completed the *Open, Aware* and *Active* work-sheet, use Figure 1 to map out where your strengths lie and where you need to develop your skills. Give yourself a score on each of the three skills from 0 to 10. Then place an 'X' on the corresponding line. You can then use this chart to monitor your progress. Come back to it after you've read the book to see how you've developed.

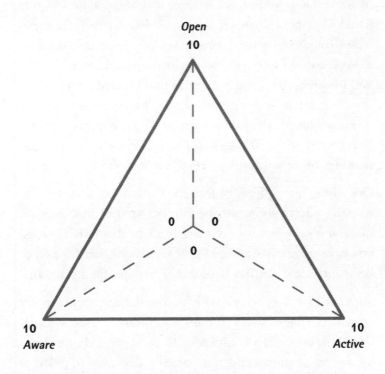

Figure 1

2 *Open*: The Skill of Opening Up to Thoughts and Feelings

Most people would probably agree that life is, at times, quite a tricky business. There are lots of obstacles to navigate, problems to manage, births, deaths, marriages, losses and traumas along the way. Of course, there is lots of fun, richness, vitality and meaning too – this is the stuff that we live for. But it's a complex, often confusing adventure. And what's more, we arrive on this planet with no manual! The average new television comes with 100 pages of instructions – we come with nothing. We're just supposed to figure it all out by ourselves.

One of the main pieces of learning for most of us is how to respond effectively to all the interesting stuff that goes on under our skin. How do we manage all the thoughts, feelings, emotions, memories and physical sensations that are part of being alive, and also live lives that are rich, fulfilling and fun?

Although we don't come with an instruction manual, there are lots of suggestions out there about how to deal with all this stuff. Lots and lots of advice from our friends, our family, our community and our society: 'Get over it!', 'Think more positively!', 'Put it behind you, don't worry, don't stress, chill out, relax!' Stop thinking. Stop feeling. If only it were that easy. This is well-meaning advice and sometimes it even seems to works. The danger comes if we apply this to all of our experiences, all of the time. Sometimes in life we need to be able to open up to parts of our experiences we'd perhaps rather not have. Let us give you an example, using bears and blueberries. This story comes from occupational psychologist, Rob Archer.

The Bear and the Blueberry Bush

Imagine you are following a path through a forest. You have been following the path for several hours and you are not totally sure where you are going. Already on the journey there have been some really cool, fun moments – things you've seen that have been weird and beautiful. But there have been some unpleasant moments too – stuff that has been scary, and at times you've felt completely lost. Right now you know that you are a little tired and very hungry . . .

Then you come to a fork in the path – it splits off in two directions. When you look down one path you see, bathed in sunlight, a tall, lush, wild blueberry bush. When you look down the other path you see, snarling from the shadows, an enormous, hulking, grizzly bear. Which path do you choose?

This is not a trick question. If you are anything like almost anybody else on planet Earth, you would pick the blueberry-bush path. Of course you would! Free, tasty blueberries! Who doesn't love blueberries? On the other hand, very few people enjoy being ripped to pieces and eaten by huge, hungry bears.

This is common sense – when it comes to human behaviour we are naturally motivated to move towards stuff that is pleasant, and to avoid stuff that is or feels threatening. And this tends to work quite effectively in the external world when navigating down actual paths with bears and blueberries at the end. But the trap is when we apply this rule too rigidly to our internal world – the world of thoughts, feelings, memories, and sensations. If we always avoid situations that are scary, frightening or that take us out of our comfort zone, our lives become very limited. It may work in the short term – there is a sense of relief, not having to put up with those horrible thoughts and feelings. But in the long term? Nothing changes. You don't connect, you don't do the stuff that matters most, you don't grow or develop or push yourself.

EXERCISE – Think of a Proud Moment

Take a moment to think of something you achieved in life that you feel really proud of. It could be something momentous, or it may be something small. But choose something that was meaningful to you. Now, think back to the moment right before you started working towards this achievement. What feelings and thoughts were present just as you embarked on this journey? Some excitement? Maybe a thrill as you thought about achieving the goal?

Chances are, it wasn't all good. Was there a bit of fear or trepidation? Worries like 'What if I fail? What if I can't do it? What will others think of me?' Memories that flood back from the past when you set out to achieve something and it didn't work out? Notice how there is often a mix of positive and negative thoughts and feelings that show up at these points. When we extend ourselves or step outside of our comfort zones, **it's very normal to have this mix.** Now, can you imagine what would happen if you spent your whole life trying to avoid having such thoughts and feelings?

So here's a key point we'd like to make. Leading a full, rich and meaningful life is not always about thinking positive thoughts or feeling good feelings. Thoughts and feelings come and go. They are like the weather, which is constantly changing. The one constant **is** change. To become more

Active, we need to learn to be guided less by our ever-changing thoughts and feelings and more by something broader (but more of this in Chapter 4: *Active*).

In order to do this, we need to develop and enhance some particular skills. Broadly, we call this skill set *Open*. In this next section, we'd like to go through some ideas about how to be more *Open* with our thoughts and emotions so we are able to be more effective in our lives.

Thoughts – What Are They Good For?

Human language: there's no doubt that it's a very handy skill. We are the only species who use it to the level we do and it is central to how we think. It allows us to do all sorts of amazing things. With it we can learn from past experiences, plan and organise for the future. We can be creative. It allows us to connect deeply and meaningfully with others around us. Also, language allows us learn from **others' experience**. For example, as children, our parents can tell us not to stick our fingers where they shouldn't go, like wall sockets and toasters, because it hurts. Most of us, if we're smart, listen and don't have to go through the actual painful experience to learn that fingers don't belong in wall sockets or toasters. Perhaps most significantly, language allows us to **cooperate**. In the process we've developed life-saving technologies, advanced science to previously unimagined levels and taken creative arts in all sorts of incredible directions. All of this is courtesy of the gift of language.

However, language is also a **double-edged sword**. These same processes are used to compare ourselves negatively to others, to ruminate over how bad our lives have been, to worry obsessively over the future. We can use it to hurt others, bring them down, judge and criticise them. At our worst, we can demonstrate phenomenal levels of cruelty, engage in acts of prejudice, discrimination and dehumanisation with the resulting acts of war and genocide. Language offers us this too.

This ability to think, to attach abstract and arbitrary sounds to objects and concepts, developed and evolved because, overall, it was very useful and gave us humans a huge advantage over our competitors in the evolution race. Being relatively short on claws, teeth, tusks, shells, horns or other useful equipment, average humans, by themselves, are a fairly harmless sort of creature. But our ability to use language gave us the edge that outstripped our competitors. As we could communicate and cooperate we were able to form ourselves into tribes, and we became a formidable force. Very much at the forefront of our ancestors' minds was, 'whatever you do today, don't get eaten'. So our minds evolved in this way, so for this kind of environment we were highly attuned to any forms of threat. First and foremost was not ending up on the menu of local lions and tigers. But second was remaining within the tribe. Early tribes were not particularly forgiving of members who did not contribute, who were greedy or lazy – for the survival of the tribe, they couldn't afford to be. These members were ejected from the group, which, for a toothless, clawless, hairless, (and, some would argue, tasty) mammal, meant certain death. The result of this is that those of our ancestors who survived were the ones who were **vigilant**. They were cautious and looked out for lions and tigers. Also, they were cautious in the tribe, vigilant for cues they were not pulling their weight. Those that weren't, who tended to be relaxed, easy-going, a little carefree and not bothered about what others thought of them, tended not to stick around long enough to successfully pass on their genes.

With that short history lesson, we get a picture of our average ancestor. They were generally an anxious type. They tended to worry a lot about the future. They dwelled a lot on their mistakes. They were concerned about what others thought of them. The more effective they were at this, the more likely they were to stay safe and connected to the tribe, and to be able to procreate and reproduce. Knowing where we came from gives us some clues about ourselves because, as a general rule, the modern human does the same! We can often be anxious. Most of us worry about the future and dwell on the past. We tend to be concerned about how we come across to others and what they think of us. We have our ancestors to thank for these qualities (and we mean that genuinely – if it weren't for these qualities, we wouldn't be here today!). While, as a general rule, lions and tigers don't threaten us these days, we carry forward this sensitivity towards threat. It's as if our minds come pre-loaded with an old computer operating system designed for a bygone era. While it was once right up to date, these days it has its limitations. It's a little slow and clunky and doesn't always work smoothly. However, knowing this allows us to build in a few handy improvements (more on this later).

Not only do we come pre-loaded with this tendency to think somewhat negatively but we also carry forward messages from our upbringing and the environments we grew up in. Some of us were fortunate to have grown up in environments that taught us how to manage unhelpful messages about ourselves, other people and the world around us more effectively. But some of us grew up in environments where the messages were more like, 'you're not good enough' or 'the world is a dangerous and scary place'. It's possible that such messages served a good purpose for us at certain points in our lives. Perhaps they kept us safe, stopped us from taking risks or kept us on our guard around dangerous people. As a result of this, we hold on to these messages tightly, even when they clearly no longer work for us.

Added to this, **our mind is a great storyteller**. It doesn't like gaps or inconsistencies – it likes things to add up, and make sense. We're powerfully driven by this need for coherence – we love it when things neatly fit together (like a good game of Tetris). Part of this is because it is hard work to maintain contradictory ideas in mind at the same time. If we can resolve things into a simple story that matches what we already know, and what we've learned growing up, so much the better. Things seem more manageable and predictable when there is less complexity.

To give an example, remember Tim from the Introduction, who was struggling with anxiety? He was asked to give a presentation to his team about a new computer software package that was being rolled out. It wasn't the most exciting topic but everyone needed to know about it. Tim didn't enjoy public speaking very much, but he was very familiar with the package and thought it wouldn't be too bad. About five minutes into his presentation, he noticed a few people in the audience yawning and checking their phones. At first he couldn't understand why they would be bored, as everyone had to learn about the software. Then his mind, filling in the gaps, came up with an old story – 'It's because I'm boring and terrible at public speaking'. After this, he rattled on through the rest of the presentation as fast as he could, and finished without giving anyone a chance to ask questions. As he took his seat, he thought, 'I'm never going to put myself out there like that again.'

Holding on to these old stories too tightly could mean we end up behaving the way we always have, missing opportunities to live a life of value. It can constrict us and narrow our worldview. This makes it difficult to remain open to new experiences, see things from different perspectives and respond to what life throws us in a flexible way. We need to keep in mind the question, **'how useful and effective are these stories in helping me build a life that I want: a life that is meaningful, rich and vital?'**

Thoughts as Tools

A sledgehammer is a marvellous tool. You can smash through concrete blocks. You can drive metal stakes into the ground. You can knock down a wall in no time. But, sledgehammers are not so great for small nails, or for gently tapping a glass pane into position. You could say the same about thoughts: great for planning ahead for the future and fantastic for solving problems. But when it comes to things like enjoying an incredible sunset, learning to play an instrument or falling in love, let's be honest here, thinking can really get in the way! 'That's a nice sunset but not quite as good as the one last week – a little more red perhaps?' Or, 'you can't play the guitar – you're just not musical.' 'He doesn't really like you so keep your distance.' Sometimes thoughts can be useful in helping us getting the job done. Other times, they are not useful at all and stop us from being effective. They can pull us off course, preventing us from appreciating, from learning, from just being in the moment.

The US comedian Emo Philips famously quipped, 'I used to think the brain was the most wonderful organ in my body. Then I realised who was telling me this.' Sometimes our minds can be a little like this, wanting us to believe they are the best tools ever! At the same time they can be reluctant in admitting their shortcomings. However, there's something liberating in the knowledge of the limitations of our minds. As we contact the edges of what this powerful word machine can do, we then really develop the opportunity to harness its potential.

Our Mind at Work

Have you ever watched an athlete take an important penalty shot (you choose the sport – hockey, football, basketball – the same principles generally apply)? Inevitably the crowd starts shouting. The home crowd will be yelling (seemingly) helpful advice: 'get it in the net! Don't miss it like last time!' The away supporters will be doing their best to distract the player: 'you're useless, you'll never make it' (usually with slightly more colourful language). The player has a choice here – listen to the crowd and get caught up in what they are saying, or argue back at the crowd and tell them they don't know what they are talking about. You could imagine the end result of either of these two approaches.

Isn't it a bit like this in our own lives, particularly at those really important moments when we're stepping out of our comfort zones and taking risks? Our minds love to wade in with all sorts of advice, commentary or criticism. How we respond at these moments is crucial. Do we get absorbed with what the 'crowd' is saying? Do we work excessively hard to fight, struggle, discount, argue with what the crowd says? Or is there scope to respond to them in a third way that allows us to effectively engage with the task at hand? Going back to the penalty-shot situation, most modern athletes are now trained to manage high-pressure situations like this effectively. They are taught specifically to focus mindfully on the task at hand and use a clear, well-rehearsed routine. In this way, they lessen the impact the crowd has (and their own minds too!) so that they can take the best shot they can. These are the kinds of skills we will be talking about more in this chapter.

Just Control Your Thoughts!

Just control your thoughts. Stop being so negative. Think more positively. If it were that easy you probably would have done that a long time ago and you wouldn't be reading this book! You might be relieved to hear that in fact, changing your thoughts or blocking them out is a very difficult thing to do. Although we can of course consciously 'think' thoughts, the vast majority pop into mind completely randomly and of their own accord, often as a result of a previous thought, or even the situation you are currently in. It's almost as if our minds have a mind of their own! We also know that when we try to control our thinking by pushing away or blocking a thought, we get a *rebound effect*. It's as if the harder we push a thought away, the more it tries to come back into our consciousness. It's a lot like trying to hold a beach ball under water in a swimming pool. The further down we push the ball, the more it pushes back, trying to get to the surface. It can take a lot of effort to push thoughts out of our minds, and while possible, the energy expended blocking out thoughts could be more usefully expended elsewhere in our lives.

So the important message is that **you probably have a lot less control over your mind than you'd like.** It can be tempting to enter into a struggle and try to change what is going on, particularly if the content of your thoughts is upsetting or very negative. The key though is learning to respond in more effective ways to thoughts. The first step is being able to become skilled at noticing the process of thinking in a **less habitual way**.

Most people spend their days being pulled all over the place by their thoughts. It's as if by merely popping up and being in consciousness, a thought deserves attention and recognition. While this might be the case for some thoughts, there are lots of thoughts that really don't deserve attention or are just downright unhelpful. It's been estimated that we experience many thousands of thoughts over a day. Which are the ones that get our attention? What are the common themes that occur? What are the favourite stories our minds like to tell us? In fact, just as you've been sitting here reading this book, you've probably had all sorts of thoughts go through your mind, some of which you may have given attention to or acted on, some that you just let slip by. How did you make that decision?

In becoming more *Open* to our thoughts, it is important to notice which thoughts we devote our attention to. It's easy to let this process occur on automatic pilot, which usually means that we're guided by whatever thoughts happen to be around at a particular moment. Remember The Bear and the Blueberry Bush? To help us do more of the important things in life, particularly when stepping outside our comfort zone, it is more effective to be guided by something broader than just whatever thought or story is current news.

So, a starting point is to get good at noticing this process – seeing thoughts for what they are – as guides, tools, sources of information, but not necessarily as fundamental literal truths that we have to act on or obey.

EXERCISE – Thought Bingo

It's often the case, in the process of thinking, that a thought occurs and we respond automatically. We may elaborate on the thought, and get drawn into it. We may push it away or attempt to distract ourselves with another thought. Let's take some time to practise slowing this process down and doing it less on auto-pilot. We'd like to introduce you to a game called

'Thought Bingo'. All you need is a pen, the worksheet below and a mind.

Sit back in a comfortable position in your chair, with your Bingo sheet and pen in front of you. We'd like you to bring to mind an action that involved doing something that matters to you. Something that's important, something that you know enriches your life, and that you're not doing at the moment. Something that has a sense of purpose. This doesn't need to be a huge thing, it could be small. It could be something like spending time with a loved one. It could be exercising or playing sport. It could involve connecting in some way with your community. But it has to be something that would be a step out of your comfort zone. Something where you feel a twinge of anxiety that tells you this action would be a challenge for you.

Take some time now to really *imagine* yourself engaging in this activity. Then, carefully start to watch your thoughts as they parade across your mind. Notice each one and register what kind of thought it is. When you see a judgement, circle 'judging' on your sheet. When you see a prediction, circle, 'predicting' on your sheet. Your job here is to simply **notice the process of thinking**. Keep going for approximately five minutes, or until you complete the line (at which point, you're free to leap up and shout 'Bingo!' as loudly as you possibly can).

Judging	Evaluating	Criticising	Remembering	Predicting
Assessing	Describing	Deciding	Worrying	Planning
Reasoning	Explaining	Reflecting	Questioning	Arguing
Analysing	Problem-Solving	Noticing	Persuading	Comparing

What did you notice in doing this exercise? What did you notice about the quality of your mind as you took some time out to watch it? Did you notice thoughts that were 'positive' and supportive of your undertaking this activity? Were there thoughts that acted to hold you back, and that said you wouldn't be able to do it? Or you won't enjoy it or it would be a waste of time? And notice your response to these thoughts. How easy was it to just let these thoughts be there? Which were the ones that tugged at you, wanting you to 'play' with them? Did you feel a pull to resolve these thoughts? To change them or move them on? **We're not looking for particular answers here but we'd like to encourage you to be curious about your mind at work.**

The Mind Is a Drama Queen

Let's face it – minds **love** drama. Anything with a bit of tension, horror, conflict, a nasty outcome – the mind is in the front row, popcorn in hand, secretly delighted by the drama unfolding in front of its eyes. If it could, it would be glued to 24–7, wall-to-wall soap operas. The mind (and we're talking purely metaphorically here of course) is drawn to drama, but as it happens, the drama it's drawn to is straight out your own life. Minds are less interested in stories where everything works out and when life trundles along nicely of its own accord. Where's the fun in that?! So, minds naturally look out for and focus on drama. And where it can't find it, it already has tons of material to work with – stitching together clips from your past or, better still, making up altogether new plot lines for a future you haven't experienced yet!

This is useful to know and points towards some tricks for effectively managing a drama-loving mind. First, it might be helpful to take what our minds are narrowly focusing on a little less seriously. Perhaps we can sit back a bit and appreciate the humour in the drama plot lines that our minds get so addicted to. A little like when you're watching soaps on the television and delighting in the slightly silly over-the-top drama.

Secondly, we can help our minds develop a broader taste in what they watch. It's likely our minds will always be drawn to drama but perhaps we can ask them to pause for a moment and consider other aspects of the story they haven't taken into account. Something perhaps with less drama, perhaps a bit more sophistication and nuance: less suspense and more subtlety. Maybe something that more accurately reflects our lives.

Fusion with Thoughts

We've been spending time talking about thoughts and learning how to notice our minds at work. One part of thinking we want to focus on is what we call *fusion*. Have you ever sat back in a movie theatre and got completely lost in the story? You can feel the protagonist's feelings as if they were your own? The outcome of the film and what happens to the characters really matters to you. This is fusion – where what you're directly experiencing (seeing and hearing) is streamed together with your thoughts, they become literally fused together. Of course, this is great when this happens in a good movie and adds to the whole experience. However, this same process can turn against us as we get fused with all sorts of other thoughts and take them literally and act as if they are true. When you're fused with a thought, it usually means you've *believed* what your mind has said to you, lock, stock and barrel, and that thought now **unhelpfully guides your actions**, making it more difficult to move your life forward in a meaningful way.

This doesn't mean you should ignore thoughts or pretend they aren't important. Sometimes thoughts are useful tools. It is, however, important to notice when we become fused with our thoughts, as these are the points at which we are most likely to get caught up in an unhelpful struggle.

How to Spot Thought Fusion.

Sometimes these thoughts are easy to spot; sometimes they're a little more tricky. Each of us will have our own thoughts that we're more likely to get tangled up in. But here are some clues to suggest you may be getting fused with your thoughts:

- Your thoughts have a same old, same old feel to them. You've heard this many times before.

- Your thoughts are very critical with lots of self-judgements.

- Your thoughts have a very 'black and white' feel to them.

- Your thoughts involve lots of comparisons with others.

- Your thoughts involve lots of negative predictions about the future.

The main thing to remember is that when we are fused with our thoughts, we are much less likely or able to activate ourselves to move towards our values. Remember Dave from the Introduction? He had recently lost his job and was struggling with depression. He decided to go and see a counsellor to get some help. Here's a piece of a therapy session, where Dave talks to his counsellor about a thought with which he often becomes very fused:

> *Therapist*: Dave, it sounds as if 'I'm a total loser' is a particularly tricky thought for you.

> *Dave*: Oh god, I know, I hate it but I just can't stop thinking it.

Therapist: What happens?

Dave: Well, it just feels so true. If I'm honest, sometimes I am a complete loser who's always screwing everything up.

Therapist: Yeah, OK, I get that. Tell me what you normally do when your mind serves these thoughts up?

Dave: Umm, sometimes I try and argue with myself. Tell myself it's not true and keep positive. But that never works.

Therapist: Uh huh. What else do you do?

Dave: Sometimes I just sort of give in and admit it's all true. I seem to have a talent for coming up with proof of just how much of a loser I really am. Then comes a pretty quick downwards spiral of self-loathing, usually followed by too much wine.

Therapist: Sounds rough. You know this pattern well then?

Dave: Oh yes.

Therapist: Let me draw your attention to a couple of things. First up, 'I'm a loser' sounds like a real good attention getter! It's dramatic and has an emotional punch behind it. Minds love this kind of drama and attention.

Dave: It certainly does that.

Therapist: So it seems this all happens pretty quickly, but after your mind serves this up, you respond in a couple of automatic ways. One is to try and argue and fight with your mind. Or drown it out – quite literally with wine. The second is to give in to what your mind says and roll over. I want to be clear, there's nothing necessarily wrong with this at all. But here's the thing, when you respond in this way, my sense is this shuts down options for you, and it doesn't feel like you have much choice in how you respond.

Dave: It's true, I feel stuck, like there's no way forward.

Therapist: Yeah, OK. So we want to develop some more effective ways of responding here so you are able to have some more choice.

But What about Positive Thoughts?

The emphasis here has been on 'negative' thoughts. These tend to be more easily recognisable as unhelpful and more likely to slow us down in life. Does that mean our job is to replace these thoughts with more positive ones? No! Because even so-called 'positive' thoughts can act as barriers to effective action. For example, someone could become unhelpfully fused with the thought that they were the *best* dancer there ever was (unless you're Fred Astaire, then in which case, you're off the hook). You would be out there on the dance floor, strutting your stuff, busting your moves, sure in the knowledge you are as good as it gets. You'd probably never practise, because, hey, you're the best, and you know all the moves. You certainly wouldn't listen to anyone else about your style or want to learn new moves, because who cares what anyone else thinks when you are the greatest?

Put like this, it's easy to see the problem with being fused with 'positive' thoughts. Even if you were a very good dancer, you would go out of date pretty quickly. And, there's a good chance that you would be pretty annoying to be around. There are lots of subtle positive thoughts we can become fused with. What about, 'I'm a great parent' or 'I'm a nice person' or 'I'm a good partner'. These may be true in a lot of instances. But what about when they are not? Holding on too tightly and being fused with such thoughts can prevent us from hearing important feedback or learning how we **actually** are.

Dealing with Fusion – the Skill of Defusion

Our goal here is essentially to be able to get moving again towards what's important to you in life. How do you do that? A central skill is learning to be able to **step back** from thoughts and defuse from them. This means that thoughts have less power over us, that they stop guiding our actions automatically, and that we get to choose what happens next. Just because a thought happens to be present, doesn't mean we **have** to act on it. It's entirely possible to have the thought, 'I'm a loser' and still engage in meaningful activity. It's possible to have the thought, 'no one likes me' and pick up the phone and connect with important friends or family.

The aim is to develop the skill of defusing from thoughts. Usually, it takes a little practice to introduce a new way of responding to thoughts. It's a bit like folding your arms. If you're like most people, you fold your arms in a particular way each time – one arm naturally folds itself over the other without you even thinking of it. Developing a new habit is a bit like learning to fold your arms the other way around. At first it feels weird and unnatural, but give it a bit of time and practice and it will start to feel natural and flow more easily.

What can we do when we notice ourselves getting caught up in 'mind-stuff' and become fused with our thoughts? The first trick is to simply notice that this has happened. Even that alone can be very powerful. We stop, pause for a moment, and notice where we are with our thinking. Just in that moment we have an opportunity to respond a little differently to how we normally do. In that pause we can ask ourselves:

- Just what is my mind saying in this moment? Are there words or images?

- Label the thought. Is it a judgement? A criticism? An evaluation? Is it about the past, the future or what's going on right now?

- How fused are you with the thought? Is this an old story? Do I feel open and vital? Or do I feel closed and constricted? Is what my mind saying helpful? What's most important in this situation – getting the job done or being right?

Use the Noticing Thoughts Worksheet to help you keep track of your thoughts. See if you can pause in those moments when you would normally become very caught up and fused with your thoughts and take some time to simply notice your thoughts and make a few notes.

NOTICING THOUGHTS WORKSHEET

Notice your thoughts	Label the thought	How fused are you with this thought?
What is your mind actually saying? Are there words? Are there images?	Is this a judgement, criticism, evaluation? Is it about the past, the present or the future?	Is this an old story? Do you feel closed or less engaged? Is this thought helpful to you?

Thank Your Mind

It's important to remember that your mind is just doing its job – even when it's serving up all sorts of disturbing, uncomfortable or distressing stuff. It's simply doing what it's designed to do and that is mainly keeping you safe. As we described before, not taking risks, being hesitant and cautious, underestimating your abilities, watching what you say, making negative judgements about the future, dwelling on negative events in the past – these are all protective mechanisms to: 1. Stop you getting eaten and 2. Stop you getting thrown out of the tribe.

So, a good starting point is to pause for a second, notice what your mind is saying and thank it for doing such a wonderful job! We don't want to mock or belittle our minds as they do undertake a serious and important task for us. Nonetheless, there is something just a little bit funny about this process. Here our minds are, working so hard to watch out and protect us, while at the same being so critical, judgemental and negative towards us! Sometimes a simple acknowledgement and a 'thank you' is enough, as we refocus our attention to the task at hand:

> *'You're not good enough and no one likes you!'* Thanks, mind – great to have your feedback.

> *'Why bother – this is never going to work out. Just play it safe.'* Thanks, mind – an interesting perspective.

> *'That was a complete failure and absolute waste of time.'* Thanks, mind – good to have you along for the ride.

Different Ways of Being with Thoughts

After you've spent some time practising noticing your thoughts, it's time to start trying out some ways to further build in different ways of responding. At times, just noticing your mind at work is enough and it's easy to get back on track again. However, sometimes thoughts can be particularly sticky and some alternative strategies may be needed to defuse from them. We may have become used to treating uncomfortable thoughts with solemnity and reverence . . . how has that worked out for you? How would it be to treat them a bit differently?

EXERCISE: Experimenting with Thoughts

Take a moment to consider two or three thoughts that you often find yourself fused with and make some notes about what these typically sound like, for example, do they normally sound high and shrill, or perhaps deep and heavy?

1.

2.

3.

Ok, now that you've done that, we'd like you to experiment with some different ways of being with these thoughts. Keep in mind, we're not trying to belittle or undermine these thoughts. Also, we're not trying to pretend they're not there or magic them away. Our aim is to add in some extra ways of being with thoughts that may open the possibility for you to have a little more freedom and choice in their presence. See if you can distil your thought into a few words that are particularly punchy. Now, in the **spirit of experimentation**, let's try either singing your thought out loud or in your head to the theme of one of these well-known tunes:

- Happy Birthday
- She'll Be Coming 'Round the Mountain
- Jingle Bells

Another way to do this is to say the thought in the voice of someone famous, or a cartoon character – try to choose one that sounds very different from how you normally experience this thought. You can really let your imagination and creativity run a little wild here. Some of our favourites include:

- Homer Simpson
- Donald Duck
- Arnold Schwarzenegger
- Yoda

What did you notice in doing this? Was there anything new or different added in? Perhaps a sense of looseness and distance from this thought that often feels really up close and personal? It's all right if you didn't experience this. We'd suggest trying it a few times and in a few different ways.

Emotions – Being *Open* to All of Your Experience

What are Emotions Anyway?

Tim was driving home after a long day at work. As he was driving, he happened to glance up at a billboard advertising life insurance, with a picture of an elderly couple who reminded him of his own ageing parents. He noticed his heart suddenly start thumping in his chest and his stomach clenched up. An image sprung to mind of him standing alone in a cemetery. He felt extremely anxious and noticed a very strong urge to call his parents to check they were OK.

As **Dave** sat down to turn on the TV, he remembered he had forgotten to call his sister the day before to wish her happy birthday. He noticed a sinking feeling in his stomach and felt very heavy in his body. A number of thoughts went through his mind, including, 'you're a useless brother, you never get anything right'. He experienced a strong sense of guilt and shame.

Emotions are particularly complex aspects of our experience that are made up of multiple parts. They are deeply personal and subjective responses to our current situation, either externally or internally. A way to think of an emotion is like a *wave* that passes through us that is made up of physical responses, thoughts, feelings and urges. Sometimes, these waves can be huge; sometimes mere ripples on a pond. Just like a wave can give us clues about the weather, emotions give us clues about ourselves and what we are currently experiencing. They tell us about what we like and don't like. They tell us about the things we enjoy and the things we hate. They help us to know what is good for us and what is not so good. They give us a sense about the things we need to do more of in life and what we need to do less of.

We can imagine that you might be reading this thinking, 'But my feelings just get in the way and stop me from doing anything! I feel too anxious, too lonely, too sad or too angry.' Our aim here is not only to help you work more effectively with your feelings and emotions, so that you don't completely cut yourself off from this very important part of your experience, but also so they don't completely overwhelm or dominate you. What we're aiming to do here is *feel* better rather than feel *better*.

We hear a lot of people say to us, 'I just want to feel less anxious/sad/angry.' One thing we're not going to be able to do is teach you how to turn your emotions off. Even large doses of strong drugs or alcohol can only temporarily numb feelings (at least until you pass out) and tend to be a little unhealthy in the long run. Part of the problem is that, if we were able to remove your capacity to feel unwanted emotions, we'd also remove your capacity to feel the emotions you do want, such as excitement, vitality, curiosity or affection! As the saying goes, there would be a real danger of throwing the baby out with the bathwater.

One way to think about this situation is to consider how 'life' is for the average zombie. A zombie is a shell of a human, returned from the dead to spend its days shuffling about the place in an endless search for human brains. Certainly, to the best of our knowledge, a zombie doesn't experience anxiety, grief or rage but neither does it experience joy, passion, thrill or love. So here's the question: is this the kind of life you want for yourself – a zombiefied existence devoid of any real feeling?

You may still say, 'Well, I'd rather have no feelings at all than have to put up with this!' Undoubtedly, some feelings are much easier to have or make room for than others. Some we welcome in and we would be entirely happy if they stayed forever. And, if we're honest, some we wouldn't mind if we never saw again. You can think of these types of feelings as being a bit like an unwelcome party guest:

Imagine, one day, you decide to throw a party for all your friends. You get out your phone and start inviting people. You want a big party so you say, 'Anyone can come!'

On the big day, you get your place ready for the party. You're really excited to see everyone. Pretty soon all the guests start arriving. After a while, everyone you're expecting has arrived and you're having a good time.

But then the doorbell goes, and you think, 'I wonder who that is – must be someone I've forgotten about.' And it is – someone who you definitely did not want at the party. It's your neighbour, Brian. Brian has to be one of the most annoying people you know. He's rude, grumpy, he moans a lot and he's not so flash on personal hygiene. He is the last person you want at your party. But before you know it, he goes straight inside, without even saying hello. He starts going up to your guests and is rude. He helps himself to the drinks, and generally acts a little weird towards your friends.

You feel pretty upset, embarrassed and angry. Before long you go over to Brian and tell him, 'That's it, time for you to go!' And you throw him out of your party. Once he's gone, you feel relieved. You go back out to the party and start to enjoy yourself. But after a while, you hear the doorbell again. When you go to check who it is, you realise Brian has come back! Before you can stop him, he opens the door and races back into the party. So you go and get him and throw him out again. This time though, you decide you're going to make sure he doesn't come back, so you decide to stand by the door and make sure he can't get in.

And this works fine – Brian can't get back in and you feel good about this. Trouble is, you realise that, all the while, you're missing out on the party! You can hear everyone else having a good time. You want to be out at the party. But, because you can't stand Brian, you can't risk him coming back in. You don't know what to do! You really want to enjoy the party but the thought of Brian being there really gets to you.

After a while, you realise that, actually, this party is pretty important to you and you want to be with your friends; in the very least, you want to make sure they are OK. So, you decide to go back out and say to yourself, 'If Brian comes back in, that's how it goes.' So, you go back to the party, and hang out with your friends.

And sure enough, after a few minutes, Brian comes back in and starts being annoying again. But this time, something's different. You don't ignore him, because he's pretty hard to ignore. But you decide just to get on with the party and talk with your friends. And you notice that, even though Brian is there, you are having an OK time. Sure, it would be better if he went home, but at least you're not stuck at the door missing out on the party.

So, we'd invite you to consider how you experience unwanted or difficult emotions. How do you generally respond to them? What has been your experience in trying to control how you feel? There are many ways that work very well to control, quieten or dampen down emotions. Alcohol, drugs, television, sex, exercise, food, music, pain, Internet use – all of these can be used to try to modify how we are currently feeling or to take away an emotional state we'd rather not have. Take a moment to consider how much of these things you have done. And here's the really important question – **how effective have these strategies been at managing that emotion?** Think particularly over the long-term – have you actually achieved more control? Or have you simply experienced brief periods of respite with increasingly more frequent and louder periods of the emotion? Perhaps more importantly, how effective have these strategies been in helping you to live a vital and meaningful life?

Clean and Dirty Pain

A helpful way to think about emotions is to differentiate between *clean* and *dirty* pain. Clean pain can be thought of as the normal and natural hurt that comes from living life: the pain when we lose someone or something close to us or the hurt and frustration that comes from life not working out as we had hoped or expected. This is going to happen to all of us at the points in our lives when reality jumps up and bites us. If you're alive and have a pulse, then chances are, you're going to feel some of this hurt and pain at some point yourself. **Dirty pain happens when we respond to this normal and natural part of the human experience in a closed way** – when we try to push this part of our experience away from us. We start giving ourselves a hard time for feeling a certain way, we compare ourselves to others who look like they're coping better and we end up working extra hard to block out the emotion. What happens? Well, we end up feeling not only the original feeling but also a lot of extra 'dirty' feelings on top of that – frustration, annoyance, guilt, shame, and the list goes on. While all this is going on, we deprive ourselves of the energy and opportunity to do things that matter to us.

It's understandable that we end up responding to these kinds of feelings in unhelpful ways – some of them are certainly not easy. But ask yourself: is it necessary to load ourselves with this extra helping of 'dirty' pain? Isn't the 'clean pain' already enough? What we're suggesting is that it could be better to develop more effective ways of responding to these kinds of emotions – ways that don't end up with our experiencing being an extra burden. How do we do that? This requires developing the skill of *Openness*.

Remember Marcia, the charity worker who was also a carer for her unwell mother? Consider Marcia's response to a set of difficult emotions:

> **Marcia** had been asked out on a date by a guy at her work. She hadn't been on a date for a long time and was nervous and excited at the same time. In the morning she told her mother that she was going out that evening and her mother had said she was having 'one of those days', her code for 'I'm depressed, don't leave me by myself'. Marcia knew from experience that if she left her mother alone, something bad could happen. She had felt a burst of anger towards her mother, thinking,

'My one night out and you do this!' Quickly, she berated herself for feeling this way, and then felt intensely guiltily for becoming angry. She knew she'd have to cancel her date as she couldn't bear the anxiety of leaving her mother at home alone or the inevitable guilt she knew she would feel. She spent the rest of the day experiencing a vague sense of sadness, from which she distracted herself by keeping busy at work. At the end of the day, she arrived home feeling both empty and exhausted.

In reading this, you can probably get a sense that Marcia finds it difficult to remain open to some emotions, particularly anger. You might also notice how she responds to such feelings: by pushing them away or distracting herself. While this is an understandable response, it seems to come at quite a cost. What would some different, more helpful responses perhaps have looked like?

Acceptance: The Skill of Opening Up

The skill of opening up to our emotions requires us to develop a stance of *acceptance* towards our internal experience. It means making room and space for that which is already there, and at the same time easing up on the tendency to fight or struggle with these feelings. Now, it's important to say, we don't mean that you have to go around feeling and accepting all feelings all of the time! But it will be an important skill to have available to you in your toolkit. There will be times in life when you feel emotions that you'd rather not have. Or times when you embark on journeys filled with trepidation and uncertainty. At these points it's important to be able to respond to the inevitable emotions that arise in effective ways. And, by effective, we mean ways that allow you to keep on track to be able to do the important things in life. So being open to our emotions is, at its heart, a very active process. We foster this sense of openness so we are able to do what we value. The process is **not about resigning ourselves** to feeling a certain way or giving up hope for things to be different, or wallowing in pain. By opening up to emotion and allowing ourselves to make room and space for the natural feelings that occur, and developing a sense of willingness in having these feelings, we have greater flexibility to do the things that we really care about.

It can be helpful to think of our emotions as small children within us. Small children that feel sadness, fear, anger or hurt. What's the most effective way to respond to a small child feeling such feelings? Well, it depends. Most often, a child needs to be heard. They need their feelings to be acknowledged by those around them. Sometimes, children need time to tell their story and explain what happened to them and why they felt the way they did. However, sometimes, what works is to scoop them up, focus their attention on something else and get them moving on with their day. It can be a bit like this with emotions. Most of the time emotions do need to be validated. Sometimes we need to take our time with them and listen carefully to what they have to say. At other times, we simply need to acknowledge them and refocus our attention to the task at hand and carry on.

Have you ever done any physical training, like running, cycling or swimming? When you first start out, your body screams at you, 'Stop this now! I don't like it!' Everything hurts – legs, arms, head, lungs, and even the bits you can't name. But, if you persist, over time, you get to know the pain that you can disregard or don't need to listen to. Like the pain in your legs as you first start running. Or the twinge in your shoulders as you take your first swimming strokes. You learn to listen to your body better, knowing which are the types of pain you don't need to worry about versus the pain that does require attention. As you develop this skill, you learn that the pain has things to say. Sometimes, it simply means that you're giving your body a good workout and you carry on. Other times, it means you need to stop, pay attention and attend to that part of your body. The skill lies in listening closely to your body and learning to tell the difference between these types of experiences. The same applies to emotions as well.

Getting to Know Your Emotions

A core skill in developing openness is getting to know your emotions. Often, as we lead our busy lives, bouncing from experience to experience in autopilot mode, it can be difficult to get a sense of what is going on inside, and how we are actually feeling. This is made all the more difficult by the fact that our internal landscape can be rich and varied, and also in a constant state of flux. So the question of 'how are you feeling?' can be a tricky one! As we start to slow down, we begin to register more of this internal world and develop a vocabulary about it. Without this, our emotional world has no depth, no features and no variation. We're left, essentially, flying blind without a map to differentiate this landscape. As we learn to put words to these different parts of our experience, we gradually build up a more complex picture of ourselves, of the things we like, of the things that upset us, and the things in life that make us angry and leave us filled with joy. So the skill is this: to notice, register and label our internal experience as it is occurring, as much as possible without criticism, evaluation or judgement. As we develop this skill, we learn to view our experience with a greater sense of clarity. It's a bit like bringing the map into sharp focus, so that we're much more able to see the contours and the way ahead.

EXERCISE – Getting to Know Your Emotions

Spend some time getting to know your emotions. Over the next week, ask yourself once a day, 'What am I feeling right now?' Describe it in as much detail as possible. Make a note of where in your body you felt the feeling. What is your body posture like? Does your facial expression change? Does the feeling tell you anything about you or what is important to you? As you notice this feeling, what automatic, habitual responses arise? See if you can do this without attaching judgements to the emotion. Describe it as it is, as if you were a curious scientist, documenting this experience for the very first time. Use the Noticing Emotions Worksheet to keep track of these.

NOTICING EMOTIONS WORKSHEET

What am I feeling?	Where am I feeling it in my body?	Does this feeling tell me anything?	As I notice this feeling, how do I respond?
How would you label this feeling or emotion? Describe the feeling in as much detail as possible: shape, size, weight.	What is my posture like? My facial expression? Where in my body am I not feeling it?	What does it say about me? What does it say I need to do? What does it say about what is important to me?	What is the normal, habitual response that goes along with this feeling?

The Emotional Radio and the Secret Openness Dial

Our emotions can be a bit like a radio over which we have no control. Sometimes the music is calming, soothing and relaxing with birds chirping and whales making their familiar noise. Sometimes it's energetic and pumps us full of motivation, making us ready to take on the world. But there are other times when the music is not what we want to hear. It grates on our nerves like the product of the latest manufactured (and we would likely to sincerely apologise if you are a fan) teen-band. It's loud, intrusive and you wish it would just stop! With a radio, you have a choice; you can easily turn down the volume or change stations. It's pretty natural to think the same rules apply to emotions; just turn down the volume and you won't be so bothered.

But (and refer to your own experience here) it turns out that this emotional radio doesn't work the same way. Sometimes it's really difficult to turn the volume button down because it's as if it's stuck at full volume. When you do manage to turn it down (often with a lot of blood, sweat and perhaps a few tears), no sooner do you turn your back but the volume has shot back up again! Here's a useful piece of information that didn't come in the instruction manual: the trick is to know about the other dial on the back of the radio. This one can be called the 'Openness Dial' and there are two very useful things to know about this dial. The first is that when Openness is at 0, it locks the volume at 10. When we are not open to the emotion content of our radio, our emotions tend to blare out at full volume.

1.   2.

The second useful thing to know is that when we move the Openness dial to 10, the volume dial is now free to move. In reality, volume dials move of their own accord depending on what is going on around you. Setting Openness to high is not a guarantee that volume won't be high, but what you will find is that it won't be locked at 10 and therefore be able to change. So the more *Open* we are to our emotions – the more willing we are to allow them to be as they are – the more likely we are to get them moving about. They are sometimes high, sometimes low and in this way you begin to make room for the natural variation.

EXERCISE: Opening Up to Emotions

Let's deliberately practise a different way of being with an emotion that in the past you have struggled with. Think for a moment about a painful emotion or feeling that often causes you problems. It could be sadness, anxiety, loneliness or anger, or any other feeling that you can get unhelpfully caught up with. Now, think back to a time when you felt that feeling. As this may be your first practice, we'd suggest starting slowly. Begin with a time when the feeling was present but not overwhelming. Read the following instructions and then go back and practise the exercise:

Sitting in a comfortable position, close your eyes or focus them on the ground on a point in front of you. Then, picture yourself in the situation in which you felt that difficult feeling. Imagine looking out from your own eyes, remembering what the situation was like. Where were you? What time of day was it? Who was there with you? Just spend a few moments really getting absorbed in the situation.

Now, we're going to ask you to do something that perhaps, ordinarily, you wouldn't do. See if you can direct your attention inwards and notice how you are feeling. Spend some time observing this feeling, with a sense of curiosity. If and when judgements about this feeling arise, see if for now you can set them aside. Notice urges to change this feeling, and see if you can set those aside too – just for now.

Notice exactly where in your body this feeling is located. It may be in just one place or it may be in several. See if you can now imagine this feeling as an object. How big is it? What kind of texture does it have? Is it smooth or rough? Heavy or light? Does it have a colour? Does it have an edge or is it diffuse? Notice if it moves or fluctuates. If it had a sound, what would it be? Spend a few moments imagining this feeling as an object. See if you can imagine it in as much detail as possible.

Now, imagine that this object moves outside of your body and sits hovering in front of you. Get a sense of it. Examine it with curiosity as it floats there. See if you can rotate it around to view it from another perspective. Keep in mind that your job is not to get rid of it or change this object. Just for now, all you need to do is bring a sense of awareness to it and allow it to be there.

Lastly, now bring the object back inside you, where it belongs. See if you can welcome it back into your body – perhaps as you would an old friend – with a sense of openness and acceptance. Allow this part of your experience to be in your body, just for this moment.

How did you find the exercise? Was it easy or hard to notice the feeling? How was it to imagine it as an object? Did you notice any new qualities about this feeling you hadn't noticed before? What was it like to bring it back into your body?

Extra Tips

Being open to emotion and feeling means cultivating a non-judgemental stance towards the range of our emotions. This doesn't mean that we won't have judgements – it's normal and natural to judge, evaluate and categorise. I like this feeling – I don't like that one. This one is good – that one is bad. Our minds love doing this. It's part of our make-up to do it. A non-judgemental stance means noticing the judgements as they happen and mindfully allowing them to pass, without becoming fused or entangled with them. Here are some common thoughts, judgements and evaluations about emotions that might invite struggle:

- I can't handle this feeling.

- I shouldn't feel this way.

- This feeling is too much.

- Why is this happening to me?

- This feeling will never end.

When we get very fused with these types of judgements, we often end up struggling with our feelings. We become much less curious about them. We can become narrow and rigid about our experiences. We feel like we know all we need to know about these feelings and that's it. Sometimes, when we make room and space for what is already there, we get the opportunity to notice qualities that we hadn't seen before – qualities that were obscured by our judgements and preconceptions.

Urges and How to Surf Them Successfully

Sometimes in the presence of emotion, especially strong emotion, it's normal to experience desires or urges to 'do something' about it. At times these urges can become pretty strong – it's as if they are demanding our attention and want to force us to do things. At its heart an urge or craving is just a strong desire to change the current situation: 'I want that piece of chocolate cake now!', 'I want to stop working and watch TV', 'Give me that extra large glass of wine, right away' or 'I'm going to tell you exactly what I think of you!' This is the mind responding automatically to the current situation it finds itself in, flowing to the path of least resistance. It's easier to have that slice of chocolate cake – it tastes good (you know it does). Why work when you could watch fun, relaxing TV (everyone else is)? It feels great to let you have a piece of my uncensored mind (as you desperately deserve it). Now, while none of these actions is necessarily wrong, in and of themselves, you can imagine the trouble you would end up in if all you did was respond mindlessly and automatically to each and every urge or craving that came up.

A key quality of urges is that they call us to action: 'If you don't do what I say and satisfy me, then I'm just going to get bigger and bigger to the point that you won't be able to stand it!' Well, actually, most if not all urges don't act in this way. They are more like waves in the ocean. They swell in size, to the point when they reach their peak, then they drop in intensity. The trick is learning to experience this natural drop. When we give in to an urge and do what it demands of us, we get nicely rewarded with a sudden decrease in the intensity of the urge, and we feel better! And, chances are, when this urge occurs again, we'll be inclined to go with it as we have done before. What we miss out on is the natural decrease that happens, just like a wave passing through.

Is there a different way to behave with urges? Well, one way is to grit your teeth and fight it. This can be effective but it tends to take up a lot of energy. Just like being in the ocean, it's possible to fight against wave after wave but it's hard work. Another way is to approach the urge with a stance of mindful acceptance. Objectively observe all the different parts of it. Notice the edges of the urge, notice the parts of your body where the urge isn't. Focus in on the natural ebb and flow as it increases, decreases or stays the same. In this way, you begin to foster a sense of curiosity towards this part of your experience, which introduces a pause between the feeling and call to action. It may be the case that you decide to act on the urge, however, see if you can do this mindfully rather than on automatic pilot.

There's good reason to practise this too. The more we practise surfing our urges, the better we become at it. It's both like a skill we can develop and like a muscle we can strengthen. As we strengthen, we end up having more and more in reserve for when we need it.

Next Steps

In this chapter we've talked about thoughts and the ways in which our minds work, sometimes in unhelpful ways, to prevent us from moving forward. We've introduced the idea of defusion as an alternative to getting stuck with thoughts. We've also talked about emotions and the skill of acceptance. Having learned more about the skill of being more *Open* with your thoughts and feelings, we're going to move on to the next key skill of ACTivating your life: developing mindfulness and being *Aware*.

3 Aware: Noticing What's Going On Inside and Connecting with the World Around You

Are You Paying Attention?

Did you ever have that experience at school of sitting in class and gazing out of the window while the teacher held court at the front of the room, only to be told off for 'not paying attention'? Well, we know it's too late now, but was your teacher actually being fair? Were you really 'not paying attention'? What was going on in your mind as you looked out of that window? Perhaps you were drawing careful fantasies of yourself scoring the winning goal in the World Cup final or picking up an Oscar. Perhaps you were just allowing your mind to wander where it wanted. What would have happened if you had said to your teacher, 'I was paying attention . . . just not to you'?

It probably wouldn't have been received very well, but the fact remains that 'paying attention' means more than just tuning in carefully to what is happening in front of you (although that is an important element of it). The **way** we pay attention and **where** we direct our awareness is fundamental to the way we experience life. If we become inflexible with how and where we direct our awareness – if it is consistently rigid and super-focused like a laser beam, or if it is too diffuse, wandering around all over the place – our lives will be diminished. But there are some simple *Aware* **skills** that we can learn that – if practised – can help us to build lives that are rich and fulfilling.

In this chapter we are going to draw a clear distinction between **thinking** and **awareness**. We will go more into this later, but by **thinking** we mean the content of our thoughts – all the words and images that our minds generate from moment to moment. By **awareness** we mean the simple act of noticing, whether it involves the thoughts that are coming and going in our minds, the sensations in our bodies, or the world around us.

A term that is of vital importance in ACT is *mindfulness*. Mindfulness is a term that we use to describe a particular **quality** of awareness. While there are many different ways of defining mindfulness, we see it as **being aware of the present moment, in a way that is conscious, curious and flexible**. Let's break this down:

- *Being aware of the present moment*. The mind is like a time machine. Often it is zooming us into the future to plan or fantasise or worry about what is to come, or cata-pulting us back into the past to reminisce or ruminate about what has been. Whether our journeys into the past or future are pleasant or unpleasant is not the issue (although as we talked about this in Chapter 2: *Open*, the human mind often tends to focus on negative or painful memories and thoughts) – when we disconnect from the present moment we disconnect from the world around us. The present moment is where we live and take action, and too much time in the past or future will have a damaging impact on our experience of life **in the here and now**.

- *In a way that is conscious.* Using these *Aware* skills is an active process – it is about deliberately and consciously directing the focus of our awareness to the present moment rather than idly hoping that it will happen.

- *Curious.* Of course, *Aware* skills are about more than simply being deliberate about how and where we focus our awareness. If that were the case then it would be no different from the voice of that teacher telling us to 'pay attention'. We can choose to focus our awareness on something and still resist and struggle with it. Using *Aware* skills means bringing a quality of curiosity to our experience – a sense of openness, acceptance and inquisitiveness about what it might have to offer, even if we notice our minds telling us that we do not like it. Of course, it is easy to be curious about something that we like – a film we haven't seen before or an exciting opportunity, for example. It's far harder to bring a spirit of curiosity to something that is uncomfortable or scary – such as going for a job interview or having to deliver a best man's speech! However, it is this spirit of curiosity that is central to all the cool and interesting stuff that can become available to us in developing a mindful approach to life.

- *And flexible.* As we will talk about later, we humans can
  be very rigid in the ways that we think and the ways
  that we respond to situations in life. But a rigid perspective can deprive us of creativity and choice. On the
  other hand, learning to be more flexible with how and
  where we focus our awareness can be extremely helpful. Sometimes it might be useful to really narrow down
  the focus of our awareness to just one particular activity
  or part of our experience – a bit like when the spotlight
  focuses on just one actor during a play. Other times it
  might be useful to actually broaden out our awareness
  to take in all of what we are currently doing, seeing,
  hearing, smelling, tasting, feeling and thinking, like
  when the house lights come up at the end of the play
  and everything is illuminated at once.

The difficulty is that most of us have learned to live life
unconsciously, incuriously and rigidly, responding to our
thoughts and feelings as if they were all equally true and
important, minds catapulting from past to future and rarely
settling in the here and now. Developing *Aware* skills is
something that needs to be worked at. As we move through
this chapter we will show you some exercises that you can
do to grow your ability to be truly mindful and aware. But
to really experience the benefit of them you have to do them
regularly – ideally, every day. A little like when you go to
the gym: if you want to build a muscle you have to exercise it consistently. Well, awareness is like a muscle too, but
one that the vast majority of us rarely use consciously, so it
needs working on!

So, notice what your mind is saying to you right now. If it is saying 'that sounds like a lot of hard work, why bother?' then you may want to simply bring some mindful awareness to that thought. Perhaps thank your mind for its contribution and see if you can spend a few moments reading the next section anyway.

What Are the Benefits?

As we said in the last chapter, thoughts can be difficult to change and control, and they often pop into our minds entirely of their own accord. Every thought that appears in our mind will have an impact – a little like when you throw a stone into a pond and, even when the stone has disappeared below the surface, it leaves behind a pattern of ripples spreading outward. Sometimes our thoughts come thick and fast – especially unpleasant or negative ones – and soon it is like there is someone throwing handfuls of stones into the pond until the surface is completely consumed with ripples and waves. In these moments we can feel overwhelmed and paralysed.

Practicing *Aware* skills won't necessarily stop those stones from hitting the water – our minds are thought-generating machines and don't even let up when we are asleep – but, as we develop them, we learn not to add unnecessarily to the ripples by adding extra thoughts, focus or attention. And over time what we will often find is that the ripples aren't quite so big. When the thoughts show up – even really unpleasant ones – they cause less of a disturbance. This can be really helpful for a number of reasons.

First, it can feel better. While feeling better isn't necessarily the aim of using *Aware* skills, most people find that they prefer a mind that is a little more like a clear, still pond than one that is in a constant state of unrest.

Also, *Aware* skills are a great way to increase self-awareness. When the surface of the pond is covered in ripples it is almost impossible to see what is going on underneath, and anything that you **can** see is distorted. When it becomes still and clear, you can see with much greater clarity what is there. By paying attention to what your mind is telling you, with a quality of openness and curiosity, you can start to identify some of the ways that your mind works – the patterns and trends, the way it habitually responds to fear and challenge, and also the way it responds to opportunity. Of course, that doesn't necessarily mean that you will like what you see when you look under the surface, but if you can also approach that stuff with the same spirit of openness and curiosity – noticing what your mind is telling you about it and being willing to allow the thoughts to come and go like the fleeting ripples on a pond – then it can be extremely useful.

With self-awareness comes **choice**. The more clearly we can see the patterns and habits of our busy minds, the less likely we are to slip back into autopilot and start to follow them unquestioningly. We can start to create a bit of a gap between what our minds tell us and what we actually do and say, and it is in that space that we create that we can really start to build lives that are rich, meaningful and fun – by making choices that are driven by what really matters to us, rather than what our minds are telling us in any one particular moment.

A Little about Connection

By the way, if all this makes it sound like this chapter is just about pointing your awareness inwards and dedicating your life to some Zen-like quest to master your innerworld, please rest assured that it isn't! Remember, this is all about doing what it takes to create a life that is **of value to you**. At times this might mean observing your thoughts and feelings with curiosity. At other times it might mean consciously directing your awareness outwards to the world around you. But sometimes we can get so wrapped up with what is happening in our heads or under our skin that we stop engaging with the world – nature, food, people we love, and all the stuff that makes up life. As the scientist, writer and mindfulness teacher Jon Kabat-Zinn said, 'The little things? The little moments? They aren't little.' *Aware* skills are as much about turning that spotlight of our awareness outwards as it is about turning it inwards. But we will come to that . . .

Some Simple Ways to Practise Mindfulness and *Aware* Skills

Undoubtedly the most effective way of exercising that awareness muscle is to commit to regular practice of mindfulness and *Aware* skills. There are a number of easy exercises you can do, some of which are quite brief and can be practised at frequent intervals throughout the day. Others are a little longer, and generally involve having your eyes closed (although they don't have to). Some of these longer, eyes-closed exercises can feel like meditation. Again, we'd like to stress than this is not about meditation in the way that most people understand it. The aim is not to achieve some enlightened state. There is no expectation of any particular religious or spiritual belief. These are simply exercises designed to help you become more aware and connected to what is going on in your mind and under your skin, and to strengthen your ability to achieve some distance from these things and really focus your awareness on what is happening in the here and now. In this way, as we begin to slow down and take a pause, we begin to open ourselves up to more of the choices that are available to us.

EXERCISE: Awareness of Breath

A great place to start is to practise becoming aware of your breath. Your task will initially be to spend just five minutes consciously directing the spotlight of your awareness towards your breath and the changing sensations in your body as you breathe in and out. Our advice is that you read through the following instructions and then put the book down and go through the exercise in silence. Don't worry about memorising the exercise – whatever you remember as you go through will be fine.

Try to find a warm, quiet, comfortable spot where you won't be distracted or disturbed. It might be useful to set an alarm so that you know when the time you have allotted for the exercise is up.

Sit down in a comfortable position – feet flat on the ground with hands held loosely in your lap is usually quite good. Closing your eyes often helps too, but some people prefer just to allow their eyes to unfocus and come to rest on a spot in front of them.

When you are ready just start to notice the sensations within your body – any areas that feel tight or sore or any areas that feel relaxed. You don't need to try to change anything – you are just noticing. Then after a while, narrow the spotlight of your awareness so that it is focused on your breathing: the changing patterns of sensation in your stomach as you breathe in and out; the gentle rise and fall of your ribcage; the feeling of the cold air passing into your body through your nose, and the warm air leaving your body through your mouth. Bring a quality of gentle curiosity to your noticing, as if you were a curious alien who had just arrived on Earth and had never observed 'breathing' before.

As you do this, your attention will wander – thoughts, feelings, memories and urges will arise naturally. Whether they are pleasant or unpleasant simply notice that your attention has drifted and, when you feel ready to do so, gently refocus your attention on your breathing. Remember that you are just supposed to observe your breath – not to try and change it or regulate it – simply to let it be what it is.

Even if your mind wanders a hundred times it's OK. Allow the thoughts, sensations and memories to be whatever they are – there is no need to change them or try to chase them away. Just gently refocus your awareness on your breath when you are ready to do so, with the same quality of gentle, open curiosity.

When it is time for you to finish the exercise, expand the spotlight of your awareness again to take in the whole of your body, noticing any sensations that are there, wanted or unwanted, pleasant or unpleasant. Expand it further to take in what you will see and notice as you open your eyes. Then open your eyes and spend a few moments reflecting on the exercise and anything you noticed . . .

Practise, Practise, Practise

Many people find this kind of exercise very relaxing. When that is the case it is fantastic. However, it is important to stress that this is not a relaxation exercise, and any feelings of relaxation are just a pleasant bonus! The aim of this kind of *Aware* Skill is simply to notice the passage of your thoughts and feelings, to practise the skill of gently unhooking when you find yourself being carried away by a thought, and to return to the here and now using your breath as an anchor. In this way, as the pool of our consciousness slowly settles, we can develop the skill of mindful awareness.

Initially, you could commit to practising the Awareness of Breath exercise for five minutes once or twice a day. Then – after a week or so – think about increasing the time by a couple of minutes every few days. Some people make a half-hour awareness practice part of their daily routine, and those who do usually find that it brings them a greater sense of well-being, clarity and choice about how they go about their day-to-day lives.

The important thing about regular practice is that it will help you to slowly build your awareness muscle, so that responding flexibly to your busy mind will start to feel like second nature in time. However, you are still only human, and there will inevitably be times when you find yourself getting wrapped up in unhelpful thoughts and emotions. When this happens you can still get back in contact with the present moment in just a few minutes by using the Three-Step Breathing Space.

EXERCISE: Three-Step Breathing Space

Step 1: Connect with what is going on for you in the here and now

Notice what is going on in your mind by asking yourself 'What thoughts am I having right now? What feelings am I having right now?' Notice any other urges, memories or other thoughts or sensations that might be there.

Step 2: Narrow your awareness to your breathing

When you are ready, focus the spotlight of your awareness onto your breath: the changing patterns of sensation in your stomach as you breathe in and out; the gentle rise and fall of your ribcage; the feeling of the cold air passing into your body through your

---

nose, and the warm air leaving your body through your mouth.

Step 3: Expand your awareness to the entire body

Gently expand the spotlight of your awareness to take in the whole of your body. Notice any sensations that might be present, scanning your body quickly from head to toe without trying to change anything.

Again, the more you practise using the Three-Step Breathing Space, the more natural it will feel to use it in moments of challenge. If you notice us persistently encouraging you to practise over the course of this book, it is for good reason! Let us explain why . . .

Watch Yourself!

The truth is that as human beings we are creatures of habit and routine, and tend to respond to situations in life in a similar kind of way, time and time again. When those ways of responding are useful in helping us to live the kind of lives that we want then it's great. But when our responses are actually contributing to our lives being less rich, fulfilling and fun then it can be a problem.

We can tend to be particularly rigid in the way that we respond when we get fused with unpleasant thoughts or feelings. Let's revisit Samantha – we introduced you to her in Chapter 1, after she referred herself for therapy to get some help managing the anger that she felt was starting to take over her life.

It's the end of a long and stressful day. Samantha had a number of difficult conversations with patients and colleagues at work but managed to keep her cool, despite feeling like she was going to blow up sometimes. Her husband is out having drinks with friends from the office and now Samantha is trying to get her two kids ready for bed single-handedly, but they aren't cooperating! She is feeling tense, anxious and increasingly angry. Her mind is saying, 'For God's sake why can't they just do what I tell them? Are they stupid? How come Colin gets to go out and have fun, when I'm stuck here? Bloody hell, I can't cope!'

After asking her son, Charlie, to go upstairs and clean his teeth for the third time, he picks up his phone and starts playing Angry Birds. Samantha grabs the phone out of his hand and throws it across the room. At the top of her lungs, she shouts, 'What is wrong with you? Why can't you just listen? If you're not up those stairs in ten seconds you are going to regret it!'

Charlie dashes upstairs, scared and confused. Samantha slumps down into the sofa, feeling a wave of regret and shame starting to wash over her. Pretty soon her mind is telling her, 'I've done it again. What's wrong with me? I'm a monster

– a real mother wouldn't shout at her kids like that.' As she gets more and more wrapped up in these thoughts the feelings of shame just intensify. It takes her fifteen minutes before she feels calm enough to go upstairs to speak to the kids and apologise, but she feels awful for days afterwards.

Without judging Samantha, can you think of other ways in which she might have responded to the situation? Perhaps ways that wouldn't have left her feeling dreadful, and that might have been more true to the type of mum she wants to be – patient, caring and *open*?

Again notice how when we are outside of a situation – looking in as an observer – it is so much easier to see the options that might be available, to see how getting caught up in her thoughts and feelings made it so much more likely that Samantha would respond in the way that she did. What if it were possible to be an 'observer' of your own experience – to notice what is going on inside you and around you in such a way that you could take action and respond to life's challenges from a place of choice and awareness, rather than a place of stuckness and fusion? Well, the good news is that you take that 'observer perspective' all the time, almost certainly without realising it. Remember, you already have the skills! But let's spend some time learning how to access that 'observer' perspective more easily when it matters.

The 'Thinking Self' and the 'Observing Self'

Part of the reason that we humans tend to get so caught up in our thoughts and other internal experiences is that – as we talked about in the *Open* chapter – we have learned to take them *really seriously*. When our ancestors were on the savannahs of Africa, they had to tune in very closely to the information provided by their minds – if they didn't, they risked being killed or eaten!

In fact, so highly have we come to value our ability to use the amazing tool of thinking that we sometimes define ourselves purely on the basis of what's going on inside us – our thoughts, emotions, memories, urges and sensations. If the predominant mood is worried or nervous then people will tend to think of themselves as an 'anxious person'. If an individual's mind often offers up negative self-judgements, then they will think they have 'low self-esteem'.

But we are more than just the sum of our internal experiences and mind-stuff. In fact, the thing that makes humans *even more* amazing than we give ourselves credit for is the fact that not only are we able to think laterally, plan, fantasise and experience a range of emotions that are beyond other creatures (so far as we know) but we are also **aware** of this aspect of our experience. The fact that you've been able to do the exercises so far in this book – noticing your thoughts, watching them come and go, noticing the sensations in your body and describing them, focusing your awareness on your breathing – shows that not only is there a part of you that thinks and feels but there is also a part of you that **notices and observes** your thoughts and feelings.

In ACT, we talk about our *Thinking Self* and our *Observing Self*. The Thinking Self is that constant stream of thoughts and images that runs through our minds, almost every moment we are awake; the Observing Self is the place from which we notice all that mind-stuff, as well as every other part of our experience – both the world inside us and the world outside. If this sounds a little bit strange, don't worry! Your Thinking Self will want desperately to analyse and 'understand' – that's how the thinking self works! – but it's easier to get to know your Observing Self by experiencing it.

EXERCISE: Noticing That You Are Noticing

Sit back in your chair and find a comfortable position. For a moment just allow your awareness to flow where it wants, settling on a thought or a feeling if it wants to, or moving on if it wants to. When you are ready, we would like to invite you to experiment with focusing your awareness on different parts of your experience. And as you do this, we will also invite you to just be aware that you are noticing these different experiences in the here and now.

- Notice the thoughts that are passing through your mind right at this moment. And notice that you are noticing.

- Notice the sensations you can feel inside your

body right now: any areas of tension or relaxation. And notice that you are noticing.

- Notice any sounds that you can hear around you. And notice that you are noticing.

- Notice any images that form in your mind. And notice that you are noticing.

- Notice the rise and fall of your chest as you breathe in and out. And notice that you are noticing.

- Notice the overall quality of your emotions right here and now. And notice that you are noticing.

Finally, allow your awareness to just flow where it wants, and to come to rest on whatever aspect of your experience it wants to. And as you notice whatever it is that your awareness chooses to focus on, also notice that you are noticing.

As you participated in this exercise you were stepping gently from moment to moment between your Thinking Self and your Observing Self: having the experience of a thought, a feeling, a sensation, a memory – being inside it – and then stepping back and *observing* the thought, feeling, sensation or memory.

The idea of there being anything more to us than our Thinking Selves is not a common or even a popular one in Western culture – we lack an adequate vocabulary to talk about it clearly. One way of visualising it is to remember the idea that we introduced in Chapter 2 (*Open*): that all the stuff that goes on under our skin – the stuff that our Thinking Selves focus on – is rather like the weather. Well, if that's the case, then the Observing Self is like the sky. The weather will change from day to day, from moment to moment – sometimes warm and beautiful, sometimes stormy. What remains constant is the sky, containing and accommodating the changing patterns of weather, unable to be harmed by it, no matter how fierce the storm or how bright the sunshine. The sky is a witness to the weather, and will be there long after even the most powerful hurricane imaginable has blown itself out, just as your Observing Self will be there always able to make space for your thoughts and feelings, regardless of how difficult or unpleasant they may be.

Here is something else that you could practise and incorporate into your day to help you to get in touch with your observing self and find that space of noticing and acceptance more easily.

EXERCISE: Noticing, Watching, Observing

This next exercise is a little like the Thought Bingo that we showed you in Chapter 2 *(Open)*. When you were playing Thought Bingo your task was to notice the kinds of thoughts that were passing through your mind and then tick them off on your bingo card as they came and went. Noticing, Watching, Observing is similar: your task will be to simply sit back and allow your mind to work, noticing whatever stuff it throws up with openness and curiosity. You are good and experienced at this now (presuming you have been doing the exercises up to this point!), so you don't need a bingo card anymore. Also, what we would like you to do is consciously approach all the mind-stuff that appears from the position of your Observing Self. To help you with this, as each thought, feeling, memory, sensation or urge emerges, say to yourself 'I notice that I am thinking x' or 'I notice that I am feeling x' or 'I notice that I am having the urge to x'.

Perhaps spend five minutes doing this exercise and then spend a few moments reflecting on what it was like. Were you aware of being in that Observing Self space? What is different about the quality of your awareness between the Observing and the Thinking Selves?

In some ways, one of the most valuable things about consciously adopting the position of the Observing Self is that it compels you to slow down for a moment – to pause and take a step back from the always-busy Thinking Self. In the space that opens up, it is possible to start making choices about our actions – choices informed less by what is going on between our ears and under our skin, and more by what matters to us in the big picture (by what some people refer to as our 'values', something we will talk a lot more about in Chapter 4: *Active*).

Let's re-visit Samantha trying to get her kids to go to bed, except this time she has been working on her *Aware* skills and is trying to do something a little differently.

It's the end of a long and stressful day. Samantha had a number of difficult conversations with patients and colleagues at work but managed to keep her cool, despite feeling like she was going to blow up sometimes. Her husband is out having drinks with friends from the office and now Samantha is trying to get her two kids ready for bed single-handedly, but they aren't cooperating! She is feeling tense, anxious and increasingly angry. Her mind is saying, 'For God's sake, why can't they just do what I tell them? Are they stupid? How come Colin gets to go out and have fun, when I'm stuck here? Bloody hell, I can't cope!'

Samantha goes upstairs into the bathroom and shuts the door. Sitting down on the side of the bath she does a quick Three-Step Breathing Space practice. She closes her eyes and draws her attention to her breathing. She then allows her awareness to focus on her thoughts and what is going on in her mind. 'I notice that I am having a feeling of frustration,' she says to herself. 'I notice I am having a feeling of anger. I notice I am having a thought about Colin not helping me. I notice that I am having a self-judgement about me being a bad Mum. I notice I am having an urge to go and shout at the kids.'

In pausing like this Samantha notices how the chaotic swirl of her thoughts and feelings gradually begins to slow down. She can see clearly what her anger is telling her and what it wants her to do next, and decides that – just in this moment – she is going to do what she want to.

When she opens her eyes, Samantha thinks about how she would respond if she were being the best mum that she could be, the kind of mum that she would most like to be all the time. She decides that she would be patient, playful and assertive. She goes downstairs and says to Charlie, calmly and firmly, 'Charlie, I have told you three times to clean your teeth. I need you to put down that phone and go upstairs. If you do that for me now I'll be up in ten minutes to read you a story.'

We will finish the story there because whether Charlie actually does what Samantha says is kind of beside the point! Much as we cannot control our thoughts and feelings – despite often believing and wishing that we can – we also cannot control how other people behave. What we can do is take a step back from the whirlwind of judgements and comparisons that our minds tend to throw up in moments of challenge and conflict and make a conscious choice about how we want to be and what we want to do. Sometimes it will 'work' in terms of getting us what we want and sometimes it won't. But, on average, it will lead to a life that feels more full, authentic and fulfilling.

Getting Some Perspective

Not only does really becoming acquainted with our Observing Self allow us more flexibility in how we choose to act but it also helps us in how we choose to view the world. Whether we realise it or not, the way that we view the world – the perspective that we take on it – undoubtedly has an enormous influence on our experience.

For example, have you ever received some kind of social invitation – to a party for instance – and noticed your mind loudly telling you 'I don't want to go!'? Maybe you went along to the party and found that you actually had a much better time than you expected? On the other hand, maybe you went along and found that that the whole thing was a slog, that you spent the whole time looking at the clock, and that you ended up looking back on it as a wasted evening?

If, like most people, you have had experience of both of those situations then ask yourself this question: what was different on each of those occasions? Perhaps the people were different, or something else happened outside of you that had an impact on what your experience was like. But was there anything different about **you** and the way you approached the situation?

Perhaps in the first instance you went into the evening telling yourself, 'I'll just go along and see what it's like. Maybe it will be fun. If not I can always make an excuse and leave.' Perhaps in the second instance you went into it telling yourself, 'This is going to be miserable. What if I get stuck in a conversation with someone boring? How long do I have to stay before it's OK for me to go?' The situation was exactly the same in both cases – an invitation to a party – the thing that was different was the *perspective* you took on that situation: in the first case a perspective of optimism and openness, in the second a perspective of pessimism and reluctance.

Most of us have particular perspectives that we drop into almost automatically in different circumstances. Some people, when faced with challenging life situations, automatically adopt a perspective that is associated with resilience and curiosity. Other people automatically adopt a perspective that is associated with fear and self-doubt. Neither one of these perspectives is wrong or right – both are quite normal and natural, even useful.

However, we can sometimes become rigid and get stuck in familiar perspectives, unwilling or unable to look at the world in different ways. Every perspective comes with its own set of opinions and assumptions that will have an enormous impact on how we view the world, how we respond to others, and the quality of our experiences as we go through life. There is a famous and old story called 'Socrates and the Road to Athens' that illustrates this point beautifully:

Socrates had gone for a walk outside the city walls of Athens. He was resting by the side of the road about five miles from the city. As he rested he saw a traveller approaching.

'Greetings, friend! Can you tell me, is this the road to Athens?' said the traveller. Socrates assured him that it was. 'Tell me,' said the traveller, 'what are the people of Athens like?'

'Well,' said Socrates, 'where are you from, and what are the people there like?'

'I'm from Argos. And I am proud and happy to tell you that the people of Argos are the friendliest, happiest, most generous people you could ever wish to meet.'

'My friend, you will find,' said Socrates, 'that the people of Athens are exactly the same.'

A few moments passed and another traveller approached. 'Greetings, friend! Can you tell me, is this the road to Athens?' said the traveller. Socrates assured him it was.

'Tell me,' said the traveller, 'what are the people of Athens like?'

'Well,' said Socrates, 'where are you from, and tell me what the people are like.'

'I'm from Argos. And I am sad to say that the people of Argos are the meanest, most miserable and least friendly people you could ever wish to meet.'

'My friend, you will find,' said Socrates, 'that the people of Athens are exactly the same.'

For the travellers in the story, their perspectives act as filters that only allow them to see certain things. Anything that doesn't fit into the narrow confines of that perspective is ignored or dismissed.

Let's revisit Tim for a moment. We met Tim in Chapter 1 – he is finding that his mind is constantly generating thoughts and feelings of worry and anxiety, and that his life is starting to become dominated by an overwhelming need to avoid making mistakes.

It's 7 p.m. on a Wednesday evening and Tim is alone in the office. Everybody else has gone home but Tim is still there frantically cross-referencing the figures in an HR report that he has to hand to his manager the next day. He has already checked the numbers a dozen times, but on a couple of occasions they came out differently, and now he feels as if he can't trust himself to get them right. His mind is telling him, 'If I get this wrong I am going to be in big trouble. I made a mistake once before, I can't afford to do that again. What if I have got this fundamentally wrong? I don't even know what I'm doing anymore.' He is locked into a very familiar perspective – Tim at one point described it to his therapist as the 'catastrophe' perspective, where he assumes that everything that could possibly go wrong will, and his life is going to fall apart because of a mistake. So, he ends up staying in the office until nearly 11 p.m., and even after he goes home his mind is still racing with images of what is going to happen the next day when – inevitably, as he sees it – his mistakes are exposed.

When Tim becomes trapped in the 'catastrophe' perspective he is unable to make choices effectively about his actions. He feels that he has no option but to keep going over the figures time and time again. Not only that but also he is unable to see his situation clearly or accurately. The thoughts keep dropping into his mind like stones into a pond, and the surface has become so obscured by ripples that he is unable to see with any clarity what is going on within him or around him.

This would be a great moment for Tim to practise his *Aware* skills and step into his Observing Self, and to get a little distance from his thoughts and feelings. From there he might notice that he is approaching the situation from the 'catastrophe' perspective and that it doesn't seem to be a very helpful one at that moment! He could even begin to explore some *different* perspectives.

Let's re-visit Tim a few days later as he talked through his late night at work with his therapist.

Therapist: That sounds like a really tough evening.

Tim: Yeah, it was horrible. But what else could I have done? I can't afford to make any more mistakes at work. There have been rumours about a takeover and that always means redundancies. If I'm always making mistakes I'll be putting my job at risk.

Therapist: What perspective are you in right now?

Tim: Well . . . it feels like it might be the 'catastrophe' perspective again.

Therapist: Sounds like it. I have a question for you – if you had to tell me somebody in your life who you really respect and whose opinion you value, who would it be?

Tim: It would have to be my dad.

Therapist: What is it that you respect so much in your dad?

Tim: Well, he's kind and he's a good listener, but he's also quite pragmatic. He's the kind of bloke who just gets things done!

Therapist: OK, what I want you to do is move so that you are sitting in that seat over there . . .

(Therapist points towards an empty chair. Tim moves and sits down.)

Therapist: I'm going to ask you a few questions and I would like you, as best you can, to answer as if you were your dad – from his perspective. OK? Bear in mind that this is just an experiment. You are not trying to psychically **predict** what your dad would say, or find the **right** answer. You are just trying out a different perspective to see what might be there.

Tim: OK.

Therapist: What would you, Dad, say to Tim about the situation he is experiencing right now?

Tim: Umm ... I'd say that he needs to go easy on himself ... that he is a very capable person *and actually hardly ever makes mistakes at work.*

Therapist: And what would you have said to him the other evening when he was checking *that report over and over?*

Tim: I would have said to him that he needs to go home and relax! I would have said to him that checking the figures three times is fine and that his report is good enough as it is ...

If your Thinking Self is puzzling over some of these ideas, that is OK. Let's do a couple of exercises to give you a taste of flexible perspective taking in action.

EXERCISE: Taking the Perspective of Another

Think of something that is currently worrying you, upsetting you or stressing you out. Really let your mind settle there for a minute or two and allow whatever thoughts and feelings arise to be there. Make a note below about anything that showed up in your mind and any feelings that arose as you allowed yourself to dwell for a moment on that issue.

Now, think of three people in your life who are important to you, and who you know care about you. They can
be alive or dead, as long as they are important to you.

Imagine that the first of these people is sitting in the
chair opposite you. Visualise them. Get a sense of
their character and their energy. See if you can make
it as rich as you can, a bit like super HD TV. You'll
probably need to use your imagination to fill in any
blanks and that's fine. Now go and sit in that chair and
answer the questions in the Taking the Perspective of
Another Worksheet **from that person's perspective**,
making notes in the first column.

TAKING THE PERSPECTIVE OF ANOTHER WORKSHEET

	Name:	Name:	Name:
What do you have to say about the situation that is worrying (your name)? Is there anything they may have missed?			

What would you suggest to (your name) to help them cope with the situation?			
What would you suggest that (your name) could do to take one small step towards a life that feels more fulfilling and meaningful?			

When you are ready, move back to your original seat and imagine that the second person you thought of is sitting opposite you. As before, visualise them, and get a sense of their character and their energy. Now go and sit in that chair and answer the questions in the Taking the Perspective of Another Worksheet **from that person's perspective**, making notes in the second column.

Finally, move back to your original seat one last time and imagine the third person. Again, visualise them; get a sense of their character and their energy. Now go and sit in that chair and answer the questions in the Taking the Perspective of Another Worksheet **from that person's perspective**, making notes in the third column.

What was that like? Remember, we said in the Introduction that ACT is all about just learning to use skills that we already have a little more consciously and effectively. Most of us have, probably on many occasions, tried consciously to see the world though someone else's eyes, with the aim of gaining more understanding of what they are experiencing. Here you are doing something different – consciously trying to see the world through someone else's eyes to understand a little better what **you** are experiencing.

We are not proposing that this is the definitive answer to all situations where you find yourself stuck, or that the 'right' perspective will inevitably reveal itself (the idea of a 'right' perspective in itself is a risky one). We are just noting how helpful it can be to open oneself up to new perspectives and information when we find ourselves in difficult situations. Sometimes just shifting into a different perspective can reveal to you that the way forward is more straightforward than you think.

Listen to Yourself!

What is so great about stepping into someone else's shoes for a moment and taking their perspective is that it shakes things up a little – it gets us out of our habitual ways of seeing the world and thinking about ourselves. As we said before, we humans are creatures of habit and routine – we can go through life on auto-pilot, stuck in just one familiar perspective and responding from that place time after time.

Sometimes we can get so stuck in a familiar perspective that we start to feel as if we **are** that perspective. The person who naturally approaches life with a spirit of adventure comes to think of themselves as 'an adventurous person'; the person who worries a lot comes to think of themselves as 'a worrier'.

This tendency to define ourselves by our most common thoughts and feelings and most frequently adopted perspectives can be really limiting. As we saw in the last section, there is more to us than we realise! We are more than just our Thinking Selves – we have access to this amazing Observing Self that just notices everything that is going on within and around us without judgement. From that Observing Self place we can see our thoughts for what they are – just words. We can see our feelings for what they are – just sensations within the body. We can see our urges for what they are – just drives to make us take one of many different available courses of action.

From that place we can also see that even if we spend a lot of our time feeling fearful or angry, or having fearful or angry thoughts, that does not mean that we are 'a fearful person' or 'an angry person'. No matter who we are there is always more to us than this – there are multiple aspects to all of us, many of which often get ignored or forgotten about when we are struggling or suffering.

Let's revisit Dave, who we met earlier. He had been made redundant from the job he held for many years. It was a real shock and now he says that he feels 'all at sea'. He has tried to apply for a few jobs but with little success, and he has come to be very pessimistic about the prospects of ever finding employment. His mind has been telling him 'What's the point? No one's ever going to want to employ a washed-up has-been.' That term 'has-been' has become incredibly powerful for Dave, and countless times a day his mind reminds him 'I'm a has-been'. Stuck in this 'has-been' perspective he doesn't see the point in applying for any more jobs; he doesn't feel like seeing his family or his friends; he doesn't see the point in doing anything. It feels like life is over.

When Dave goes to see his counsellor, she is curious to find out about some other aspects of him:

> *Counsellor*: So what I hear from you when we talk, loud and clear, is that right now you see yourself as a 'has-been'.
>
> *Dave*: Because I am . . .
>
> *Counsellor*: Well, I'm not actually going to try and persuade you that that's not true, but I am interested in getting a sense of what else there is to you. When you're really living life to the full, what do you like to do?
>
> *Dave*: It's been a while, but I like going to the theatre.

Counsellor: To see what kind of things?

Dave: I quite like musicals – *Chicago*, that kind of thing.

Counsellor: OK, what else?

Dave: Well, I'm a football fan . . . I used to go and watch Crystal Palace most weeks. I still watch them whenever they're on TV.

Counsellor: OK, so a theatre-goer, a football fan. Tell me about some of the roles you play in your life . . .

Dave: Well, I'm a friend, a son, a brother . . .

Counsellor: It was actually your sister who suggested you come to see me wasn't it? What kind of a brother are you when you're at your best?

Dave: I'm fun . . . Sally and I have always had the kind of relationship where we laugh a lot. I'm supportive . . . I'm the kind of brother who's there when you need him. Dependable.

Counsellor: OK, that's interesting. You know, sometimes it's useful to remind ourselves of these different parts of ourselves. It's like holding dice in our hand and forgetting that there are other sides that have different numbers! It's not like any side is more 'right' than the others. They are all essentially true. But we often focus only on what is in front of us and forget what we can't see at this exact moment . . .

Dave: I get what you mean ... most of the time these days I can only see the 'has-been' bit. It's like that's all there is to me.

Counsellor: I understand. When life gets tough, that's one of the ways that our minds will start to beat us up – reminding us of all the stuff about us and our lives that we don't like, and urging us to forget anything else. But here we have it – you are a theatre-goer, a football fan, a caring supportive brother. All these are as relevant as you as a 'has-been'. I wonder what it would be like to look at what is going on in your life from the perspective of 'Dave-the-brother', rather than 'Dave-the-has-been' ...

The United States of You

With all these perspectives available, in a way it's kind of as if you are the President of a country – the United States of You! – and all these different parts of yourself – the optimist, the pessimist, the father, the daughter, the music-lover, the critic – are like government advisers.

What many of us find is that there are certain advisers – often the loudest, most aggressive or most negative ones – who we seem to listen to more than any others, and we end up following their advice and doing things their way almost all the time. But being a good President means taking in a broad range of input and advice, and being open to all opinions. Unfortunately, most of us have certain advisers that we barely ever call on. It may be that we don't trust them, or maybe we don't even know that they're there. It pays to really get to know your trusted team of advisers – all of them: the loud ones and the quiet ones, the ones you like being around and the ones you don't like being around. The more familiar you are with them, the better and broader the advice you will receive, and the clearer and more accurate the picture you build of reality will be.

EXERCISE: Getting To Know Your Advisers

If each of us has all these different parts of ourselves – this team of advisers, each of whom offers us a unique perspective on the world – then it pays to get to know them. Now you have an opportunity to do just that . . .

Get comfortable in your seat and take a few deep breaths. You can close your eyes or keep them open, but when you feel ready, allow your mind to start to explore the question 'who am I?' knowing that there cannot be just one simple answer. Think about all the different qualities that you possess as a person. Think of all the roles that you inhabit every day, the parts you play in the lives of others. Think about parts of you that are there and maybe don't get expressed that often, but that you would like to see more of.

Start to give names to these parts of yourself – like 'the comedian', 'the appreciator', 'the runner', 'the worrier', 'the son', 'the mother' – whatever means something to you. Come up with as many as you can and make a note of them in the space below.

Just for now, choose six from the above that you would like to get to know a bit more about. Imagine these as your team of advisers, each one absolutely exemplifying the qualities of that part of yourself. In the space below, describe those qualities (we've given you a couple of examples to start with):

Adviser	
The Runner	**Helpful**: Determined, relentless, loves a challenge, keeps on going even when tired, does what it takes to reach the finish line. **Unhelpful**: Can be relentlessly demanding, doesn't know when to quit or take time to relax.

The Worrier	**Helpful**: Future-oriented, always trying to keep me safe from harm or embarrassment.
	Unhelpful: Focuses almost exclusively on the negative, keeps me anxious all the time.

Now, think of a situation that is currently worrying you, upsetting you or causing you stress. Let your mind settle completely there for a minute or two and allow whatever thoughts and feelings arise to stay there.

Now, select three of your new team of advisers and one by one consciously take on their perspectives.

Start with the first one: what are the qualities of this adviser? What is their energy? How do they see the world? As best you can, allow yourself to settle into this perspective just for a moment and answer the questions in the Consulting Your Team of Advisers Worksheet below as if you were this adviser, making whatever notes you want to in the first column.

Now call on your second adviser: what are their qualities? What is their energy? How do they see the world? As best you can, allow yourself to settle into this perspective just for a moment and answer the questions in the Consulting Your Team of Advisers Worksheet below as if you were this adviser, making whatever notes you want to in the second column.

Now call on your third adviser: what are their qualities? What is their energy? How do they see the world? As best you can, allow yourself to settle into this perspective just for a moment and answer the questions in the Consulting Your Team of Advisers Worksheet below as if you were this adviser, making whatever notes you want to in the third column.

CONSULTING YOUR TEAM OF ADVISERS WORKSHEET

	Adviser:	Adviser:	Adviser:
What do you have to say about the situation that is worrying (your name)?			
What would you suggest to (your name) to help them cope with the situation?			
What would you suggest that (your name) could do to take one small step towards a life that feels more fulfilling and meaningful?			

Remember, in this exercise we are not interrogating our advisers in the hope of finding the 'right answer'. We are just trying some different perspectives to see what wisdom might be available in each. Just as each one will have something of value to share, the biggest mistake many of us make is becoming too attached to one particular perspective. Dave started to associate himself powerfully with the 'has-been' perspective and it had a big impact on his life. An important lesson when he gets a new job will be to ensure that he doesn't start to associate too strongly with the new perspective that is likely to emerge of 'Manager' or 'Bread-Winner' or however he might think of it. He did that before, and when he lost his job it felt as if his whole identity had been stripped away. There is more to us than any one of our perspectives can represent. Why not try to hold all those parts of you with an equal sense of lightness? Then as life twists and turns we can move with it, flexibly and effectively.

Try a Little Tenderness

There's a particular adviser that very few of us tend to call on consciously or with any frequency, despite the fact that they could be an extremely useful vice president. We call it 'self-compassion'.

We are all familiar with the idea of compassion: that feeling of empathy for someone who is in distress, and the desire to do whatever we can to reduce their suffering. We place a great value in society on showing kindness and compassion to others when they are struggling, and yet very few of us extend that kind of treatment to ourselves. So many of us respond to our own disappointment, adversity or pain with tremendous harshness – beating ourselves up, criticising ourselves, applying degrees of harshness we would never dream of with anyone else, rather than holding ourselves gently; offering consolation rather than criticism. In doing so the entirely normal 'clean pain' that is an inevitable part of a life fully lived swells and mutates into the crippling 'dirty pain' that ends up burdening us even further, and making it so much harder to live the kinds of lives that we want. Perhaps you went out on a limb and asked someone you like out on a date, only to be turned down. Naturally, this is a painful experience, but taking a chance like this is almost always necessary if you want to find someone to share your life with. The disappointment, sadness, maybe even embarrassment that would usually accompany this kind of experience for most people would be what we describe as 'clean pain'. But if you then went home and spent the next couple of days telling yourself that you are pathetic for getting your hopes up, and even more pathetic for letting yourself get so disappointed, that you are never going to find a partner if you always get upset when things don't go your way – this would be an example of 'dirty pain': the pain that our minds create for us when we are unwilling to experience uncomfortable – but inevitable – thoughts and feelings.

Imagine for a moment that you are sitting with a small child. She is desperately upset and in floods of tears because she was teased at school. How would you respond to her? Would you praise and affirm her? Would you put an arm around her and remind her of all the wonderful things about her, and that being teased doesn't make her any less of a worthwhile and special person? Or would you sternly criticise her, tell her she is a loser and that she needs to get her act together?

Witnessing a child suffering is sufficient to evoke deep compassion in virtually all of us. And all of us were ourselves once children. Remember that while the content of our thoughts, the roles that we play, the bodies that we live in may have changed significantly over the years, there is a part of us that is untouched and unchanged. The children that we were so many years ago are still alive within us, and in need of care when they are suffering. A powerful way of getting in touch with that elusive quality of self-compassion is to get in touch with that part of you that is still the child that you were many years ago.

EXERCISE: Extending Compassion towards the Child Within

Call to mind a situation in your life that is currently upsetting you or causing you some pain. Allow your mind to explore the situation in whatever way it wants. As painful thoughts and feelings arise resist the urge to struggle with them or push them away, just allow them to be as they are. Even allow yourself to fuse with them a little.

When you are ready, allow your mind to begin to build a picture of yourself as a child. Perhaps there is a photograph or video clip that springs to mind and really reminds you of what you were like when you were young. Spend a moment recalling what it was like to be that age, what you were like as a child.

Now, imagine that you then were suffering in the way that you are today. Imagine the child that you were being assailed by the painful thoughts and feelings that you are experiencing.

How do you feel towards the younger you? In what way would you want to respond to the younger you if you could see yourself right now? What would you say?

Self-compassion is about learning to treat yourself in a way that is open, encouraging and kind; recognising that life can be hard and that you are only human. It's about really practising the skill of opening up and making room for those unwanted feelings that are like the Unwelcome Party Guest we talked about in Chapter 2 (*Open*).

Dave's counsellor took him through the Extending Compassion Towards the Child Within exercise and encouraged him to practise, to really get to know the self-compassionate side of himself, and to develop the skill of stepping into that perspective. While Dave said that he really benefited from it in the moment, his face suddenly fell and he seemed almost annoyed: 'This is all very nice, but I can't go through my life being all "kind" to myself and saying "there, there" when I mess up! I can't afford to go easy on myself, I'll never get another job if I slack off now!'

Dave is not alone in this. Many people think that self-criticism is vital to getting things done, and that self-compassion means letting yourself off the hook or being self-indulgent. There is a fear that developing a self-compassionate perspective will deprive us of our motivation.

However, we would ask you again to think back to that small child – perhaps this time she is upset after getting a disappointing test result. How would you motivate her to move forward – with praise and encouragement or with a barrage of harsh criticism? In fact, research evidence clearly suggests that self-compassion actually enhances motivation and helps people respond positively and actively to setbacks. A self-compassionate response doesn't only have to mean self-soothing and comforting. A self-compassionate response may well be one that calls for action, for actually **doing** something to look after oneself after a painful experience or disappointment. Self-compassion is not about wallowing in feelings – it is about **acknowledging them and responding to them in a way that is most likely to keep you moving towards what matters to you in life**.

More importantly, the belief that self-compassion will lead to a life of self-indulgence is based on the misunderstanding that what we are proposing is that you move to one side and allow the 'Secretary of Self-Compassion' from our team of advisers to take full control. But, as always in ACT, the key words are 'flexibility' and 'workability' – developing the ability to try on different perspectives and choose the one (or more than one) that is going to be most helpful and effective in helping you build a life that is rich and fulfilling **in the present moment**.

This is crucial – **there are no 'right' or 'wrong' perspectives!** Every perspective has something to offer, each one contains potentially important information. It's a bit like when you are buying a second-hand car and you walk around it, looking at it from every angle, crouching down to check underneath, kicking the tyres, looking under the bonnet. Only when you really look at it from a number of different perspectives can you know what you are getting. In the same way, if we only approach the world from one perspective we are never going to get a clear and accurate picture of how things actually are.

It is when we get stuck in a particular perspective and unable to see any others that we start to experience problems. It may seem obvious that somebody who was locked into a perspective on the world and their experience as fearful and pessimistic will find that it has a negative impact on their life. But imagine somebody who only ever approached life from a perspective of joy and optimism. What if you wanted to talk to them about something painful or something that had upset you – how good a listener do you think they might be? How effectively do you think they might respond if they were about to be mugged? A little fear is probably quite useful in those kinds of situations!

So don't waste time trying to find the 'right' perspective – there is every chance that you will quickly find yourself caught up in your mind, filtering through options and unable to take action until you find the one that is going to be just **perfect** for the situation you are facing. Be experimental, be playful and try stuff out!

Getting Connected

If you spend enough time practising the exercises we have shown you so far, and developing the skill of becoming more flexible with your awareness, the chances are that you will find that you are more connected with what's going on under your skin and between your ears than ever before. Our hope is that this will free you up to do more of what matters to you and live the kind of life you most want for yourself. Because what is life if not for living and enjoying? And yet, it is so easy to get locked into a pattern of rushing through our days on auto-pilot, heads down, barely noticing the world around us.

Learning to become more flexible with your awareness is not just about becoming more acquainted and connected with your internal world, it is also about really getting to know the world around you. In ACT we talk about 'engagement': the state of really being totally present and connected with the world outside your skin via your five senses – what you can see, hear, smell, taste and feel. You have surely heard the phrase 'stop and smell the roses'? It is such a well-used sentiment that it's in danger of becoming a cliché, and yet there is a very fundamental truth in there.

Do you ever eat dinner in front of the TV – but with most of your attention on the show you are watching? When you eat a TV dinner, to what degree do you really taste the food that you've prepared? How engaged in the experience of eating are you?

What about when you are wrapped up in the content of your drama-loving mind? When you are really fused with your thoughts what impact does it have on your appreciation of the world around you and your overall experience of life? Imagine if you were forced to go through the whole of your life with your eyes glued to a screen playing endless episodes of a dramatic soap opera, or a stressful thriller. How could you possibly do any of the things that you care about that bring a sense of value to your life, whether it be reading a book, enjoying the feeling of the breeze on your skin, chatting to a good friend or hugging a loved one?

When we are fused with our thoughts, struggling with our feelings or fighting our urges it is exactly as if we were trapped watching that never-ending TV show. We disconnect from the world and our lives are diminished. Practising the *Aware* skill of engagement can help you to re-connect. In doing so not only will you find that more of the richness and sweetness of life becomes available to you but also that sticky thoughts and unwelcome feelings tend to be a bit less sticky and bit less unwelcome.

Woody Allen's classic film *Annie Hall* was originally entitled *Anhedonia*. He was persuaded by his producers that this might not be the most audience-friendly of titles: partly because many would simply not know what it means, and partly because those who were familiar with it would know that it is the clinical term for an inability to experience pleasure from things that were once enjoyable, a symptom often experienced by people who are suffering from depression.

While not everybody who is depressed will experience anhedonia, many people who are not depressed will be familiar with the feeling of somehow not getting the best from life – of rushing through our days, and missing out on the experience of really living: of physically being in one place, but mentally and emotionally somewhere else.

Aware skills are about switching out of auto-pilot and starting to become fully conscious and intentional about how and where we direct our awareness, so as to create lives that are really of value. The exercises we are going to take you through in this next section are all about taking the spotlight of your awareness and turning it outwards into the world.

Why don't we start by going back to that TV dinner example and practise connecting with something that for most of us is a source of pleasure, but one that we often don't fully experience because our awareness is elsewhere – eating!

In this exercise we are going to ask you to do something that – if you are anything like us – you have done a thousand times before: eat a sweet! But we really want you to be fully aware of the experience as you do so, bringing the qualities of awareness that we described earlier –consciousness, curiosity and flexibility. Really be conscious and intentional in the way that you connect with the experience through all of your senses. Bring a sense of childlike curiosity to this familiar experience, taking nothing for granted. Be flexible with your awareness – inevitably, you will find that at times you will disconnect from the experience and your Thinking Self will start getting involved. When that happens it's OK – just gently draw your awareness back to the sweet and whatever it is you are experiencing through your five senses.

Our advice is to read the instructions below once and then do the exercise yourself without looking at the book. Don't worry about trying to replicate the instructions perfectly, just give yourself two minutes to really explore the sweet with all of your senses, focusing your awareness on the experience.

EXERCISE: Awareness of Eating a Sweet

You can do this exercise with any piece of food – a raisin is great, as is a segment of orange or tangerine. But a way that we love to do it is with a wrapped sweet or hard candy. See if you can find one, and then try out the exercise below.

Pick up the sweet and place it in the palm of your hand. Slowly examine it . . . turn it around in your hand to see it from a different angle. Drop your hand into your lap so that you can see it from above. Examine it as if you were a newborn baby, seeing it for the very first time. Feel the texture of the wrapper . . . examine it with your hands. Allow your fingertips to travel into the folds and creases.

Now turn it upside down so it is resting on its other side and examine it from this angle . . . trace the outline with your eyes . . . notice the different colours and how they change slightly where they are in shadow or where the light is hitting them.

Now unwrap the sweet but slowly. As you do so, hold it up against your ear and listen to the noise that it makes.

Now hold the sweet in the palm of your hand again. Again, examine it from every angle. Pick it up in your fingers. How does it feel? Rough or smooth? Squeeze it a little – is it hard or soft?

Now raise it to your nose and smell the sweet – really notice the smell.

And now place it in your mouth but don't chew just yet. Just notice the feeling of it on your tongue. Move it around your mouth and notice every aspect of it. Notice the urge to chew and swallow and what it feels like to resist it. Notice it if it begins to melt and lose its shape.

Now bite down and chew the sweet and notice the sensation of it between your teeth and tongue, the clenching of your jaw whilst you slowly chew. Notice the taste of the sweet as if you were a curious scientist examining it for an experiment. Notice the taste that remains in your mouth when the sweet is gone and any feelings, sensations, thoughts, memories that you are left with.

What was that like? What was different about that compared to how you normally eat a sweet? Many people find it quite a surprising experience – that there should be so much more to experience in an activity that we normally engage in so unconsciously: flavours, smells, sensations that have been there all along but have slipped under the radar of our always-busy minds. It's almost as if we spend most of our time travelling through life with our eyes fixed on the floor – only when we lift our heads to connect with the world around us do we notice how much there is to marvel at.

A great exercise to really get you connected with what's available in life at any moment is to remember an acronym that our colleague Suzy Dittmar came up with: BIF. This stands for:

- Beautiful

- Interesting

- Funny

As you move through your day try to be aware of what is going on around you – in particular look out for things that strike you as funny, interesting or beautiful. You could even get into a habit of making a note of any BIFs you have seen or experienced at the end of each day. These are the parts of life that often become lost to us when we are stuck in our thinking selves, or being zoomed by our amazing minds into the future or the past. Many people find that as they start to practise these and other *Aware* skills more regularly, a sense of gratitude and appreciation for what they have starts to develop, and life starts to feel that bit richer than it did before. Try it!

Ugly, Boring, Unfunny . . .

In looking out for the BIF moments in life, you will inevitably notice that a fair amount of what is out there in the world is neither beautiful, nor interesting, nor funny – sometimes it can be ugly, boring and unfunny. And while you may find yourself really relishing the opportunity to connect with the stuff that you love, you may similarly notice an urge to disconnect from the stuff that you hate. Maybe you find that getting stuck in traffic starts your mind pumping out judgements and comparisons; maybe you find that having to speak in public throws up lots of uncomfortable emotions and sensations that you'd rather get rid of or suppress. But as we know, ignoring this stuff isn't possible for long, and struggling with it usually only serves to make the thoughts more insistent and the feelings more powerful. Consciously engaging with stuff that we don't like feels extremely challenging initially, but what we find is that it stops that process of clean pain becoming dirty pain as we struggle with or try to escape it. Also, we start to learn that not only is it possible to endure uncomfortable stuff but also that a lot of the time it is nowhere near as bad as we think.

Let's revisit Samantha for a moment. One of the things that really tends to trigger her anger feelings is getting stuck in traffic, but every day involves a drive to work that as often as not ends up with her sitting in her car and going nowhere for twenty minutes at a time. Soon her mind begins to start making all sorts of judgements and comparisons and demands. 'Every damn day this happens! Why are there always roadworks on this particular stretch? I'm better off selling this car and just taking the train. Late again! I'll be playing catch-up again all day . . .' She begins to feel increasingly frustrated and annoyed, gripping the wheel ever more tightly in an attempt to control the feeling.

Imagine someone else who also hates getting stuck in traffic – we'll call her Sandy – who also has to take a route to work that frequently involves getting stuck in long traffic jams. However, Sandy has been working on improving her *Aware* skills and realises that struggling against the uncomfortable thoughts and feelings that her mind throws up tends only to intensify them. She realises that, no matter how much she fumes and rails at the injustice of the world, the traffic isn't going to move any faster so she has developed the habit of consciously connecting with this experience, and other ones that she doesn't like. She notices all the different colours of the cars around her – not just saying 'red car, green car' in her head, but really taking in all the different hues and shades, the metallic, the shiny and the matt. She winds her window down a little and takes ten deep breaths, noticing whether the air is warm or cold, the different smells depending whether she is in the city or the country, taking it all in with a spirit of real openness and curiosity. Sometimes she just tunes into the sensations she can feel in her body – the roughness of the steering wheel on her palms, the point of contact where the ball of her foot pushes down on the clutch.

Both Samantha and Sandy end up getting to work at the same time. But Samantha arrives annoyed, frustrated and fused with the idea that the world is against her and that she is a fundamentally unlucky person. Sandy arrives feeling calm and connected with the world around her, ready to face the day ahead. While Samantha's mind is like a pond overcome with ripples, Sandy's is still and clear.

Spend a few moments thinking of three activities that you really don't like, but that you have to engage in regularly – at least once a week. Write them down in the space below:

1.

2.

3.

Our challenge to you is that you commit to engaging in these activities mindfully at least once each over the course of the next week. Practise defusing from judgements and comparisons and making room for feelings you don't like. Practise gently escorting your awareness from the world of your thinking self into the world of your observing self and – from there – just noticing what is going on around you using your five senses. When your thoughts wander and when you find yourself struggling –which you almost certainly will – don't worry, just notice what has happened and softly return to the input that is available to your from your senses.

Next Steps

In Chapter 2 (*Open*) we introduced some skills that will help you to get a bit of distance from unhelpful thoughts, and to open up and accept uncomfortable feelings. In this chapter we've talked about what it means to be *Aware* – how we can sometimes become a little rigid with how we view the world, and the freedom and choice that can come from taking different perspectives on our own experience and the world. By getting in touch with your Observing Self you can just notice what is going on inside you and connect with the world around you. The more *Open* and *Aware* you are, the easier it is to start living the life that you want, and really get *Active*.

4 *Active*: Knowing What's Important and Moving in That Direction

Where Are You Going?

You have this life to live. For all of us, it is lived one moment after another – whether we carefully make plans for the future or just let things happen in their own time. No doubt you've had moments that you'd choose to live over and over ... and ones that you'd rather not have experienced at all. Sometimes you have been bold, sometimes you have just done your best to cope with what life has served up to you.

So what guides you? If you could be free to choose to act like the person deep down you want to be, what things would you be doing?

Being asked these questions can be challenging. If you are like many human beings you may just be doing your best to get by. It might be life is like white-water rafting: you might be so busy trying to get from moment to moment, just keeping your head above water that the idea of setting a direction doesn't really come into it. It may seem that these questions would be more appropriate at another time, when you are struggling less, when there is more free time, and when you feel better (in some way) than you do now.

It could be that you are clear about how you want to act, but there seems to be a gulf between the person who can do that and the person you are today. Perhaps there were times in the past when you acted as the person you wanted to be, but they seem a long time ago . . .

Values – What Are You Guided By?

In this chapter we are going build on the skills of setting directions for yourself, and flexibly persisting with doing things that are important to you.

These are the skills of being *Active*, and provide purpose for practising the *Open* and *Aware* skills.

Active skills help to 'set the scene' for how your life will expand. We will describe a number of different ways in which you can organise and shape your actions creatively so that you can keep broadening out and live more fully, and also manage the times when things don't work out.

Here are two questions to hold in mind as you read:

1. Do you have a clear direction forward in life? Do you know what is important to you?
2. Or do you feel lost and confused about the direction in which you want your life to be going?

It may also be useful to check this: your actions are guided by *something*, even if they are **reactions**. So far, in this book we have been discovering what can guide you: (a) the struggle that can sometimes happen with feelings, thoughts and other experiences that you do not want and seem to stand in the way, and (b) the 'sticky' judgements and critical thoughts that call for your attention and can seem important when making decisions and deciding on which actions to take.

In ACT we explore what can happen if you sit with these questions and make room for the thoughts and feelings that may bubble up.

All of our actions as human beings are for some purpose or another, although sometimes it is hard to work out why people act the way they do. It may even be difficult to work out for yourself why you act the way you do: we can spend a long time trying to work this out . . . and come up with answers that in the end don't actually help us to move forward anyway! We've already described what can happen with some of these 'answers', like the stories that our minds tell about us – that may fit the 'facts' but keep us trapped and stuck in patterns of action that are limiting our lives. (See Chapter 3: *Aware* for some more discussion of this.)

We have explored what it is like when you are guided by your fears and those times when you are *unwilling* to have the feelings, thoughts and urges that turn up in your daily life. We have looked at what it would be like to do something that seems perhaps counter-intuitive, such as being willing to have these experiences in order to expand your life rather than constrict it further. In this chapter we are going to explore the **purpose** for practising the *Open* and *Aware* skills described in this book:

• What would you hope to be in your life (that reflects that you've made bold choices)?

• We are interested in helping you connect with the 'big picture' for your life. Where do you want to go? What do you want to be about, if you really could choose?

What Are Values?

In this book we are going to talk about 'values'. Simply put, these are **chosen life directions**. There are two parts to values: 1. they are chosen, by you and 2. they are directions, rather than goals or destinations.

When we act on our values, we **demonstrate what is important to us**. This means that our actions have a quality of **purpose**. In this moment what purpose would you choose to serve? What purposes do you serve through your choices and actions? Is there are difference between what you would **choose** and *what you are actually doing*?

One way to learn from the process of acting on your chosen directions is to notice the *vitality* that comes from doing the things that you do. *Vitality* is the sense of meaning and purpose that you have from acting on values. A vital life is one where you are having moments that are highly meaningful, which have come from moving in the directions you have chosen to take. These moments may be pleasant and even joyful.

However, they may also be painful at times. But what makes them vital is the fact that they are evidence of a life fully lived, moving in a direction that is consistent with your values.

Some examples of chosen life directions may help to illustrate what we mean by values and vitality.

Choosing to *act in a caring way toward yourself* in terms of your health may be a value. This direction could involve doing things such as exercise, regular health checks, eating health food, and finding ways to manage your stress. You can imagine that there are moments when these activities may be pleasurable (enjoying increased fitness, relaxation after a busy day) and also moments that may be scary or unpleasant (having medical tests, having root canal work). There may be a sense of vitality in choosing, on purpose, to live in this way, as a person who cares about their health through choices and actions.

Another example of a value could be in the area of relationships. A person might choose to *act in a loving way* toward the people in their life, including their lover/partner, family, and friends. The **ways** that this person could act lovingly will be different for each of the people in their life (e.g. responding to a lover in an intimate way, gently setting limits to a child, listening and providing support to a friend) and across situations. The quality of acting in a loving way will involve both pleasure (feeling loved in return, trust, closeness) and pain (showing vulnerability, the possibility of loss, concern when bad things happen to someone close). It could be seen that a vital life involving an intimate relationship may include the exciting early days of meeting someone new, the years of companionship (sharing both hopes and disappointments), and, if 'until death do us part', watching your loved one pass away and grieving their loss. (This is why many people find the first ten minutes of the Pixar film *Up* so moving and profound – a man's story of meeting the love of his life, sharing their lives together through thick and thin, until she passes away, leaving him alone – as it reflects the vitality of living by chosen directions. The film is worth seeing for this part alone.)

A Five-Year Perspective

To get started, it may be helpful to use a broader perspective from the day-to-day one that we usually have. We are going to ask you to imagine you have a time machine and could travel into the near future, being able to visit your future self. From this vantage point you can look at the effects of your choices and actions.

EXERCISE: Looking Back on Five Years of Acting on Your Values

As you have practised before, use your *Open* and *Aware* skills to connect with this moment, to feel in contact with your body and the way it feels right now, and notice what is going through your mind, the emotions, feelings and urges that you have. Take a minute to really connect with being here now, with you as you are, making room for the experiences that you are having.

We would like to invite you to imagine that it is five years from now. In this time you have been bold and made choices guided by the directions that give you purpose and meaning.

Imagine where you would be, with whom you would be, what your day-to-day life would look like. Really picture this scene. Notice your connection with it and what this feels like right now.

From this perspective, we would like to invite you to reflect on these questions:

- What would you be able to look back on (decisions and choices that reflected your values)?

- In making these choices and acting on them what feelings and emotions would you need to make room for?

- What would be the same in your life?

- What would be different?

- What would you really like to stand for in your life?

There are various ways of responding to this exercise. It may be the directions that you want to follow in your life are very clear to you. Or maybe you have drawn a blank, or that the directions are unclear. These are all understandable responses to this exercise.

In this part of the book we were going to invite you to: (1) **strengthen your connection with purpose** and (2) **find ways to commit to doing the things you care about**.

What Values Aren't

Sometimes it can be clearer to understand what we mean by 'values' by understanding what they *aren't*. Again, as in other parts of this book, our minds can make something more difficult to understand because it doesn't fit with the usual way of doing things.

Values Are Not about Feeling Good

So, this may not be what you want to hear, but the fact is that by heading in directions you care about, you may well end up welcoming more discomfort into your life. While acting on your values can lead to a great sense of meaning and purpose, it may also increase your contact with the things you care deeply about, which can sometimes involve a sense of vulnerability, pain and unwanted feelings. We hope that through learning the skills of *Openness* and *Awareness*, you will be more willing to accept that these experiences should exist and also play a part in choosing valued directions.

The psychologist Carol D. Ryff, who studies ageing, described a difference between the psychological well-being that comes from flourishing, belonging, life purpose, personal growth (what is called *eudaimonia*), and merely chasing pleasure for its own sake (*hedonia*.[2]) There is a body of research to suggest that there is greater well-being and quality of life with lifestyles based more on eudaimonia than hedonia. Values (although not always) can tend to have qualities that bring longer-term, slower-burn satisfaction (i.e. rather than short, quick-fix hits). We are, of course, suggesting that the eudaimonic lifestyle may involve experiencing discomfort in the service of your valued directions. This may mean that these uncomfortable feelings are *given the dignity that comes from living a purposeful life.*

This is not to say that pleasures won't materialise from basing your choices on values. In fact, the experience of opening up and being aware of pleasure may be part of chosen directions (such as a direction of becoming more sensual, expressing yourself sexually, appreciating moments with your five senses, etc.).

Values Are Not about 'Uncovering the Answer', 'Finding the Truth' or 'Being Sure'

The process of acting on values can at times involve profound moments of uncertainty, ambiguity and discovery. Choosing to be open to experience and setting a direction can frequently mean being in uncharted personal territory.

2   Ryff, Carol D, 'Happiness Is Everything, or Is It? Explorations on the Meaning of Psychological Well-Being', in *Journal of Personality and Social Psychology* **57** (6): 1069–1081 (1 January 1989)

Remember Tim from the Introduction (the man who is struggling with worry and isolating himself from others)? Think about the situation that Tim is in, with his challenges in loneliness and lack of connection with others. For Tim, who has avoided getting close to people, starting to make steps in the direction of connecting with others may involve a number of moments when doubt will be part of the experience.

So, rather than your values being like an *archaeological dig into your soul*, uncovering layers and finding the answer to a long-held mystery, instead what we are doing is more like **construction**.

We're going to invite you to create and build a life of purpose. Like designing and building a new home this may involve experimentation, trying new things out, seeing how they fit, and considering the construction as a whole. There are likely to be moments when things don't work out. Through the process of this construction you may learn things about yourself and about the directions that you choose. The beauty of this approach is that every day you have the opportunity to be creative with your life and choose what your purpose is. Instead of waiting for a perfect answer, you're gaining experience and approaching life like a work in progress (more on this later).

We are encouraging you to engage in the process of discovering what works for you when you just decide to live by the directions you choose. We can bring our curiosity to bear on how to live in this moment, in a way consistent with the ideals that we hold dear.

If you have been the type of person who has sought to find answers in yourself about what the best ways to deal with life are, then you may find that the *Active* approach of choosing a direction and taking some steps, without having everything 'worked out', is going to be unusual. As we discussed earlier in this book, our minds like to have absolute certainty, even when this is not always so useful for living a vital life. You may find that there is a liberation that comes with choosing a direction and acting like the person you want to be, *and* not needing to have it all worked out before you do this!

Values Are Not Goals

Values can never be fully achieved. This quality of acting on values means that while you may or may not achieve particular goals, the value, the broad direction, is there throughout. It is there because you choose this direction to guide your actions and choices.

As values can never be fully achieved, they also *can't be totally failed*. Mistakes and wrong turns do not cancel out a value: it is still there, whether or not you make progress in your goals. It may be that through the mistakes you become more skilled, and more attuned to what is required to complete a goal. An example of this would be learning a musical instrument, like the guitar, perhaps as part of a valued direction of being creative or expressing yourself. Learning a musical instrument involves making *heaps* of mistakes! Through playing the wrong notes when learning a musical piece, you become more skilled in noticing where you are placing your fingers, can hear the harmonic difference between notes that fit with a melody and those that are from the wrong scale, and develop a sense of timing. Throughout all of these experiences of becoming a fluid and skilled guitarist, there will be the valued direction – and as you become more skilled, the options will open up further about how you may express yourself creatively on the instrument. But you can only get there by being willing to make all those mistakes.

Although setting and pursuing goals can be useful, there is a downside to having goals without broader directions. Goals are binary: you are either pursuing a goal or you have completed it. When we focus on goals alone, we can sometimes end up in a pattern of 'catch-up', with the goal there ahead of us, and feeling the distance between where we are and where we want to be. This distance can be painful and invite a variety of unhelpful responses, such as trying to be a perfectionist about achieving the goal, or 'analysis paralysis', where you spend time being indecisive about what actions to take, and become stuck in your head with various reasons and stories why you did or did not do something.

Instead, values provide the direction, and goals are like signs that you are heading in the way that you have chosen. As directions are not goals, this means that the direction is beyond and around any particular goal that you set. Values provide flexibility: there may be a lot of different ways in which you can embody the qualities of action that are important to you and, because you are choosing this, you can always make another and different choice as you learn *from your own experience* of what it is like to live by the direction you set.

So, you can ask yourself these questions about your **goals**:

- What purpose is this goal serving?
- What will it enable me *to do* that is meaningful?

Hopefully, this can clarify the **purpose** for pursuing a goal. Sometimes we can become so focused on achieving goals, that we lose sight of the purpose. Asking these questions can allow for that 'bird's-eye view' of the purposes for all the choices and actions, striving and discomfort that may come with living your life. In our experience it can be useful to check the purpose of your goals.

Goals or Values? Finding the Direction

Here are some answers people have given us about their purpose for living:

- 'I want to be rich'.
- 'I want to be a psychologist'.
- 'I want to be loved'.
- 'I want to be the fastest runner in the world'.

How do these sound to you? Notice that each of these is a **goal** (with varying degrees of difficulty required to achieve them!). What makes each of them a goal is this binary quality of *either it is done or it isn't*. While there is nothing necessarily wrong with setting goals and devoting your energies to achieving them, what is missing from each of these is the **purpose**.

For many of us, our life goals may be *unexamined*, and asking simply 'In what direction am I going by doing this?' may help us to gain a perspective about how we are choosing to spend our life energies.

A further question that can help to get a clearer view of purpose is to ask yourself what you would be *doing* after you achieved this goal. What are the life directions of those actions about?

In our experience, when exploring and constructing valued directions with people, we sometimes hear them describe dearly held goals where the direction is unclear. It can be that a goal has been pursued for a long period that was a *means to an end*, but has become the purpose for living.

For example, we asked Dave – who wanted to be rich – about what he imagined would happen when he achieved this goal. Dave described that he would be comfortable, never have to worry again, be able to provide for his sister and elderly parents, and be considered a success by other people. Interestingly, it was hard for him to imagine what he would be doing day-to-day if he were rich.

When we explored what pursuing this goal was like, Dave said that the goal was constantly on his mind, so that it was difficult to consider other things important to him. Dave also admitted that he felt that he was a 'loser' until this goal was achieved. Life was passing him by as he spent his hours trying to find ways of working harder and thinking of ways to become rich.

In this case, while *caring for his family* through providing a monetary safety net was important, there were also other, escape-based purposes to Dave's goal (such as trying to avoid being seen as a 'loser' by himself and others, and not having to worry again). On reflection, it also appeared that pursuing this goal was resulting in Dave not being very in the present with his family, and spending a lot of time worrying and ruminating. Placing a high importance on the approval of other people (which, as we will explain further, we have little influence over), also meant that Dave was dependent on something out of his control.

We could explore whether there were broader and more flexible ways to pursue at least one of the directions that this goal was about: acting and making choices that were concerned with caring for the family. This perspective appeared to help construct a number of ideas of things that could be done *now, in line with purpose.* For example, rather than scheming about various ways to get rich, Dave could instead be spending time, appreciating the present moment; listening more carefully and supporting his sister rather than saying 'I'm too busy for this now', and connecting with others. It seemed that rather than putting *life on hold,* and waiting until he was rich, there were moments now where vital, purposeful choices and actions could happen.

For your own goals, it can be useful to slow down and connect with the actual purpose. Is the purpose of this goal to escape from thoughts and feelings about yourself, where life is incomplete until you achieve the goal? If so, is there the possibility of finding a goal connected to a purpose that would involve you **approaching** life, even if this involves discomfort, uncertainty, pain?

There can be times when we have pursued goals over a long period and yet, when we reflect, it was unclear what all this striving has been about.

Noticing purpose also helps us to recognise those times when **doing less may mean more**. If you have been a strongly goal-oriented and 'busy' person, it may be useful to see what the *purpose* of all that activity has been. Has it had a sense of vitality? Or has some of it been about 'staying busy', keeping you from thinking about things, or coming into contact with worries or issues that are painful? As in our earlier discussion of auto-pilot, has 'staying busy' meant that you have been out of contact with the present moment, missing out on experiences and opportunities that might have been available to you?

An example of a purpose that leads to a goal might be to 'act in a loving way'. This is a value because it is broad: there are many ways to act lovingly. It is a value because it will never be fully achieved – there will always be more moments that offer the choice of acting lovingly. In contrast, a goal stemming from this value might be something like: 'When I get home tonight I will focus on sharing with my partner how my day has been, and listen carefully to how it has been for them.' This is a goal because there is a clear choice or action being taken, there is a place when the action will happen, and a person that the action will happen to. It will either be achieved or not, and if it is part of a broader direction of acting lovingly, then it is a values-based action.

Later on we will discuss some ways to use goals as part of choosing and acting based on your values.

This neatly brings us to another point about using values to guide behaviour.

Values Are Not about Pleasing Other People or 'Fitting In'

Values are *personally chosen* life directions. While our societies and cultures have values, they are not chosen by us, although you may find that you would choose a number of them. Many people find that their lives have been largely defined by pleasing important others, such as their parents and extended family, so that it is difficult to think of their own personal values.

There are also actions that we take to 'fit in' with others. Again, some of these you would choose to do, while others are driven by habit or a fear of standing out. You may find that in some ways your struggles lead you to **play small** in your life, in order to draw attention away from yourself and to avoid risking criticism and rejection from others.

There is also a big disadvantage in always focusing your life on pleasing important others, to the cost of other sources of meaning: other people may not be as reliable or consistent in noticing your efforts and rewarding them. It sometimes can be like being *held hostage to whether or not someone notices and acknowledges what you are doing.* While you wait for acknowledgement (if it ever comes) you are missing out on discovering ways to free yourself, by learning how to please yourself and try out other directions you would like to take.

Earlier in the *Aware* chapter of the book we talked about living a life more deliberately in the moment, and less on auto pilot. As we live more in the moment, we have the opportunity to *choose* more how we want to act, and what qualities of action we wish to show: this means that we have the chance to act differently in those moments where we automatically do things to 'fit in'. You may discover as you live more in the moment, that many of your previous actions were about pleasing others (or at least not risking experiencing their criticism), and from the position of choice, you would not do as many of these things. Focusing your actions on your own personal values can enable you to be in contact with a source of meaning and purpose, available even when others aren't around.

Marcia tends put her own needs after everyone else's. This means that while she acts as a caring daughter, friend and work colleague, it also meant that she would frequently become overwhelmed and stressed about the amount of stuff that she agreed to. Marcia would spend her time worrying about whether she was doing enough so that other people would like her. It was hard for Marcia to even think about what she wanted out of life – she just knew that she couldn't keep living this way. Marcia was held hostage to other people's approval, and scared of doing anything that would lead to disapproval. So she wouldn't take any chances. To help Marcia, we explored the *difference between being 'nice' and being kind*. From this perspective, kindness might be doing the caring thing, even if it means that someone is not happy with you. And being nice was really a way of escaping from anxiety. By slowing down and getting in touch with the ways that she could be kind, Marcia discovered that there were areas of her life that she had neglected (an intimate relationship, interests, her own self-care) due to the fear of being rejected. By using the *Open* and *Aware* skills she was able to make room for the possibility of rejection, and act assertively when it was necessary.

So for yourself, an important question to consider is the degree to which you are doing things to avoid upsetting others, trying to make sure that they are pleased with you, or to fit in or look good. What is the cost of that for you? Are there things you would do, even if no one ever knew that you did them? Are there things that are important to you that may even invite the disapproval of significant others? If no one else could ever see you doing these things, would you still do them?

And Finally, Values Aren't (More) Rules!

If you have noticed the way your mind works, just like the rest of the human race, then it is possible that you have noticed how it seems to change values into rules! Instead of living your life the way that you have been, NOW YOU MUST ACT ON YOUR VALUES! The other variation is when it seems that considering values just seems to add another burden, and your mind says, 'Well, here's another way that you are messing up things. As well as your problems you are also not being true to your values.'

We think that you have enough rules in your life. Instead, we are inviting you to consider the rules that you live by. Do they help you to act like the type of person you really hope and dream of acting like? We aren't big fans of rules that tie you up, give you more burdens beyond what it is like to be a feeling, living, breathing human. Life is tough enough!

So, values aren't more rules. Instead, values may be considered *guides* (the direction thing again), like a small light on a path, or a compass point (more on this later). There may or may not be a clear direction ahead of you: sometimes it will involve a leap of faith. Values are not shackles: instead, acting on them is about exercising *your freedom to choose*. Being connected to your life directions can mean that in each moment you are free to choose.

A useful way to describe values is to think of them as being similar to compass points. Choosing a life direction can be like deciding to head west. A compass will provide you with an orientation toward a direction and you may be able to point the compass toward something westwards (like a tree on the horizon) to maintain your bearing. Reaching the tree will mean that you have gone west, although the direction also extends beyond where you have ended up – in fact, heading west never ends! So, when choosing a life direction and taking steps, it may be that there are markers on the journey giving you clues that you are heading in the direction you have chosen. For example, if your direction is acting like a loving person, then goals like being in a relationship may be a marker, although there are plenty more loving actions to take beyond finding someone to love! So, as we described above, values are directions – guiding our course, but never actually achieved. There is always more to do in the directions we choose. And, of course, we can always decide to choose a different direction.

Constructing Values

The ability to connect with important life directions, to imagine the type of person you would want to act like, and choose to act in that way, is the essence of valuing. As we described above, choosing life directions is more like being a builder than an archaeologist, you are *constructing* rather than **uncovering** your values. Values are chosen life directions: you are free to choose *right now* so that your actions can be about something bigger, more vital and more important. What life purposes would you choose to construct?

In the rest of this chapter, we're going to cover some ways in which you can be inspired in your constructing, by being aware of your own experiences, the perspective-taking of others, and connecting with highly meaningful moments in your life.

Connecting with the Observing Self

One way that we can connect with valued directions we'd like to pursue is through *perspective-taking*. As we described in the *Aware* chapter, flexible perspective-taking is a valuable skill to strengthen. It enables you to source the wisdom of a greater variety of ways of looking at life, rather than the usual version that the Thinking Self serves up. We are going to guide you through some exercises that are about different forms of your own perspective (cultivating your Observing Self), and then through some exercises that are about other peoples' perspective.

Your Own Perspective

You may have noticed in the course of your life that your perspective about some things has changed, no doubt influenced by the experiences you have had, and just through getting older. We are going to invite you to take the perspective of yourself from a later point in your life, let's say from your eightieth birthday (if you haven't got there already).

EXERCISE: Your Eightieth Birthday

Imagine that it is your eightieth birthday and on this day you are looking back on your life, the choices you have made and what they were about. All of your memories, the people around you, the way your body feels, and the place where you are reflect these choices.

Take a moment to connect with your desires in the here and now: who and what would you really hope would be there, as you look back on your life?

For example, there may be memories of acting in a loving way, or connecting with others, or making a contribution with work. You might have memories of consistently striving toward something, courageous moments where you took some bold actions, or simply took the time to switch from being on autopilot to living your life more deliberately and purposefully. If you could imagine that you had acted boldly, and made your actions be about something important in your life, then what would you be able to look back on as an older person? For a few moments stay with that . . .

Let that scene dissolve in your mind. Now let's imagine that instead, on your eightieth birthday, that you have lived a life where you did not act on what's important to you, that instead you were guided by avoiding feeling uncomfortable, trying very hard not to have unwanted feelings or doubts. From this honest perspective, now that you have lived a long life, what would you **fear** has made up your life, if you did not act on your values?

Now let that scene dissolve, and come back to the here and now. From these perspectives – imagining a life of purpose and a life ruled by your fear – what would your choices be now? What would you use to guide your choices and actions?

_____

_____

_____

_____

_____

_____

_____

_____

Everything Changes

You have lived for this long on the planet – have you noticed how things continue to change? And how you are continuing to change too? Your body is getting older, second by second, you learn more, perhaps get a little wiser each day. You can look back at photographs and videos of you and see a younger version, who had not experienced as much as you have now.

And one day you are going to die. There will be a day when you take the last of all the breaths you've taken, at the very end of your life.

Notice now that breathing is something you have done all your life, throughout all the experiences that you have had. From this perspective notice how much has changed and already passed in your life. Already most of what you have worried over and thought about has ceased to exist (like a comment someone made that upset you last year, or an argument with someone recently).

From this current breath, what do you want your life to be about now? What are the things in life that matter, in a deeper sense? What could you imagine from this perspective doesn't matter? From this broader perspective, and using the wisdom you have in knowing what lasts and is of value, and what isn't . . . what would you choose for the precious energy of your life to be about?

_____

_____

_____

_____

_____

_____

The Perspective of Others

Another way to develop a helpful perspective for your chosen directions and actions is to get in touch with how other people may view them.

In the *Aware* chapter of the book we introduced the idea of using a Team of Advisers to help develop flexible perspectives on the experiences you are having and the stories that your mind tells you about yourself. Here are some further ways that you could do this.

EXERCISE: Your Best Friend

We want to invite you to get in touch with how your closest friend would describe what you are about. If we were able to interview your best friend, a person who knows you very well, and ask them to describe you at your best, what would you hope that your friend would say about you? What things do you stand for in your life? What kind of friend are you, when you are at your best? Imagine that this friend is looking at you with kind eyes, knows what you can struggle with, and gently and lovingly describes the moments when you are acting with the qualities that your friend appreciates ... what would they say? Write this in the space below.

_____

_____

_____

_____

_____

_____

_____

_____

_____

_____

EXERCISE: Your Heroes and People You Admire

It can help to focus on the people you admire – your heroes and inspirations. The qualities that these people display may point to the type of person that you would like to act like. This could be someone in your family or community. It could be someone who has achieved something amazing.

For example, many people admire Nelson Mandela, both for the sacrifice he made to the struggle for the end of Apartheid in South Africa, and for his stance on promoting reconciliation after his release from Robben Island and when he became president of South Africa. Mandela's response to his imprisonment and release was to stand strongly for a process of reconciliation among the people of his country. This was a remarkable set of actions, considering the circumstances of the treatment of people under the Apartheid regime, and his personal struggle. Mandela could have endorsed retribution, but didn't. If you can, imagine what it would have felt like to be systematically discriminated against in the land of your birth, to be imprisoned, to be away from your partner, family and friends for twenty-seven years. What feelings do you think Nelson Mandela experienced? How did he manage to make room for anger, sadness and memories, while standing for a peaceful path to a united South Africa? Mandela was not a super-human, although his choices and actions are admirable. Instead, he was a human being, with the same capacity as we all have to struggle with experiences and to feel the pain of making sacrifices. We'd like to suggest that in many ways Mandela demonstrates what it is like to live a value-driven life.

Think about the person you admire. What qualities do you appreciate about this person? What values do they embody for you?

Again, you may notice that your mind might make the process difficult, possibly by saying things like 'you could never be like that', or 'this person is special/ talented' or reminding you of the times when you have not lived up to the values that this person displays. As before, we would like you to gently notice what your mind is saying, and just observe it as you would a butterfly on your hand or the wind rustling through trees. If you are willing for this experience to be part of getting in touch with the inspirations in your life, there may be room for your mind to generate these thoughts and images.

And now think about how your heroes and inspirations engage with their values in the face of the challenging experiences that they have? (As all humans have.)

Imagine that there have been times when your hero may have found it hard to persist with their plans or to change direction when things did not work out. Think about how this person may have had occasions when they found it hard to face the day, or get out of the bed in the morning, or may have been worried about something. How do you think they connected with their purpose, at these times? Imagine your hero taking a deep breath, connecting with their valued direction, and stepping forward ... taking their doubts and fears with them. Those doubts and fears are part of your hero's experience, while they did the things that you admire them for.

Now, shift your attention to where you are today, the moment you are in, what you are noticing in terms of how your body feels, what you can sense from the sounds, sights, smells around you, what you can touch, and the mental experiences from your mind. Notice that the value that your inspiration displayed is also here in this moment, through you taking these moments to connect with them. . . . Now what opportunities are there in this moment to take action in this direction? This could involve the smallest step. Look for a way that you can embody the value that your hero demonstrates; now it is your turn to take steps to show you care about this direction too!

Trying on Different Fashions

As we described above, there are times when we can be unsure about whether a direction is where we want to go, and *trying out* acting from a value will put us in contact with the experience to inform our choice. At these times we are suggesting that choosing directions and taking action may be more like trying on different clothes and seeing how they fit. Like fashion, you can always change your 'look' another time. By seeing what works as you try new things, you can let your experience be your guide: it might be that choices that your mind says 'aren't you' open up your life in ways that your mind could not imagine! Just like changing your clothes you could try out being free to choose to act in different ways.

Guiding Stars

What are your guiding stars? Another way of approaching values is like they are 'guiding stars' – in ancient times sailors used the stars to navigate the oceans, setting a course by the location of constellations.

For you, what are the stars on the horizon in the directions you would choose to head? Some of your stars may be bright and clear, while others are faintly glimmering through the clouds. Could you set the course by them?

The Light on the Hill

A similar idea is to think of the steps in your life as toward a Light on a Hill. Australian Prime Minister Ben Chifley used this metaphor at the Labor Party conference in 1949, as a way of describing his party's ultimate objective – to improve the lives of people in Australia and beyond:

> I try to think of the Labor movement ... as a movement bringing something better to the people, better standards of living, greater happiness to the mass of the people. We have a great objective – the Light on the Hill – which we aim to reach by working for the betterment of mankind not only here but anywhere we may give a helping hand. If it were not for that, the Labor movement would not be worth fighting for.

When you look to the horizon of your life, beyond this moment, then what is the Light on the Hill for you? In what direction are you stepping in order to take a step closer to the Light? The Light on the Hill can be anything you choose – what would make that light burn brightly so that even in the darkest times there is some illumination for your steps?

There will be moments where it may help to look up to see the Light on the Hill: when you are experiencing sadness, regret and turmoil. Some of these moments will be like going through a swamp full of dirt, rubbish and leftovers, where things look ugly and smell awful! And on top of that, being bitten by lots of nasty little insects! You may have thoughts like 'This is unpleasant and boring' or 'it's not worth the effort' or 'why didn't anyone tell me about the swamp?': all invitations to give up on the direction you are taking. We'd suggest that using your *Open* and *Aware* skills you could notice your Light on the Hill and freely let your feelings and thoughts go in whatever way they want to, while moving forward in the swamp.

Sometimes a purposeful life may be helped by choosing to experience what you are experiencing, being open to it, not fighting it or needing it to be different than it is!

Learning from the 'Peak Moments' of Your Life

What are the moments when you feel most alive, vital and engaged?

Sometimes understanding what you would choose as

directions in life comes from paying attention to the wisdom of the 'Peak Moments' that you have experienced.

Peak Moments are times when it has seemed like your life had purpose, when you felt that there was nowhere else you needed to be, that you were fulfilling something important. They might be big, significant moments that had an important impact on your life. Or they might be small moments that have been highly meaningful to you personally.

Paying attention to these peak moments and what they may say about what is meaningful to you, could be part of the 'getting of wisdom' and 'living a rich, full life'.

In reflecting on your Peak Moments, consider also the times *when it has hurt to care*. It can be that the moments when we experience pain are also moments linked to our valued directions.

To help you with connecting with your own Peak Moments, imagine how each of these examples could be occasions where it 'hurts to care':

- Taking a risk by asking out on a first date someone you find super-attractive.

- Persisting with completing a difficult project, despite your doubts and fears.

- Standing up for something important (morals, a social issue, politics).

- Deciding and committing to stop doing something that helped you escape but also involved personal cost (stop drinking, taking drugs).

- Deciding to change jobs and taking a pay cut, to do something that had more 'heart'.

- Telling a parent that you loved them (when you hadn't done that before).

- Coming out to your family (telling them that you are gay).

- Making a commitment to do something that involved courage (becoming a parent, having an operation).

- Holding your newborn child.

- Savouring a sensory experience (admiring a beautiful place, drinking a great cup of coffee, listening to moving music, smelling a flower, stroking a pet).

There have probably been moments in your life when you have been brave, been at your best, stood for something important . . . even if it may not have 'felt' like it at the time. Here is an example of a Peak Moment that one of us (EM) experienced:

Several years ago I took my mother on a road trip to visit her eldest brother, who was in a nursing home and didn't have too long to live. My mother had not seen her brother in five years, since he had become disabled and moved into the home. My elderly mother isn't so great with travelling by herself, so there wasn't much chance of her going to visit her brother, who lived about a six hours' drive away. I offered to drive her – knowing that it was going to be a hard trip: my uncle had been a central person in both of our lives, a kind and intelligent man who had put his family first. It was going to be upsetting to see him in poor health. My mother was hesitant, but then agreed to my offer. The trip to the town my uncle lived in was good – spending hours talking and connecting with my mother, probably the first time in many years that we had spoken so deeply about our lives. We arrived late, stayed with some relatives and planned to see my uncle the next morning.

The next day we went to the nursing home. The staff were friendly to us as we walked into the main room where all the residents were sitting in their chairs, having breakfast and getting ready for the day. I looked around the room for my uncle. At first I could not see him, neither could my mother. And then I did: in a corner of the room, sitting hunched and pale in a chair that dwarfed him, was my uncle. He looked so different from the man I had known: frail, much thinner, with sunken eyes. These eyes showed recognition of us, just as my mother realised that this was her brother. She broke down in tears as I put my arms around her. I held her as we sat down next to my uncle, taking in how he was, his eyes tearfully connecting with ours. This moment, as painful as it was for me to see my uncle like this, and my mother so bereft, I would choose all over again. It was a vital, peak moment full of purpose, as I chose to be caring toward my family, while knowing it would probably involve deep sadness (which it did).

EXERCISE: Peak Moment

We are going to invite you to connect with a moment where you had a real sense of vitality – a moment when you were really engaged with life; when you seemed truly to be living. This moment can be a big, significant occasion or a small time of connection and purpose.

So, use your *Open* skills to first be in the present moment, getting in touch with where you are, the position your body is in, what you can hear, the way that you feel. See if you can make room for whatever you notice in this moment.

And now we invite you to remember a moment that seemed vital, important . . . when you felt connected, that this was what life was about. . . . Notice if your mind, and bodily sensations, make this seem difficult or complicated.

Notice where you were in this moment. What did you see around you? Were you by yourself or with other people? What posture was your body in?

Notice what you were doing in this moment. Were you engaged in action, or simply appreciating what was happening?

Notice what it felt like to be there, in this moment. How did your body feel? What emotions did you notice?

And now connect with the meaning of this moment for you. What makes it vital and gives it purpose? Breathe in and around that, let yourself connect with it, even if it involves gently noticing and opening up to feelings and thoughts that you would usually struggle with.

If this moment were part of a broader direction in your life, if it extended in front of you in that moment, and is still here today, just ahead of you, providing direction for your choices and actions . . . then what would you call that broader purpose or direction? It's OK if words are hard to find, just let yourself connect with this.

If you were to be guided by this direction today, then what choices would that involve? How different would this be from how you've been acting today? In terms of being *Open* and *Aware*, what experiences may it involve making peace with, or being willing to have, to act like that person?

Finally, if you can imagine that the direction is connected to you, and is just in front of you, as you get in touch again with the present moment, what do you notice?

It may help to write some impressions below about the Peak Moment you connected with. What are the moments when you feel most alive, vital and engaged?

_____

_____

_____

_____

_____

VALUES EXERCISE: Choose Four Areas of Life

We are going to invite you to consider four areas of your life, and reflect on the qualities of action you would choose to engage in these areas.

For many of us there are probably four main areas of life (there may be more, of course): what we do with those closest to us (Relationships), what we do to make a contribution and maybe make a living (Work), how we look after ourselves (Health), and what we do for pleasure and enjoyment (Fun). At different points in our lives we can regard these areas as more or less important, maybe making choices and taking actions in the direction of our values, or doing things that are not taking us forward, or perhaps even moving away from the direction we would choose!

There are also other life areas that can be important to people, of course: such as how they act in a spiritual way, as an engaged citizen, or by striving to do their best in athletic, intellectual or creative areas.

We would like you to reflect on each of these four areas of life, in the worksheet below.

First, we would like you consider, at the moment, how **important** taking action in each of these areas is. You can rate this with a score from 0–10, where 0 signifies that it is unimportant to you, and 10 that it is highly important. The importance of this area, of course, can change – this is just how you see it today.

Next, choose one of the areas that you have rated as more important than the others – don't worry if there are areas that are equally important because you will be able to describe each of your important areas in this exercise.

Once You Have Chosen an Area:

Now we would like you to connect with how you would like to act in this area of your life. Take a few moments to get in touch with this life area, and the ways that you have taken action in the past: the actions you have been pleased with, and the moments when you really lived close to your values. Picture one of these scenes: imagine the way your body felt, what you were experiencing with your senses, the way you held and moved your body, while acting in line with your chosen directions. You could think of this as a Peak Moment.

Get in touch with those 'Peak Moments' when you have acted like the person you would choose to act like if you had had more opportunities. Connect now with your hopes and dreams for this part of your life: what direction would you be heading in, and where is it possible that more Peak Moments could happen? What actions and choices would be part of this direction?

And now, consider your actions over the past week or so. How **consistent** have you been in heading in the direction that you would choose? You can rate this with a score from 0–10, where 0 signifies that you have done nothing in the direction of the value, and 10 means you have been acting as close to this direction as possible. And again, your consistency in acting in this area can change, as it has in the past and will in the future.

Watch Your Mind Work Its Magic

Now, notice what your mind may be saying about how consistently you've been living according to your chosen directions. If your mind is like ours, then thank it for the comparisons, criticisms and other things it is bringing up that can make this exercise difficult to do! Also notice the emotions and feelings that you have while connecting with your chosen directions and actions this week. We are going to suggest that you make room for any experiences that invite you to struggle or get caught up: connecting with your values involves connecting with the things you care deeply about, and your pain will be close by as a result. Being *Open* to your experiences and *Aware* of your thoughts can be particularly helpful when connecting with your values so you can get *Active*.

Now Make Some Plans!

We would like to invite you to connect with your values, and consider how you would take a step in the direction you would choose in the next day or so. This could the smallest step, yet would still mean you were acting more consistently with your values. What will this small step be? Imagine where you would be when you took this small step. Who would you be with? What movements would your body be making? Imagine taking this action and notice what may show up in terms of thoughts and feelings. Could you make room for these? Could you be willing to feel this way and think this way while you are going on this journey? Practise your *Open* and *Aware* skills and see if the answer could be yes. Now make a plan for when you will take this action.

AREAS OF LIFE WORKSHEET

Life Area	Small Step	Importance (0–10)	Consistency (0–10)	What Is Your Mind Saying to You about This Step?
Relationships				
Work/Making a Contribution				
Health				
Fun/Leisure				

**EXERCISE: Noticing the Opportunities to Take
Your Valued Actions Now**

We want to invite you to start noticing your daily life, and the amount that you are acting on your values now. This exercise should also help you to notice the *opportunities* to act on your values from day to day.

From moment to moment you are here in the present, even at the times when your mind engulfs you so that it is difficult to see that you are here, now. If you slow down, you can experience how each breath you take is a link to the present moment. Your body feels what it feels in this present moment: this is the difference between the experience of our bodies and where we can disappear to in our minds!

So, building on the *Aware* and *Open* skills, we are going to use the anchor of your breathing and the connection you have with the sensations in your body, to practise becoming open to the opportunities in the present moment to act on your values.

Imagining waking up in your bed with the day before you. You feel the way you do when you wake up in the morning, and you can notice what it feels like for your body to be lying in the bed, the way that your mind starts up with thoughts about this moment and the day ahead. Before you get out of bed, come into contact with a valued direction. Imagine it like a path extending before you, where various moments in the day ahead will be like little destinations on that path. Notice, if you can, whether there is a pull to be acting on this value, any bits where you mind is telling you that it must be like this or that, or that you have to act like this. Notice the pull of this, and see if you can soften around it, to just let it be there like the other experiences that you have practised willingness toward before. Notice anything that seems to make this harder than it is: the choice to just be with how it is to care about what you are doing.

Acting on Your Values

Here are a few different ways that you might think about consciously acting on your values.

The Ripple Effect

Our colleagues in Scotland, Gordon Mitchell and Amy McArthur, talk about how acting on values can create a 'ripple effect' in your life. Have you ever dropped a stone into a still pond? The ripples in the water extend out from where the stone has broken the water, sometimes going out very far. When you act on your values you can see how far the ripples in your life extend. Sometimes simple actions can produce far-reaching ripples! From taking action and then seeing the effects, like the ripples on a pond, your life space may extend. Your life expanding like ripples on a pond is more likely to happen as you take more actions based on your values, rather than on your fear.

Video Gaming

What is your high score today? Another way to approach acting on values is to think of them like **getting a high score on a video game**, where each day you start at zero and see how high or far you can go. If each day is approached in this way, the pursuit of your personal best is more like a game rather than an examination you **have** to pass. And there is always the chance to see how high a score you can get the next day, even if today's score is not near your personal best or a high score.

The Daily Charge

What activities in your life recharge you, and which ones drain you? By using your *Aware* skills you can pause and assess where your energy levels are, and think about *how to* create a life that charges you up more than it drains you. Notice here that we are talking about a life with both kinds of activities: acting on your values at times will be energising, and also at times be tiring, exhausting. For example, connecting with friends may recharge you at times (e.g. a great conversation, enjoying your friend's wedding, getting closer to someone), similarly, connecting may tire you (e.g. an honest conversation about a problem in a friendship, caring for a friend during a challenging time). Reflect on your daily life, the feelings and experiences you have, and the connection with your chosen life directions. It may surprise you about the activities that drain and recharge you, when you pay attention to the effects in your life.

Useful Metaphors

Sailing Metaphor

Sailors use the energy available in the moment from the wind, to head in the direction they wish to go. Acting on chosen values may be like the process of sailing, where a **sailor** adjusts the sails to make the most of the wind that is available, and may plot a course, tackling with the wind, which may not be blowing in the direction that is intended. Acting on values is like this: you use the energy of the situation you have, rather than the one you wish for, just like using the wind that is available, rather than the wind speed and direction that a sailor would wish for. There will be moments of plain sailing, when you can hoist the spinnaker to make the most of the moment; there will be moments when there is exhilaration and fear from catching the energy available when acting on values – where your feelings will be mixed, not always 'positive'; and there may also be moments when you are in the doldrums! Again, this points to a quality of values-based actions, which is that they sometimes need to be considered separately from the feelings that arise when carrying them out. There are times when feelings can be a useful guide, but there will definitely be times when it is useful to hold those feelings, which show up when sailing in the direction you have chosen lightly, so they are not taken too seriously.

Garden Metaphor

Acting on your chosen values, and expanding your life may be like **tending a garden**. When you are starting a garden, you choose and prepare the ground for growth and plant the seeds. Then you need to stand back and have faith that the seeds will germinate. While at first you may not see the evidence, if you tend them consistently the green shoots will break through the soil in time. If you are impatient and break open the soil to check, or decide to plant more seeds somewhere else in the garden, you will not see the fruits of your labours (planting seeds can be like the early stages of learning an instrument, trying a new hobby, socialising with new people or starting a new job). During the time the seeds have taken to produce flowers you will have been looking after the garden, by paying attention and working steadily (e.g. changing a habit such as exercising more, not acting on urges). There will be times when you need to give up your control to the weather and environment supporting the process of growth (e.g. opening up in a relationship, taking a risk, trusting someone, letting go of control). There will also be times when you are acting against the weather (either it's raining too much or not raining at all). You will notice that some plants take a little longer to grow and require nurturing a little more to bring forth their potential. A garden needs seasons to vary for the plants to grow, so it may be that the times when you can take certain actions may depend on what is available and happening around you (e.g. applying for a job when there is a vacancy; travelling when you have a holiday). Like a garden there may be a process of weeding out and concentrating your energies on the plants you want to develop. It may be about balance: you can't have it all, and certain things involve a greater investment of time and energy than you can offer at the moment, due to your other commitments. This may mean some tough choices about what you want your garden to look like.

MAKING A COMMITMENT WORKSHEET[3]

'I am here now, *Open* to the way I feel, *Aware* of my thoughts, *Actively* doing what I care about.'

I am	Notice if you are getting caught up with any unhelpful stories about yourself. Let go of these stories if they seem to be in the way of acting on your values.	Indicate when you are Noticing.
Here now	Get in contact with being Here Now – noticing you are breathing, what you are feeling in your body, where you are. Let go of distracting thoughts about things that are not in your present control.	Indicate when you are Here Now.

3 Adapted from Moran, D.J., *Building Safety Commitment* (Valued Living Books, 2013).

Open	Allow yourself to feel what you are feeling, without trying to control your emotions. Open up and be willing to have these emotions while doing what you care about.	Describe these feelings.
Aware	Notice the thoughts that show up while you are doing what you care about. Let them float by if they are not part of what you are doing; let them come along for the ride if they are. They are experiences rather than guides.	List these thoughts.
Actively doing	Move your body to do the thing you planned.	Describe the things you were going to do. What will others see you doing?
What I care about	What direction are you choosing to step toward?	Describe this chosen life direction. What are you wanting to stand for, in this moment?

Keep Going: the Essence of Committed Action

Committed Action involves using the *Open* and *Aware* skills.

As we have described earlier, pursuing a full life, rich with meaning, is perhaps **more about the journey than the destination**. It can be useful to notice when we hold on too tightly to pursuing achievements and completing goals. This can lead us to lose contact with the present moment and get further entangled with our minds. An extension of this is when the storytelling that our minds engage in, invites us to focus on the importance of achievement as *part of who we are*. As we can see, when our own stories get in the way of doing the things we care deeply about, it may be an opportunity to hold these stories lightly so we don't take them too seriously, like we would hold a balloon tied to a string.

EXERCISE: Visualising Goals[4]

A brief exercise at this point may help you to get in touch with the quality of acting that we are talking about.

Think about an important goal that you would like to achieve: really get in touch with what is important to you about this goal, and imagine that you are now at the moment of achieving it. Get in touch with what it would feel like in terms of your bodily sensations,

---

4 Adapted from Ciarrochi, J., & Kashdan, T. B. (Eds.), *Mindfulness, Acceptance, and Positive Psychology: The Seven Foundations of Well-Being* (New Harbinger Publications, 2013).

emotions, thoughts and urges. Notice what the experience of achieving something important is like. It may be that you have experiences of feeling proud, relieved, a sense of accomplishment or of having turned a corner in your life.

Now, let that scene pass and get in touch again with being here now, with whatever anchor lets you get into this moment (for example, your breathing, posture or the experience of simply sitting in your chair).

Now get in touch again with the important goal that you want to achieve. Imagine that you are going to take the very next step toward this goal today . . . in fact, you are going to put down this book and carry out that action *now*. Get in touch with the experiences you are having in imagining this step – what does this feel like in your body? What urges are you experiencing? What thoughts are going through your mind? What emotions are you experiencing?

Now, unless you did actually go and carry out the next step toward the goal, it is probable that **you might have noticed some experiences that could invite you to struggle**. If you did, see if this is similar to your experience of pursuing goals in your life. It may be that sometimes pursuing goals and taking steps is an experience that does not invite you to struggle; at other moments the very thought of taking the step brings along strong feelings and urges to struggle. There may be wisdom in noticing the difference between the experience of stepping closer to achieving a goal and what comes at the point of achievement.

Qualities of Committed Action

How does it feel when engaging in *Active* skills?

As we discussed earlier when talking about Peak Moments, taking committed action can lead to times when you feel vital, connected, and have a strong sense that what you are doing is **purposeful**.

An important part of the wisdom of committed action is to use your *Open* and *Aware* skills to notice that there are times when the feelings that you have are not pleasant or wanted. You may experience sensations, thoughts, memories and urges that invite you to struggle or that get you very attached to stories about yourself or the situation. For example, feeling vulnerable or more insecure when you go into 'uncertain' situations (such as a new job or starting a relationship).

So, thoughts and feelings may not be the best guide while acting on values. However, there will be an increased number of times when things are *meaningful*. You can notice your actions are for the purpose *you have chosen*, rather than for the purpose that fear or unwillingness would choose.

This is **a life of approach, rather than running away**.

Your Life as a 'Work in Progress'

If life can be approached more like a *work in progress*, experiences of failure, frustration and uncertainty are a part of progress rather than threats to it (despite how much they feel like that). In this book we are suggesting that rather than trying to achieve a *state of perfection* (which is highly unlikely to happen, and you may have even learned so far that it can cost you dearly), an approach to life may be to let your experiences **shape you**. By practising the skills of being *Open* and *Aware*, you are better able to *learn from experience*. This increases the chance that you will stop doing things that don't work, as well as when situations change, you have the flexibility to adjust and make the most of them. Noticing that your mind makes predictions about how things will turn out, and comparing this with experience can be an interesting exercise.

We are suggesting that it may be useful to redefine what is a *successful* life. The Work in Progress Life redefines 'success' as **working toward something** (i.e. living by your chosen life directions). Compare this to a life that defines success by 'winning', or the outward appearance of success. If you have tried to live that type of life, how has it worked out? If you find that the rewards have been few and far between, or do not last, and your worth as a person is on the line each time you either succeed or fail, there may some benefit in living as a Work in Progress.

Life as a Work in Progress may mean that you are practising **flexible persistence**. This approach is about noticing the moments to use the *Open* and *Aware* skills, to learn from experience *and* stick to acting on your values. A value-driven life may mean that you become more skilled over time, that you become wiser in your choices, and that you appreciate the moments that you have.

Persistence can sound like a 'thing' you have (like having red hair or being tall). Just like we have suggested at other times in this book, it may be more useful to consider descriptions like this as *qualities of action*. Persistence is simply a collection of actions that have occurred, across changing circumstances. We would propose that making actions part of heading in a valued direction can help you to keep on track, both in moments when it feels easy to do, and in moments when it is hard to do. Over time, as you act on your values in this way, you will be demonstrating **persistence**!

How We Organise Our Lives to Engage in Valued Actions

We are going to suggest that choosing and acting on values is going to involve changing some habits. One way to think about habits is as if they are like water channels that are carved into sand over time. They take time to develop, and the erosion of old channels remains, even as water is diverted elsewhere. So, your old habits will remain a part of your history. There may be times when you engage in old habits or at least feel the pull to do so. This is like an old channel that water (your energy) can flow down. By being *Open* and *Aware* to this, you can devote your energies to organising your daily life to support your *flexible persistence*.

Here are some ways to organise yourself to show 'flexible persistence':

- Break tasks down into smaller steps; make a goal about a step and just focus on that for today.

- Make SMART goals (Specific, Measurable, Achievable,

Relevant, Time-Bound) – frequently we can set goals that are vague, unrealistic for the time available or the resources around us. It can provide clarity to ask the following questions about the goal:

◊ Specific – what do I want to achieve? Who is involved? Where will this happen? When will this happen?

◊ Measurable – how will I know when this is accomplished? Is it a matter of how much, how many?

◊ Achievable – how can the goal be achieved? Can this be done now, even when you're stretched; is there anything that needs to be in place before it can be done?

◊ Relevant – is this in the direction I want to go (my values)? Does this matter to me?

◊ Time-bound – what can I do today? In a week from now? In six months?

• Use a diary – schedule things, have reminders.

• Create cues for actions – do you use reminders or alarms to signal what to do? You could use post-it notes around the house, or notes on your phone to provide cues and remind you of commitments.

• Keep a to-do list – but make it small for each day, choose three easy and one hard thing to do every day. A common mistake people make when writing to-do lists is that they make them too long, and then become caught up with feeling overwhelmed and demotivated with the giant pile of things they have to do! Instead, slow down, notice what you want today to be about, choosing one hard thing to do, along with three easy ones. Various systems for productivity (such as the Getting Things Done method) are built around the observation that there is an advantage in limiting the amount you have to focus on, making small steps, and filing away tasks that don't require your immediate attention (reviewing at a regular point later on).

- 'Don't break the chain' – The comedian Jerry Seinfeld has a much-celebrated productivity method that demonstrates persistence. It is simply to put a cross on a calendar for every day that you do something related to your goal (e.g. exercising, writing). As the days pass you end up with a collection of crossed days, making a chain. Your goal becomes 'don't break the chain'; if you do break the chain, start another chain and see how long the next one can be.

- Take a regular time each day (possibly the evening) to reflect or record what you have done during the day, and make a plan for tomorrow. Some people find that keeping a journal or notebook helps with reflecting in this way. It provides a reminder of the values-based actions you have already taken, moments of opportunity to choose or act on values, and a way of building your *Aware* skills, to observe yourself and what your daily life offers you. Deliberately make the time to reflect on the process of living a value-driven life.

- Celebrate the small wins – our minds like to entangle us in thoughts and images about the future, when we have achieved goals, or worries about failure. While noticing these thoughts and making room for them, we encourage you to celebrate those occasions when you choose and act on values, no matter how small.

- Notice the difference between the 'getting of wisdom' and ruminating or worrying, by using your *Aware* skills. Emphasise learning from experience – when do you change course? By choosing a path of Purpose you could notice that 'it's the Journey, rather than the Destination'.

- Tell a friend or your family about your commitments and report in, share the changes you are making, and discuss the experience of committing. Making commitments to other people can increase your motivation to get things done, along with helping you step back from the feelings, urges and thoughts that appear to get in the way making value-driven choices.

- Encourage yourself and be kind. It is difficult being a human being, more so when you are being a human who makes choices based on values, rather than fear. Your *Aware* skills can strengthen your self-compassion and perspective-taking about what you are doing. What would your best friend advise you about the path you are taking? What would someone you loved say about where you are headed? There will be moments when your ability to soothe yourself will be valuable: practising this skill will enable you to keeping going, and to pick yourself up when things get tough.

- If you have trouble stepping out of your comfort zone, particularly if your mind is coming up with lots of judgements and worries, it may work better if you just tell your body what to do. Focus on the movements your muscles need to make to engage in values-based action: be specific. In ACT we like to say that the only things you can control are the muscles that move your hands, feet and mouth. Sometimes acting on your values is *just being there*, instead of somewhere else in your head!

• Remember you are always doing something. Ask yourself: what is this action or choice at the service of? Does this put me in touch with Purpose, or am I being driven by fears, playing small or just fitting in? Each moment provides the opportunity to connect with a valued direction.

The Link between 'Feeling It' and 'Doing It'

One of the interesting things that happens through engaging with the skills promoted by Acceptance and Commitment Therapy, is that the link between feeling and doing *can be weakened*. Where before you either had to have motivation, or make sure that you felt good before doing things, by practising the *Open*, *Aware* and *Active* skills you may discover that:

1.   Difficult and unwanted feelings don't have to stop you making choices and acting on your values (they aren't barriers).

2. Lack of feeling, such as those moments when you feel unmotivated, bored or numb, doesn't have to stop you either.

This is because you have introduced an additional, powerful way to motivate yourself: **Purpose**. *You are strengthening the link between valuing and doing.*

Dial 'P' for Purpose

One way to consider the Life of Approach, is that you are choosing to add another 'dial to your dashboard'. Imagine that we all have a dashboard that gives us a current read-out of how things are going (like the dashboard of a car but, instead, it is ourselves).

Due to your mind's ability to judge the experiences that you have, you already have **a dial that measures whether something you have is wanted or unwanted** (a Mind Judgement Dial). For example, you can notice how your mind judges whether a shameful memory or a painful feeling is wanted or not. As we have previously described, there may have certainly been times when you have acted on getting rid of or controlling unwanted experiences. In this book, we have encouraged you to notice that tendency for your mind to judge and evaluate experiences, particularly where acting on it has cost you dearly in terms of the directions you care about. The *Open* and *Aware* skills help you to notice this tendency for your mind to get you ensnared in these costly efforts at control.

We are now suggesting that you notice another dial on your dashboard. This dial is set by you, unlike the Mind Judgement Dial.

This dial we can call **Purpose**, and is a measure of how much you act meaningfully in the moment, based upon your values. The Purpose dial can be set high, medium or low by you, and is only set by you, rather than your experiences or your mind. Being *Open* and *Aware* does help you to set how much Purpose you want to use in any particular moment.

The Purpose dial can also help you to approach situations where your Mind Judgement Dial is already set high. For example, if you are socially anxious, then meeting new people can invite a whole number of unwanted experiences, such as feeling self-conscious, having critical and pessimistic thoughts about the conversation, and urges to limit eye contact or even leave the situation. By engaging in your *Open* and *Aware* skills you have the opportunity to set the Purpose dial to high (if you wish), for example, if meeting new people was about a value of connecting, or part of acting as a loving person. You could set the Purpose dial and choose to go into the situation, noticing that your actions and your experiences are now part of a direction you have chosen (connecting/acting lovingly).

**EXERCISE: Identifying Times That Involve
Deliberately Setting the Purpose Dial**

Imagine the next time you are likely to have lots of
Mind Judgements, and allow yourself to get caught up
with controlling your experiences. Now imagine that
while observing all these Mind Judgements (using
your *Aware* skills), that you can also notice where the
Purpose Dial is set. Is it set low? Could there be a way
of acting with Purpose in this moment, turning the
dial up? Imagine doing that. What will that involve
you practising in terms of *Open* and *Aware* skills?

Situation when my Mind Judgements are HIGH:

_____

Purpose Dial reading   LOW   MEDIUM   HIGH

Skills to expand (*Open*, *Aware*):

_____

Choices and Actions with greater Purpose:

_____

Bringing It All Together – Taking the Long Journey up a Mountain

Acting on your values can be like a journey to the summit of a mountain, spiralling around the outside of a tall spire. Each time you circle around, you go through one side that is bright and sunny. It's clear, you can see a long way ahead and the going is easy. On the other side, away from the sun, it's dark, a bit misty, icy and treacherous. Understandably, you don't like this side as much. But to reach the summit, you need to follow the track as it circles upwards, which means going through both the sunny part and also the shaded part as well. Sometimes it is difficult to see the path ahead, sometimes you feel tired and unsure of whether taking another step is what you want to do. It can be easy to get caught up with the experiences of the moment, so that you lose sight of the direction of the journey. We would invite you to approach acting on your values like it is a journey – along the way there may be wonderful moments, and there may also be times when you'd rather be anywhere else! Acting on your values may be like this, at times it is easy going, while at others it is a tougher process. There will be times when the way is clear, while at others it may seem as though the way is hidden or a real challenge. Notice that you have a choice here; you don't have to keep striving upwards. You'd be well within your rights to set up camp and never move on. But if you do want to continue on this journey, it means you will need to spend time on the side of the mountain you don't like as much. What will enable you to take another step in your direction is practising being *Open* and *Aware*, and reminding yourself that each step is a connection with your chosen direction. And, as you continue to ascend, you learn how to manage this section of the climb more effectively. You learn to go a little more slowly on the ice. You remember to be more gentle and to take your time. Also, you learn from experience that your time in both the sunny section and shaded section always eventually comes to an end, although the journey always continues.

5 Getting Unstuck from Depression and Activating

> When we're talking about depression, we're not talking about being in a bit of a bad mood ... I have been in a palace, or been meeting a president ... and I've had to pinch myself so hard on the thigh it scars ... I've done whole episodes of *QI* where I've wanted to die ... to not be.
>
> **Stephen Fry**

Depression has often been referred to as the 'common cold of mental-health problems'. It's been estimated that between 10% and 25% of women and 5% to 12% of men will experience at least one episode of major depression in their lifetime. Although depression most often occurs between the ages of twenty-five and forty-five, it can affect people of all ages, cultures, incomes, education and marital status. High profile people like Stephen Fry and J.K. Rowling have been very open about their battles with depression. As the quote above from Stephen Fry indicates, depression may be common but it can have devastating effects on individuals and their lives.

What Is Depression?

But what actually is depression? Often, when we are thinking about depression, the first thing to spring to mind is a feeling: a low, deeply sad feeling. Winston Churchill famously described his depression as the 'Black Dog', which captures the ever-present nature of depression that can take over and dominate all aspects of a person's life. Other hallmark emotional features of depression include intense feelings of hopelessness and despair. Interestingly, people who are depressed also often find they experience an increase in other unpleasant emotions such as anxiety, irritation and guilt. However, people sometimes report that, as depression advances, they experience not so much the presence of emotion but the distinct inability to experience any positive feelings towards other people, themselves or things they used to once enjoy. It's as if all the fun, enjoyment and pleasure has been completely sucked out of life.

We also know that people's thinking tends to change when they are depressed, both in terms of what they think and also how they think. When people are really depressed they tend to be generally more negative and pessimistic about themselves and the future. They often say they feel hopeless and can't see any way out. A very natural thing that happens when people become depressed is that they try to make sense of the experience and understand it. Why did I become depressed? What's led to this? What did I do to deserve this? As we discussed in Chapter 2 (*Open*), minds like to have answers and solve problems. Alongside this, our culture reinforces this. In this scientific, rational age, we must have answers! This can lead to a pattern of thought called *rumination*, which we'll talk more about later.

As if all this wasn't enough, depression usually creates a number of physical symptoms as well. This can include feeling tired or exhausted with people often experiencing a change in their sleep patterns: either they can't sleep as they normally do, or they feel as if they need to sleep all the time. Other sources of pleasure can be interrupted too such as a reduction in people's sex drive. It's quite common for appetite changes to occur – either feeling the need to eat more or less.

So, the picture here is that depression can be hard-hitting in terms of the symptoms. As you can imagine, all this leads to some pretty big changes in behaviour: this is a central part to understanding depression and, also, finding our way out of it. The number one thing that tends to happen in depression is a **reduction in activity** – people just start doing less. With the combination of negative thoughts, unpleasant emotions and a catalogue of physical symptoms, the natural inclination is therefore to do less, both of the things that were difficult already, but also things that used to be fun. Understandably, with all these symptoms of depression, life becomes a lot more difficult. And humans being that we are, we usually don't like things that are difficult and we will naturally avoid them. We are, if not anything else, creative when it comes to avoidance. Here's some of the main ways that people use to avoid doing something when they are depressed (see if you recognise any):

• Procrastinating – putting off doing something.

• Sleeping too much.

- Rumination – going over and over something in your head so that it stops you actually doing anything useful.

- Using alcohol or drugs to excess.

- Complaining or moaning to friends and family.

- Zoning out, for example, in front of the television.

- Staying away from difficult or distressing situations.

As we start to paint a picture of depression, we see it can be rich and multi-faceted, made up of many different components. At this stage it is important to say that the presence of any or all of the above isn't enough to say someone is depressed. There's a good chance that most of us will have experienced some or all of the above at some point during our lives. To get a diagnosis of depression, a mental-health professional would want to know if you had any of the above symptoms *and* whether they stop you from doing the things you would normally do such as working or being with your family and friends as you normally would.

What we are more interested in is whether these experiences have an impact on your life. Do they stop you doing the stuff that is important to you? Does it get in the way of leading a full and rich life?

What Causes Depression?

So, what is it that causes depression? This is a good question to ask and one that doesn't have an easy, straightforward answer. The lay view of depression is that it is any of a number of things. You've probably heard that depression is just a neuro-chemical imbalance in the brain and therefore a correction to this imbalance (i.e. an anti-depressant) is the answer. If you've had depression, there's a fair chance you've heard from well-meaning friends or relatives a message that essentially boils down to, 'pull yourself together and stop feeling depressed and try being a little more positive.' You may have also heard the idea that someone who is depressed is just made that way, as if it's an unalterable part of their personality.

All of these explanations touch on aspects of depression and its causes. A key message we'd like to get across here is that depression is not simple and the most up-to-date evidence we have points to multiple, complex pathways that can interact in many different ways from person to person. Although there is a danger in spending too much time focused on trying to understand the causes of depression, it's important to know a little about what can drive it. It's important to keep in mind that very often the causes of depression can be quite different from the factors that actually keep the problem going.

There are many pathways into depression and, for some people, it appears that stress plays an important role. This can include two types of stress: past or long-standing stresses or current, triggering stresses. The past and long-term stresses that are often most important and relevant to depression involve early childhood experiences, particularly related to the kind of parenting you received. Parenting that is cold, uncaring or abusive has been found to be strongly related to depression. It seems that this kind of parenting affects the kind of beliefs that children develop about themselves – in some ways affecting their personality and particularly, how effectively they respond to stress in the future. For example, factors that seem to be important can include having excessively high standards or being a perfectionist. This can mean that a person finds it very hard to be satisfied with their lives and may be driven to achieve more and more. These people are great for getting lots and lots of work done but probably not the kind of person you would want as your boss. Another personality style that has been linked with depression (and, in fact, lots of other problems) has been the tendency to worry and ruminate. Worriers and ruminators are people who spend a lot of time in their heads, endlessly going over past failures or future concerns. It's a habit that is particularly damaging as, on the surface, it can look like it's helping ('I'm planning and anticipating future problems!' or 'I'm just trying to learn from my past mistakes') but, in fact, it can be very damaging as it takes people out of the present moment and, in a never-ending way, keeps them in contact with the negative aspects of their lives.

Current stressors are also very important. Many people, when they become depressed, can look back and identify a specific event that seemed to trigger off their depression. This could include a range of things such as the death of a loved one, or a stressful life event, such as a job loss or relationship break up. Stressors can also result from changes in the environment that mean a loss of support (for example, a close friend moving away) or no longer being able to do an activity that brought fun or gave meaning. It can also include a more gradual accumulation of stresses that go with poverty or social deprivation, which suggests that it's important to recognise some of the social factors that can lead to depression.

Research has shown that the risk of developing clinical depression is increased if you have a relative who has been depressed, and studies of twins indicate that there is a genetic or inherited risk of developing depression. It's also likely that with most instances of depression the neurotransmitter functioning in the brain is in some way disrupted and may have an impact on the development and maintenance of depression. Hence, medications have been developed that have been designed to address this. It's important to note, that while the current research evidence indicates that genetics and neurochemistry play a part in depression, our understanding of the exact role these play remains quite limited.

One thing that seems to be clear from all this is that there is often not a single cause of depression and, for most people, it is likely to be a complex interplay of all these factors together. As we think about depression, it can be easy to build an image of its being a thing that resides inside people. However, a group of psychologists, including Neil Jacobson, Michael Addis and Christopher Martell, have developed an approach known as *Behavioural Activation*[5] and this has an interesting perspective on depression. They talk about depression as not an entity, but rather a **relationship** that exists between the world and the person. This emphasises a

5 Michael E. Addis, Neil S. Jacobson and Christopher R. Martell, *Depression in Context: Strategies for Guided Action* (Norton Professional Books, 2001)

different way of understanding depression that focuses not so much on changing thoughts and feelings but changing behaviour (and therefore the relationship).

The most interesting question for those in the middle of a depressive episode is not actually how they ended up there, but what is it that keeps it going? Imagine you see a huge boulder rolling down a hill that seems to be gathering momentum, heading towards some small but quaint village at the bottom of the valley. What we now know is that, in situations such as these, the correct question is not, 'Why is that boulder hurtling down the hill at such speed?', although this is perhaps an interesting question and has its merits. The correct question is in fact, *What can I do to slow this boulder down and stop it*? And the answers to each of these questions are actually very different!

Let's return to the concepts from earlier in the book – *Open*, *Aware* and *Active* – and think about how each of these can be applied to working your way out of depression.

Getting Stuck in Depression

As we described in Chapter 2 (*Open*), our minds are master problem-solvers and when a problem such as depression comes along – surprise, surprise – the natural tendency of our minds kicks in. Not only that but also our culture supports this tendency to seek answers to depression. Friends and family will want to ask, 'Why are you depressed?' But here's the thing about depression – when someone is depressed, they tend to have more negative, pessimistic thoughts. It's like someone has dropped a big, dark rainy cloud over their minds and all that can be seen is doom and gloom (picture Charlie Brown from the *Peanuts* cartoon). So a mind equipped with this information, which largely has a negative aspect to it, will tend to come up with reasons and explanations for a person's current depressed state that are probably not going to be very helpful.

This relentless search for answers tends to send people back into the past, to mull over past mistakes and failures in an attempt to make sense of why this happened. On the surface it makes sense to do this – perhaps this will lead to some answers about how to get out of this mess. But there are two things to keep in mind here. First, remember the boulder hurtling down the hill? What started a problem is often very different to what keeps it going. So attempting to answer the question of 'why am I depressed?', while important, may not be the most helpful question. Secondly, a mind that has access to mostly negative information is likely to therefore come up with mainly negative, highly judgemental, critical explanations. See if this sounds familiar:

- I'm depressed because I'm a loser and a failure.

- I'm depressed because I've always been like this – it's who I am.

- I'm depressed because I'm weak and can't cope with life (unlike every single other person on the planet).

- I'm depressed because my brain is wired that way.

- I'm depressed because there's just something fundamentally wrong with me.

For anyone who has experienced depression, these are the kind of answers minds love to throw up (for some reason about 4 a.m. is a favourite time). Although it's possible that some of these reasons may in fact be correct, it's highly probable that they are not the kinds of reasons that would enable most people to tackle the state of depression successfully. Notice this too – these are not the kinds of reasons that are actually very easily proved. They are probably the kinds of answers that would lead someone to just give up trying! Our minds may try to convince us that they are right, particularly as they can *look* very consistent with how we are feeling, but, as we outlined in Chapter 2 (*Open*), we have good reason to be suspicious of at least some of what is going on between our ears.

Along with this is the central issue that when people become depressed they can become closed to certain types of emotions. This is understandable – feelings such as sadness, grief and anger are not always easy to make room and space for, particularly when life is feeling difficult already. So it's not a surprise that when people become depressed they tend to work hard to avoid certain types of feelings and emotions. Here's an example of what happened to Dave:

After Dave lost his job, he experienced a lot of unpleasant and difficult feelings. He felt sad and also angry at the way he'd been treated. These are pretty normal and natural emotional reactions. However, Dave didn't see it like that. When he was growing up, he'd always been told that it was a sign of weakness to be anything but positive and happy, and he was set up to respond to such feelings with avoidance. As a result, he quite understandably worked very hard to not have these feelings. He used alcohol to block them out and he watched lots of TV. He also avoided situations such as seeing work colleagues because he knew they would ask difficult questions about his lack of work and he would feel ashamed. He gave up on searching for new jobs because he felt despondent each time he sent off his CV. He had a huge stack of unopened mail that he hadn't touched for fear there would be a bill he couldn't pay. He knew he had to face these things but found he just kept putting them off. In the end he stopped going out and completely cut off from any family and friends. It all just felt too much to be spending time with other people and who would want to be with such a sad-sack anyway? He said one day to his therapist, 'If only I could just get rid of these feelings, then I could get on with my life!'

With the benefit of having a perspective outside of Dave's depression it's easy to see that, while avoidance was an understandable strategy in the short term, it meant that he was missing out on lots of good stuff in life. He was depriving himself of opportunities to do fun and meaningful activities. He was also letting problems build up and worsen over time.

As we talked about in Chapter 2 (*Open*), there are a million and one ways in which humans can avoid emotions: drugs, alcohol, sex, box-set television series, Internet use, and food to name just a few. But there are more subtle ways as well. We can use procrastination to avoid the unpleasantness of engaging in what we think will be a difficult task. We can use our minds to escape by daydreaming about a better future. Or we can ruminate on the past in the hope of finding the key that will unlock our depression, and we can trick ourselves into feeling that at least we're doing something.

Other ways include trying to maintain ultra-high standards or striving for perfection in order to avoid the feelings that go along with being perceived as not being up to scratch. Brené Brown,[6] a researcher into the emotion of shame and vulnerability, refers to perfectionism as the **twenty-ton shield** that people use to protect themselves from such feelings. The problem is when people become depressed, it can be very difficult to meet such high standards so the temptation is just to give up completely, rather than face the feelings that go with doing an 'average' or 'just good enough' job.

Out of the Moment and Autopilot Engaged

What we see in depression is that the content of a person's thoughts tends to be more negative and usually becomes increasingly so as their life is reduced and diminished.

6   Referred to in Brené Brown, *Daring Greatly: How the Courage to Be Vulnerable Transforms the Way We Live, Love, Parent, and Lead* (Penguin, 2013)

But alongside this is a way of relating to thoughts that means people get very much taken out of the moment. In depression this usually means ruminating about the past or worrying about things that are going to happen in the future. The effect of this is that a person becomes wrapped up in their internal world and, therefore, out of touch with what is actually going on around them. Often, when depressed, it may be the case that the present contains so many difficult or painful thoughts and emotions that it's understandable to be tempted to 'time travel' out of the moment. However, there are two important consequences of this. First, it means that you are not in contact with what is actually going on in front of you. This is particularly important in terms of registering how you are feeling. If you're not mindful of what you're feeling, it becomes difficult to get a sense of when you're moving towards your values. It's a little like all the dials on the dashboard of your car being switched off – you don't know how fast you're going, how long you've been travelling for or how much longer you need to travel. Also, when we are in autopilot mode and wrapped up in our thoughts, it's much more likely that we will be guided by these thoughts, which can reduce the amount of choice we have in any given moment. This is important information and, when moving through a period of depression, it is important to be able to have the flexibility to contact the present moment when needed.

Secondly, it also becomes very hard to appreciate things when we're wrapped up entirely in our minds. Our experiencing of the world is dominated by our minds rather than what is right in front of us. To truly appreciate the important things in life, we need to engage with our five senses as much as possible rather than our (judgemental, critical, pessimistic) minds. These moments could be playing with your children, listening to a favourite piece of music or enjoying a sumptuous meal. When you are depressed, life is often stripped of the things that provide enjoyment and being engaged with our Thinking Self, rather than our Observing Self, does not help.

When depressed it can be easy to become fused with an identity that is dominated by depression. Dave described being engulfed by depression to the point it felt as if that's all there was to him. He **was** depression. Because of this it became very hard for him to act outside of anything that wasn't depression. Friends would ask him out and he would think, 'I can't do that; I'm depressed.' In this way, he got so caught up in this identity of depression that it would become hard to do anything that might be inconsistent with being depressed. Even though acting in a way inconsistent with depression would have been helpful, when he was deeply in it, it *seemed* wrong!

The Inactivity Trap

One of the hallmark features of depression is a reduction in activity. The things in life that are important to us become obscured behind a cloud of negative thoughts and painful emotions. It can be as if a virtual fog descends, making it very hard to know in which direction life should go. More often than not, life becomes about avoiding painful thoughts and feelings and meaningful activity drops right off the agenda.

Life with depression typically ends up being harder. You have less energy. Your appetite changes. You experience an increase in painful thoughts and feelings and a decrease in feelings you like such as joy and happiness. Doing activities that were previously easy suddenly becomes a lot harder. Work becomes more difficult. Being around people is more challenging. Things that you used to enjoy are no longer fun. A combination of these factors means that it's highly likely that you will stop doing a lot of these activities. And this, in a lot of respects, makes sense. We humans are wired in such a way that we tend to gravitate towards things that make us feel good and move away from situations that don't. However, while this is reasonable, it can become a *trap*. If this situation goes on for too long, you can end up stuck, and then this pattern can be fuel to the fire. It can happen that by overly focusing on avoiding difficultly all the time, it in fact becomes part of the problem.

One way to capture this experience is to imagine driving a car and you're being chased by a huge zombie horde (or some other suitably scary horde). Understandably, you're really scared, you don't want to get eaten alive and so you keep your eyes glued to the rear-view mirror to make sure you're making your escape. While this might make sense on the surface, you can imagine how difficult it would be.

In this way, you could be sure that you're getting away from the horde that is behind you, but overall in terms of setting a direction, sticking to it, and effectively negotiating the various obstacles that come your way, it's not the right solution. Managing depression based on avoidance is exactly the same. It's helps you get away from things you don't like (painful thoughts and feelings, or difficult situations) but it's of no help in setting a course in life that moves you in line with the things that are important to you. As we talked about in Chapter 4 (*Active*), being guided by what is important in life (your values), rather than unwanted thoughts and feelings (and avoidance of these) is especially important in setting a course out of depression.

It can be easy to listen to what our minds say an upcoming situation is going to be like. We know that our minds like drama and, given that a depressed mind will have access to generally more negatively biased information, that drama is likely to be pretty grim! The thought of going out to meet friends for dinner? *It will be awful, terrible, you will hate it.* The week ahead at work? *It will be a nightmare and full of stress and demands that will be impossible to meet.* Going for a run tonight? *It will only drain your energy and you will end up feeling ten times worse than when you started.* This is perhaps an exaggeration but check with your mind as you approach these kinds of activities. How does your mind generally respond to the thought of increasing activity? We're not saying your mind is wrong here but there's a fair chance that your mind overestimates the likelihood that these events will be negative, unproductive, or just not enjoyable.

Behaviour guided by whatever thoughts and feelings are occurring in the present moment is one of the main ways that depression is maintained. In the short term, it undoubtedly helps as you are able to get out of difficult situations and avoid having to experience painful emotions and thoughts. However, there are a few longer-term consequences that are worth bearing in mind. First, and most importantly, is that as you avoid activities, you end up inadvertently depriving yourself of the very things that often make life worth living for. Things such as being with family, spending time with friends, undertaking meaningful work or having fun. A life without such activities is inevitably going to be less enjoyable.

The second key consequence is that such deprivations often represent a big shift in your routine. Routine is something that is super-important to humans – we are creatures of habit. Routines and habits provide us with stability, predictability and reassurance. With depression, there are commonly huge changes in routines that have been in place for many years. These routines can include sleep, eating, work, self-care: these are natural rhythms and cycles that both provide an anchoring sense of stability and also help us to get through day-to-day life.

This leads us to the last consequence. When these routines change and we avoid difficult activities, typically, things build up. Bills remain unpaid, deadlines loom and phone calls go unreturned. This means that tasks that were once minor annoyances or irritations build up, sometimes into overwhelming piles of scary proportions. And if you were inclined to avoid the smaller stuff, there's a good chance that you will end up avoiding the bigger stuff.

A key part of depression is that all of these factors tend to interplay at the same time, creating something of a downward spiral that can take some work to slow down after momentum has built up. So considering these altogether, you can start to see how they could create a significant problem. Let's see if we can zoom in on some of the things you may be doing that keep the problem going. First, let's take a look at changes Dave has noticed in his behaviour since he became depressed:

DEPRESSION ACTIVITY WORKSHEET

Since becoming depressed, what do you do less of?
See my family
Play or watch football
Talk to my sister on the phone
Go running
Go to the theatre
Reading

Since becoming depressed, what do you do more of?
Watch TV
Drink (alone)
Staying up late and sleeping late into the day
Using the Internet

What do other people tell you to do more of/less of?
More irritable and distant
Don't talk as much
Don't reply to messages
Moan about getting made redundant

What is the overall impact of what you are doing (short-term and long-term)?
Short-term life is a little less stressful
Overall, feel worse about my situation
Feel stuck like there's no way out – feel hopeless

EXERCISE – Depression Activity Worksheet

Fill in a Depression Activity Worksheet for yourself, taking note of what you do both more of and less of since you have become depressed. Ask friends and family if they have noticed any changes in what you do. Lastly, take some time to think about what has been the overall impact of what you have been doing since being depressed, keeping in mind both the short- and long-term impact.

Since becoming depressed, what do you do less of?

Since becoming depressed, what do you do more of?

What do other people say you do more of/less of?

What is the overall impact of what you are doing (short-term and long-term)?

Let's make a controversial statement: in ACT we're not so much interested in depression itself. What we are interested in is **how you respond to the different parts that make up depression:** the thoughts, emotions and physical experiences. There is no question of apportioning blame because depression is by its nature unpleasant and tricky to get out of. In our experience, people who are depressed are often working extremely hard to get themselves out of very difficult situations. One definite thing is that it is not a lack of hard work or effort that is the problem, in fact, quite the opposite:

Imagine you have a carriage with four horses attached. And imagine that, instead of the horses being attached all in a line as they should be, that they are attached so that they pull on the carriage in four different directions.

You can guess what happens? Each horse does what is natural and expected, starts pulling and the carriage goes nowhere, despite all the effort of each individual horse. The horses keep trying their hardest to get moving, but the harder they try, the faster they get nowhere. Eventually the horses give up. We think that the problem of depression can be a bit like this. It's not a problem of 'not enough effort' at all. In our experience, most people who have experienced depression are highly motivated. But they are also acutely aware when what they are doing is not working and therefore do what is, in fact, very reasonable in reducing the amount of inactivity. The issue is about getting all the horses facing the right way to harness the energy most effectively. It may not be immediately obvious how to do this and it naturally takes a little time to coax the horses to start pulling again after they have given up pulling. But once all their energy is harnessed effectively and momentum starts to build, some very interesting things can start to happen!

First, let's return to the story of Dave and think about how his depression developed, and what got him stuck. As we spoke about above, for a lot of people, depression, at least to some extent, has origins in the past that may continue to have an affect.

> *Whenever Dave was asked to think back about his family, he always responded the same way, 'My 'childhood was fine.' In a lot of ways he was right – his parents*

stayed together, Dave had not been abused and his parents had provided for all of his physical needs.

However, Dave did recall a sense from very a young age that he always felt '*not quite good enough*'. *His parents, who were both successful professionals, often pushed him to succeed and better himself. His report cards from school always said there was room for improvement, his friends were never quite good enough, and his room was never tidy enough. His parents were never directly critical of him but he developed the sense from a young age that he always needed to be constantly striving in order to avoid disappointing them.*

To make matters worse, his mother used to frequently compare him to his older sister, Laura – usually to point out how much better she was at virtually everything and why couldn't he be more like her. It was true, from Dave's perspective; Laura seemed to sail effortlessly through life. She was attractive, popular and intelligent – all qualities Dave did not feel he had. He found it difficult to make friends, as he felt different to his classmates, so tended to spend long periods of time on his own. While he did well at school, he found the academic work difficult and put his success down to the fact he worked extremely hard rather than any innate intelligence.

Dave remembered having little to do with his father, who was a remote and cold man. He only ever raised his voice once, an experience Dave recalled vividly. He had come home after school one day in tears after an older boy had beaten him up, while Dave's classmates had watched, cheering the boy on. His father's response to this was to bark at him, 'For God's sake David, stop crying and being so pathetic. It's embarrassing; grow up!'

As a result, Dave learned to carefully conceal any signs of weakness from other people. He couldn't stand the thought of being seen as weak and would do virtually anything to avoid being seen in this way. Dave was also very adept at sniffing out any feelings of weakness in himself, usually associated with emotions such as anxiety or sadness. At such points he would become fiercely critical of himself, telling himself, 'Don't be so pathetic — you don't deserve to carry on like a child.'

Dave found he actually came out of his shell once he went to university. He joined some clubs and made good friends. But somehow his relationships were nearly always lacking in depth, probably because he kept a good part of himself well hidden. He always felt as if he was 'standing on the outside, looking in'.

Dave also developed incredibly high standards for himself in life, and particularly with his work. He would work long hours after school and then later in his work. He relished the challenge his work brought to him, and experienced intense happiness whenever he hit a big target or received a promotion. The only thing was that this feeling was only fleeting and he was otherwise left with a deep sense of unease if he felt he was not achieving. It was nearly as if he was left chasing his next 'hit'. This also meant that he tended to seriously neglect other areas of his life, such as spending time with friends or developing intimate relationships. As a result, he became extremely successful in his role – his job eventually came to mean everything to him.

You can probably get a sense of the inevitability of what happened to Dave when he lost his job. It was unlikely that Dave could have responded in a different way. Growing up Dave had learned the lesson well. He knew it was wrong to have certain types of thoughts of feelings and he worked very hard to get rid of them. When these came surging up after his redundancy, he was simply not prepared to respond effectively to such a huge life change and the attendant, normal (but painful) thoughts and feelings that came along as well. The result was he was unable to respond to such a significant life change in a flexible manner.

Bringing It All Together: The Depression Trap

This may sound a little funny to say but depression, in many ways, is a habit, just like any other habit such as smoking, pulling on our socks in the morning, or driving home from work. Unfortunately, the depression habit comes with a lot of devastation and destruction. However, as we begin to recognise the habit-like qualities of depression, we begin to open up the possibility of breaking the habit.

If you remember from Chapter 3 (*Aware*), we talked about the importance of being able to recognise when we switch into autopilot and to try to develop more mindful and aware responses, so that we are able to inject more choice into our lives. This process is critical in recovering from depression.

One way to think in more detail about what happens in depression is laid out in Figure 2, and describes a central process that occurs within depression. Let's break these down a little. First of all, *Triggers* are anything that can affect you or have an impact on you. As the name suggests, triggers are what start off a process and get it underway. In terms of depression, there are many things that can act as triggers. Some may be historical or be strongly related to events that have happened to us in our lives. If you have ever experienced a traumatic event it may be that anything associated with that event will act as a trigger. Similarly, if you have ever lost someone close to you, it could be that anniversaries, photographs and even smells will act as a trigger for you, reminding you of your loved one. Triggers may be unrelated to personal history and be in your external environment. This could include a critical comment from a co-worker, or something going wrong in your life, such as dropping your new smartphone and breaking its screen.

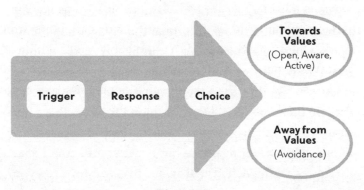

Figure 2

Following a trigger comes a *Response* and for the most part, responses are often emotional. The obvious emotions that are associated with depression include sadness, hurt, disappointment, loss or grief. But it is also important to remember that these aren't the only important emotions related to depression. Often triggers will produce all sorts of emotional responses, including anxiety and anger.

The other part of a response is, of course, what your mind says about both the trigger and also the resulting emotion. Here are a few common examples:

- I can't stand this.

- I can't handle this feeling.

- I want this feeling to stop.

- There's something wrong with me.

- Why am I the only one?

Now, all these responses are completely normal and natural and there are no right or wrong ways of responding to triggers. However, as you've hopefully picked up through this book, because of our culture and messages about emotions we receive growing up, it can be very easy to judge certain responses as bad or negative and, therefore, we somehow shouldn't have them. What is most important is what we do afterwards. Do we respond in ways that move us towards our values or away? Have a look at Figure 2. You will see that once a response happens, you have a *Choice*, in terms of taking action that will move you towards your values or taking action that will move you away from your values. Admittedly, in the middle of the storm of depression, it may not feel as if you have much of a choice. Everything can happen so quickly and on autopilot so that, before you know it, you end up doing what you've always done. Well, the very first starting point is learning to mindfully slow this process down a little and begin to recognise the choices that are available to you in what you do.

With depression, the main way of moving away from values is often underpinned by avoidance. So, you experience a trigger, you have a response that you don't want and this leads to *Avoidance*. In depression, avoidance can happen in many subtle and various ways as we've described above. Each of these patterns works super-effectively at avoiding difficult or painful emotions (in the short-term) but each also has the effect of either compounding the emotion that you are trying to avoid, putting off a difficult task that will only get more difficult with time, or cutting you off from an important source of enjoyment, vitality or meaning in your life.

As we outlined in Chapter 2 (*Open*), we're not saying that all avoidance is bad per se. Sometimes it can be a very healthy thing to do. Avoidance becomes unhealthy when that is the only tool you have in your toolkit and you use it to fix every problem you come across.

To summarise, this is how the Depression Trap works: a trigger occurs that produces some form of unwanted emotion and, this is the most important bit, you end up reacting in a way that is primarily concerned with avoidance. Overall, this makes it hard to be working towards your goals and building a life of meaning if your main pattern of behaviour is based on moving away from something rather than towards it. The good news here is that these kinds of patterns can be broken and it's by breaking them that you will find your way out of depression. But first of all, you need to slow these patterns down a little, bring that spotlight of awareness to them and become used to recognising them.

EXERCISE – What Is Your Depression Pattern?

We would like you to take some time to think about your own Depression Pattern. Think back over the past few weeks to points where you have experienced strong emotional responses. Consider what happened before this emotion, and what was the triggering event? Then, what happened after? Did you find yourself engaging in unhelpful avoidance that took you away from what is important to you? Or did you use your *Open*, *Aware* and *Active* skills to stay on track with your values?

DEPRESSION PATTERN WORKSHEET

What were your Triggers?

What were your Responses (emotions and thoughts)?

What did you do? Did you move away from your Values (Avoidance) or move towards your Values?

Curious Explorer into Depression

Wayne Gretzky, former Canadian ice hockey player and, arguably, one of the greatest ever, once said, 'You miss one hundred percent of the shots you don't take.' What Gretzky means is that in order for it to possible to succeed you have to take chances and **participate**. It means taking some risks and opening up to things not working out as you had hoped. However, as you begin to examine how your depression has trapped you, and begin to consider there are some alternatives, we would like you to bring to this a spirit of experimentation. We would like you to practise trying out new, less automatic ways of approaching depression and at the same time, very carefully, observing what happens. What is it like? What do you notice? What feels new and different? With this emphasis, the importance is not necessarily the actual outcome but the process of trying out new and different ways of responding to your depression.

Opening Up to Depression

If you remember from Chapter 2 (*Open*), a key skill is learning how to be more open with regard to all parts of your experience. All the stuff that goes on under your skin – your thoughts, emotions and physical sensations. As we talked about above, depression comes with its own set of emotions and physical symptoms. Let's start to bring all of this together. There is a lot about the experience of depression that can make it hard to be open about it.

As you start to become more active, it's fairly likely that one of the things you will notice is that your mind will start working in overdrive, throwing up all those familiar thoughts that go along with depression. As you've probably gathered now, we are interested in thoughts, but only to the degree that they are helpful and get us moving in the direction that's important to us. The trick here is not to change our thoughts or to be able to think more positively. Instead, we want to *de-emphasise thoughts* so that they are not so much in charge.

We want you to become a top-notch expert in recognising your depressed mind at work. To do this, it's good to know a few tricks that depressed minds do. Once you learn to spot them, it can become relatively easy because, first, minds only have a limited number of tricks up their sleeve and, secondly, minds tend to become very repetitive. But we need to be aware that our minds aren't doing this because they are bad, nasty or broken. Most often, they use these tricks because they want to keep us safe and protect us from becoming even more depressed. It's just a coincidence that this is the very thing that keeps you stuck. So, here are a few Mind Tricks to watch out for:

It Will Never Work out, What's the Point? You Won't Enjoy It Anyway

This is a great trick that minds play and is vital for keeping you inactive. Minds love to make negative predictions anyway but when depressed, this tendency goes in to hyper-drive. At its heart, this can be thought of as your mind doing its best to stop you from stepping outside your comfort zone and taking a risk. Minds will often work hard by making lots of predictions about the future and when we get hooked on such thoughts it can be easy to see them as true.

The key here is developing a more useful perspective. Rather than getting caught up in trying to determine whether such thoughts are true or not, the more important question is, 'Does this negative prediction help me become more active? Or does this just stop me moving forward?' Particularly because there may indeed be some accuracy to a thought such as 'I won't enjoy it'. Often, people who are depressed don't enjoy activities – certainly not as much as they used to.

No One Cares I'm Depressed Anyway

Minds do have our best interests at heart and this mind trick is great for ensuring that you don't connect with people; in order to protect you from being hurt. This can be particularly relevant if you have indeed been hurt or let down by other people in the past. However, you can imagine the impact this kind of thought might have on connecting with people or receiving important sources of support. Here is a real challenge – how to open up and be vulnerable with other people in the midst of depression, when your mind is yelling at you that people are not interested in how you are genuinely feeling on the inside.

We would invite you to simply listen out for this mind trick with that sense of openness and curiosity. Notice when this thought comes up – does it help you move towards or away from your values of developing connections with others?

Opening up to others about your depression is without doubt a difficult task and requires some thought and good timing. If you choose to, we would suggest that it is best done slowly and gently. See if you can do it in a fashion that facilitates this. Here are some tips from people who have experienced depression:

- Choose people who you think are going to be good listeners and will genuinely want to hear about your experience.

- Pick a good time. Perhaps ask, 'I have something important I'd like to talk to you about, can you spare some time?'

- Find words that you are comfortable with to describe your depression. These could include, feeling a bit low, blue, feeling stressed – use whatever captures your experience for you.

- Be clear why you want to talk about your depression. Is it because you need help? Do you just want someone to know?

- Let others know how they can help. And also how they can't help.

You've Always Failed in The Past

Another trick that minds pull in order to keep you inactive is to remind you of all the ways in which you've failed previously. As we mentioned above, minds tend to be somewhat negative, but when you are depressed, chances are that this tendency will increase and it will just about feel as if your whole life has been one big failure. And if you're not convinced, your mind will trot out all the examples from your memories as evidence of your lack of worthiness. Again, it is important to remember the aim is not to get into a tussle about whether these are true or not, but more to remember that this is simply a mind trick that happens when you are depressed and can be held lightly and not taken quite so seriously – 'there goes my mind again, dredging up all that stuff from the past'; 'thanks for your help, mind'.

It's also important to note that this mind trick can have something of a seductive quality. It's almost as if it feels good or correct. Partly, this is because doing so is usually very habitual and automatic. It can feel comfortable to ruminate in this way – like slipping your foot into an old, worn, familiar shoe. There is something to be said for what feels familiar – it can be oddly reassuring. Also, by going back and recalling past failures it can look like you are trying to solve the puzzle of why you are so depressed. And if you can work that out, you will be able to get yourself out of this mess! At least that's what your mind would like you to believe. Minds are great problem-solvers and depression, on the surface, is a huge problem to be solved. So, doing something that feels like you are working to figure out this mess of depression is going to feel at least slightly good. But again, ask yourself, in your own experience, how much does trawling through your own back catalogue of personal failures help you move forward? Now, this is not to say that there is nothing to be gained from understanding and making sense of where your depression came from but, if you are going to do it, it is best done in a mindful and considered way.

Responsibility Bias – You Always Mess up Everything

This is a variation on the 'You're a failure' mind trick and comes from a particularly unhelpful but very subtle habit that occurs when people are depressed. Deep down the trick is to do with responsibility. When people are depressed, their minds will be very quick to pile on the responsibility for all the negative things that have happened in their lives. You are the number one sole cause of all failures – no one else had anything to do with it and there are no mitigating circumstances whatsoever. And to add insult to injury, minds apply a cunning double standard so that they will discount or attribute any success or positive outcomes to circumstances outside of you. Anyone could have got that job. Most likely it was because they felt sorry for me. People don't really like me – they are unable to see what I'm really like.

It's Not Fair – I'm Not to Blame!

Whereas you're definitely not to blame for your depression, this is a particularly pernicious mind trick and is a little like the reverse of the *'responsibility bias'*. It can be easy to search out and blame others for the state we find ourselves in and, when we do, we may end up placing the responsibility for our situation on them: 'They did this to me, they caused this situation'. It's almost as if by placing responsibility for the situation on to other people, you end up giving up any opportunity for you to be active in changing. Once again, with these thoughts we are inviting you to focus less on whether they are true or not, but more on how well they help you move forward in your life. These kinds of mind tricks can be particularly difficult to ignore so read through Chapter 7 (*Anger*) for some further tips.

One thing that we want you to become skilled at is noticing when your mind is trying to catch you with mind tricks. It's important that in lots of ways these thoughts 'work' for you. There is a good reason why these thoughts have the tendency to catch your attention and for the most part it is because they, in some way, serve to protect us. We play small, we don't take risks, we don't expend energy – all things that are important for someone who is feeling depressed. But this comes at a price. As you practise *Activating* yourself, and moving out of depression, there is a good chance that some of the thoughts mentioned will become more frequent or more intense. Your job is to respond differently to such thoughts: rather than giving in to the thought or fighting and struggling, practise an alternative response, which is to defuse from it. See if you can notice the thought and see your mind at work. Focusing on allowing the thought to be there while directing your attention towards doing what matters to you.

EXERCISE – Mind Watching

As you start to contemplate activating we would like you to practise watching your mind at work and being alert for any of the above mind tricks. Take a moment to think about one thing you are not currently doing that you would like to do again. See if you can imagine in detail – what would be involved in doing it? Where would you be? Who would be there? How would you feel? Now, imagine it was a little like you were sitting in the cinema, not too close, perhaps to the back of the screen. On the screen, you can see the mind tricks popping up. The goal here is just to notice your mind at work and catch the thoughts as they occur, particularly ones that sound like any of the mind tricks from above. And keep an eye on the impact that they have: what would be the old, habitual way of responding to these? What would a new, perhaps more helpful way look like?

What Valued Action were you thinking about doing?	What type of Mind Trick did you notice?	Old, habitual response?	New, more helpful response?

Self Compassion – the Importance of Kindness

A word on self-compassion: in starting this process of being more active, it's going to be important to be kind to yourself. In our experience, this is not always an easy thing for people to do who are depressed. What we often hear are comments such as: 'I don't deserve to go easy on myself', 'I'm lazy, I've brought this on myself', 'If I stop giving myself a hard time, I'll never get out of this mess!' We would like you to pause for a moment and ask yourself how well does this approach work? When your mind is engaging in a solid twelve rounds of 'beating yourself up', do you feel invigorated, creative, ready to tackle new challenges? Or do you feel drained, exhausted, guilty and defeated? Chances are, the latter. Imagine you were talking to a dear friend, who was experiencing a significant life challenge that they were struggling with. How would you respond to them to be most supportive and encouraging? Compare this to how your mind can often be at your lowest, most vulnerable points. And, most importantly, notice the impact that this can have on what you choose to do.

We're not saying that you can just simply switch off this critical self-talk – that would be a hard task. But what is important is to become more aware to the degree your mind engages in this style of thinking. Notice and listen in to it. And also notice that you have the choice with regard to how you respond. You could act as if what your mind is saying is completely true and give up. Or, alternatively, you can notice what your mind is saying and choose a course of action that is based on taking a step towards what is important to you – your values.

Remember the 'team of advisers' we spoke about in Chapter 3 (*Aware*)? Well, there are a couple of adviser perspectives that can be particularly important in the midst of depression: these are the compassionate and critical adviser perspectives. For most people who are depressed, the critical adviser tends to become much more prominent and the compassionate adviser often takes a back seat. Now remember, we're not saying that either of these advisers is necessarily better or worse that the other. However, for most people, the key is having a balance and being flexible in terms of which adviser is most prominent in guiding behaviour.

The critical adviser usually comes across as quite harsh and judgemental and will be quick to point out mistakes, failures, negative comparisons with others or unmet expectations. On the surface, this is the one who does not always come across as pleasant: you probably would be reasonable in thinking that this adviser is the last person you need when you're feeling low and depressed. However, in the interests of flexibility, it's worth considering what this adviser brings to the table. First, this one is often interested in change and improving things and therefore loves to let you know when things are not up to scratch. Buried within the criticism is a desire for things to be better for you, although this may not be immediately obvious! Secondly, this adviser may be very familiar: they may have been around for a long time. As such, there may be a degree of comfort in keeping this adviser close and taking on board what they are saying. It may be painful, but, as the saying goes, better the devil you know than the devil you don't.

The self-compassionate adviser presents a contrast. This is a perspective that people who are depressed often struggle with. This is curious because, in our experience, many people who are depressed are often acutely aware of other people's needs and tend to be extremely compassionate people. However, when it comes to the time to direct that same level of compassion towards themselves, these standards are thrown out the door. See if you recognise any of these types of thoughts:

- If I'm not hard on myself, I'll be stuck like this for ever.

- I don't deserve to give myself a break.

- If I'm too soft, I'll be exploited.

It's quite possible there may be elements of truth to these types of thoughts; however, holding on tightly to such thoughts may not have the desired effect. Here's Dave describing such an experience to his therapist:

D: So, I decided to revise my CV again before attempting to send it out. I sat down at the computer and noticed straightaway this heavy gloom descend on me. It was pathetic – I mean come on, it was just a bloody CV. I can be so soft sometimes.

T: What happened then?

D: I feel so embarrassed saying this, but I couldn't face it. I started to cry. I switched off my computer and went to bed.

T: How were you feeling as you switched off the computer?

D: Even worse. Low. Sad. I remember thinking that I was a total loser. I mean, what's the point of applying for jobs if I can't even control how I'm feeling? I'm a joke.

T: Sitting here, it sounds like you were pretty hard on yourself.

D: Well, someone has to be. If I'm not, then this problem will just keep getting worse.

You can see from this that Dave has taken a particularly critical stance towards his feelings in this situation. You can also get a sense of the impact this stance had on Dave and his ability to persist with this task. It was like the wind had been completely taken out of his sails.

Bringing the *self-compassion adviser* into the mix with depression can add a quite radically different perspective. This perspective has a sense of gentleness towards thoughts and feelings and is more relaxed as far as judgements and criticism are concerned. It encourages you to make room and space for feelings that often accompany depression such as sadness, despair or hopelessness. This **does not** mean resigning yourself to these feelings, in fact, quite the opposite. The focus is on reducing the pull towards struggling with the feelings that are uncomfortable and taking a courageous stance that involves acknowledging the painful emotions that are there – allowing them to be there even if they are painful. It's also important to turn towards these feelings, holding them with a sense of kindness that acknowledges the experience as it is, without adding anything to it or taking anything away from it. This stance is seldom 'weak' or 'soft'. Neither is it a move that means giving up. In fact, this can be the very thing that allows for genuine movement to occur. As you ease up on fighting and struggling with the emotions of depression, you have the opportunity, in this space, to begin to ask yourself, 'What is actually important to me?' and 'How would I like to lead my life if depression were not in charge?'

Through this self-compassionate stance we learn to know what we are feeling, how we are feeling it and in what situations we feel. When we try to fight against depression, we are saying to ourselves, 'This feeling is not OK – you need to be different, better.' With this in mind, it becomes very hard to open up and be vulnerable with other people. When we hold on tightly to these kinds of thoughts, it's hard to imagine that anyone else would have a different perspective! But, of course, by doing this, we end up cutting ourselves off from key sources of support from our friends and family.

It takes considerable courage to work through depression in order to be able to turn towards difficult experiences and slowly start to reactivate our lives again. A gentle, compassionate stance is especially important, particularly during periods that are especially tough. The story of Steven Callahan provides an apt illustration of this.

Callahan was a boat builder and sailor whose boat sunk off the coast of Africa, possibly after being struck by a whale. He spent the next seventy-six days lost at sea, drifting in a life raft. During this time, his survival hung in the balance as he struggled to find fresh water and use his spear gun to catch fish. He recalled many times on his journey that he made mistakes or made the wrong decisions, some of which could have easily cost him his life (including tearing a hole in the bottom of his raft with his spear gun, while attempting to land a fish). Despair and self-criticism were always just around the corner. When asked how he hadn't simply given up, he said he kept telling himself, 'You're doing the best you can.' This allowed him to persist and keep on doing all that he needed to do in order to survive. At the end of his journey, he had travelled nearly 3,000 kilometres across the Atlantic ocean, before being picked up by fishermen from the island of Marie Galante, south-east of Guadeloupe.[7]

Openness – Self-Soothing

A core skill that people who are depressed are usually not very good at is **self-soothing**. This is the act of emotionally and physically looking after yourself, and doing things that are gentle, settling and nurturing. Overcoming depression

7 Callaham, Steven, *Adrift: 76 days lost at sea*, Mariner Books, 2002

is a hard road and, like anyone embarking on an arduous journey, you are going to need breaks to recuperate. Think of self-soothing as a little like that. Here are some different ways you could consider looking after yourself by self-soothing:

Allow yourself to have time alone. Actively choosing to be alone, rather than avoiding others, may be a necessary and healing activity. See if you can practice allowing yourself to be alone in the interests of taking care of yourself.

Soothe your senses. Listen to a piece of music that engages you. Focus on your sense of smell as you move about during your day. Notice everyday beauty that you can see about you in your environment. Slow down and bring your attention to what you can taste as you eat your daily meals. Bring your awareness and mindfulness to what you can feel, as you're showering, walking, sitting and lying down.

Allow yourself to rely on the help from others. See if you can both ask for help and then accept it when it is offered to you. Your mind may say you don't deserve it but practise noticing such thoughts and making active choices to look after yourself.

Allow yourself to feel what you are feeling. As you may with a small child, allow yourself to feel the emotions that are with you for today, be it sadness, joy, hurt, disappointment, connection, excitement or grief. Practise the skill of noticing the evaluations and judgements that come along with such emotions, tuning into these and making room for them while connecting with your valued actions.

Shame – the Unspoken Emotion

Shame is a central human emotion that is one of the most basic and primitive. It connects us strongly and deeply to other people around us and serves to remind us when we have done something that might threaten our membership to the group. Aside from the few people that are completely disconnected from others or have psychopathic traits, most of us experience shame when we have done something that we fear would be negatively evaluated by other people. In depression, shame is particularly prevalent. It comes from the notion that to be depressed means there is something wrong or defective with us and that the experience of depression is inherently shameful. This is largely driven by a culture that sees mental-health issues as deviant, dangerous or abnormal. As a result, when most people become depressed, they feel ashamed, which leads to the second thing that fuels shame – they hide their depression away from other people. Shame loves this, as it's in the dark recesses of our minds that shame thrives. It reinforces the view that you're alone, you're the only one with these issues and everyone else around you is coping perfectly well. If shame had its way, you would never tell anyone about your depression and never open up about how you are actually doing. And by doing this, shame deprives you of key sources of support from those around you. It drives you to put on a good front and make it appear that you're always coping and managing.

Well, here's the thing with shame: **it hates being talked about**. It can't stand it when you let other people know about it because by doing so, you deprive it of its very power. By opening up to other people about how you are actually feeling on the inside, you say to shame that you are not going to be bossed around and do everything on its terms. There is a risk involved here in opening up to other people. It's possible that others may not understand you or may not want to hear about your experience. However, it is also possible that opening up may be the key to getting the help and support you need.

Awareness – Disengaging the Autopilot

Dave picked up his phone and saw he'd received a text message from his friend Danielle. She was inviting him to a dinner party she was having later in the week. She hinted that Claire, someone Dave quite liked, might be there. Dave experienced a bit of a thrill at this prospect and this was closely followed by a thought, 'Why would she be interested in you?' Straightaway Dave felt a surge of sadness but did his best to fight against this thought. Instead of making any headway, his mind reminded him of the last time he'd asked someone out on a date where he'd got turned down. 'I'm such a loser – why do I always do this?' He spent the next twenty minutes sitting on the couch, thinking back over the past, going over and over in his mind, trying to answer this question.

Rumination has this quality. It tends to be very 'mindy', a highly technical term meaning that the mind is on overdrive. It is very common to believe that this kind of thinking is useful. This may be related to the belief that depression can only be dealt with once the underlying root cause is identified. Or that a deep and careful analysis of your problems and emotions will provide the key to unlocking the puzzle of depression. There is some truth that understanding and insight is a useful thing but it can be dangerous, especially in the case of depression. Let's explain why.

Psychologists are often interested in the difference between the content of thoughts as opposed to how they function (or their purpose or outcome). This is particularly the case for rumination. The content can often look quite important ('why am I like this?'; 'why does this always happen to me?') but when we look more closely at how these thoughts *work* we see two things. First, this type of thinking has a circular quality; it doesn't help you move forward. This type of thinking also doesn't provide any new information and tends to make you become even more stuck. Think of the wheels of a car stuck in mud – a great deal of noise and spinning but no forward movement whatsoever. You can get a sense of this in Dave's example above. The second part to rumination often works to help you avoid situations that are difficult or bring you in contact with painful emotions. In Dave's case, you can get a sense of how this rumination reduced the chance that he would go to dinner and possibly get rejected.

Here's a couple of other interesting facts about rumination. Psychologists have shown that ruminating actually makes people *worse* at problem-solving. When we are completely wrapped up in our heads, going over and over a situation, it doesn't often help us deal effectively with a situation.

The second fact is that when people ruminate, they will invariably feel more anxious, depressed and stressed. This style of thinking will bring your mood down dramatically. So, not only does it not help, it makes you feel worse.

EXERCISE – Rumination vs Problem-Solving

What kinds of topics do you find yourself *ruminating* about?

_____

_____

_____

_____

_____

Does ruminating help you to avoid anything?

_____

_____

_____

_____

What are the consequences of ruminating? (In terms of how you feel and helping you move forwards.)

_____

_____

_____

_____

_____

The exercise above will help you to spot when you are ruminating as opposed to when you are problem-solving. Key signs that you are ruminating will be that you are going over and over certain topics (usually old and familiar ones), that rumination helps you in some way to duck or avoid difficult tasks or emotions and that ruminating doesn't help you move forward and it makes you feel worse.

The Present Moment – the Rumination Antidote

In Chapter 3 (*Aware*), we outlined the skill of awareness: the skill of coming back into the present moment, in a conscious, curious, flexible way. When our depressed minds are busy whirring away, we are very much out of the moment. Practising this skill, sometimes known as mindfulness, will allow you to disengage the autopilot more effectively, spot rumination at work and come back to the present moment. There is, in fact, good evidence now to indicate that a regular practice of mindfulness may be particularly helpful in preventing the recurrence of relapsing depression.

EXERCISE – A Mindful Alternative

Consider below the mindfulness exercises we introduced you to in Chapter 3 (*Aware*). Think about how you could integrate these into your daily life so you are able to practise them routinely. Remember, this is like any other skill, the more you practise it, the greater the benefit you are likely to gain from it.

1. Awareness of breath.

2. Three-step breathing space.

3. Eating a sweet exercise.

4. Notice that you are noticing.

Use the record sheet below to keep track of when you practised, and what thoughts, feelings and sensations you noticed. Also, make a note of any benefits you encounter that help you keep on track with getting active.

Date	Exercise	What I noticed (thoughts, feelings, sensations)	Benefits
5 May.	Three-step Breathing Space.	Heaviness in my legs and tightness in my chest. Worrying about interview next week.	Noticed that I needed to rest. Also realised I was worrying a lot – which I hadn't noticed before.

There are a few common mind tricks that people often report as they practise mindfulness that you may want to look out for:

I feel too depressed to practise

We would say this is the perfect time to practise. It's often at these points that your Thinking mind is super busy and you are often immersed in the stream of thought. What better time to pause, slow down, and take time to step back from thinking and notice the choices that are available to you.

I don't feel any benefit – it's not working

Remember, mindfulness is the practice of coming into the present and noticing when our minds hook us and take us out of the present. Just as simple as that. Therefore, the practice is not about chasing a good feeling or being relaxed (although that can happen, which is a bounus). The results you gain are likely to come later, when you need to be able to step out of autopilot, catch your mind at work and continue with a valued action.

I can't do it; I'm terrible at these kinds of things

Great, notice that thought. Thank your mind for doing just what it's designed to do. Just noticing that you had that thought is perfect and a great example of mindfulness. Certainly, this practice is simple but not easy. Any task like this is fertile ground for minds to spring into action with judgements, evaluations or self-criticisms. See if you can simply notice your mind at work here.

Whenever I come back to the present, I feel so low and sad

This can sometimes happen as we slow down and ease up on avoidance and distraction, and it is normal and natural. See if you can, as best as possible, make room and space for the feelings that do bubble up. You don't have to like these feelings or even want them. Be gentle with yourself as much as you can. It's also all right to soothe and take care of yourself.

Increasing Activity – Getting Active

As you will have seen from our discussion above, when we are depressed the effects of our thinking can lead us to engage in patterns of avoidance and be out of contact with choices, actions, people and places that provide us with purpose and vitality. In depression, the key is **being able to increase the amount of purposeful activity you are doing**. As you've probably got a sense of now, reducing activity is a key issue in depression and working to change this cycle is essential. Now we know that this is easier said than done. In fact, if *depression* were to have a say, it would take exactly the opposite view! Depression would argue that, before you do anything, you need to deal with depression first. You need to feel less depressed, more motivated, less negative and more positive, more energetic. Instead we are going to invite you to become active, thinking about ways to reduce avoidance that takes you away from your values and increase activity that takes you towards what really matters. Let's go back to Dave to give an example of what we mean:

In talking with his therapist, Dave realised there was a key pattern that kept coming up for him He found that anything to do with work acted as a trigger for a strong set of emotions. Triggers were broad and included his family asking him about work, hearing friends talking about their jobs, speaking to recruitment agents or spending time looking for jobs. Any of these could result in feelings of sadness and shame, quickly followed by strong negative thoughts, judging him for feeling this way. Dave also noticed thoughts such as, 'I can't deal with this. It's too much.' It was at this point he realised that avoidance would start and this occurred in lots of different ways. Mainly, Dave would withdraw and isolate himself from others and engage in activities that would numb him, such as watching TV or occasionally drinking. Together with his therapist, Dave began to see this pattern happening repeatedly and realised the cost it had on him. Although, initially, he usually felt better when he withdrew, he usually always felt worse later. He ended up feeling lonely and disconnected from others. In particular, he had begun to realise the impact this had on his relationship with his sister, with whom he wanted to foster a closer relationship. With his therapist, he decided to experiment with trying out a new behaviour the next time he experienced a trigger related to work.

Connecting with Values

It's important to keep in mind that as you start to re-activate your life, it may not immediately 'feel good'. It's in fact entirely likely that being more active may lead you to feel more tired, more fatigued, experience an increase in negative, pessimistic thoughts. At this point, it will be useful to keep in mind the swamp light on the hill metaphor from the *Active* chapter. At times, increasing activity may not feel good, but keep in mind that **it is in the service of something broader and larger** than just whatever thoughts and feelings happen to be current right now. Sure, these thoughts and feelings are not pleasant, and we're definitely not saying you should like them or want them. But perhaps, from this broader perspective, it may be OK to make a little room and space for them as you start on the journey of becoming more active. Ask yourself, what would make it worth trudging through this swamp of depression? What are the important things in life that taking these steps will reconnect you to?

EXERCISE – Beginning to Get Active

Having read Chapter 4 (*Active*), what are the key values that you would like to guide you through your depression? Consider these different areas:

Relationships

_____

_____

_____

_____

Health

_____

_____

_____

_____

Work

_____

_____

_____

_____

Leisure and Fun

_____

_____

_____

_____

_____

Pick out one of these areas and below, write down one small way in which you could take an action towards one of these values over the next week. Be as specific as you can. When would this happen? Where? With whom?

My Action

_____

_____

_____

_____

_____

As a starting point, we'd like you to commit to undertaking this activity, but remember, the key here is to start small, so choose something from the bottom of your list. Remember you're learning a new skill and see if you can approach it as such. This isn't about getting it right straightaway, but developing new, more effective ways of working in the presence of depression. As you're just starting to think about committing to doing this activity, no doubt your mind is becoming busy, making predictions about what it will be like and, probably, reminding you of what it's been like in the past when you've tried to become active (or even just thought about it!). That's absolutely fine – what we're most interested in here is doing these activities in a different, less automatic way.

So, to begin with, make a note of all the thoughts that are coming up, just as you consider this activity. And make a note of the feelings, emotions and sensations that are arising too. We would like you to approach this activity with a sense of awareness, as we described in Chapter 3 (*Aware*). See if you can foster a sense of curiousness about this process. What is it actually like when you complete this activity? How do you actually feel? What sensations are actually there? When we are in autopilot mode, we often just go along with how our minds tell us the situation is going to be. In this case, we are inviting you to develop your curiosity to find out, a bit like a scientist, to see how it actually is, rather than how your mind is telling you it is going to be. As a general rule of thumb, it is important to become more active, rather than passive.

Rewards

As you start to become more active, it will be important to give yourself some rewards along the way. Sometimes the very act of moving towards your values will often come with its own intrinsic rewards. It can feel exciting and vital to be once again doing those activities that are meaningful for you. At the same time, when you make an effort and achieve something, a reward can be a simple yet highly effective way of providing yourself with some encouragement and, more importantly, making sure you maintain the new behaviour. It's often very easy to focus on when things are going wrong or where standards haven't been met, and while this is important, it's also essential to make sure that any changes are met with encouragement. This may be an actual, tangible reward or simply saying to yourself, 'Well done.' This will help you to foster a sense of kindness and appreciation towards yourself as you start out on this journey.

EXERCISE – Noticing and Evaluating Worksheet

When you try out something new, we'd like you to take some time to make a note of how it went. Make a record of how you felt before you did the activity and then how you felt afterwards. Just give a rough estimate – it doesn't have to be perfect.

NOTICING AND EVALUATING WORKSHEET

Date	Situation	How did you feel beforehand?	New behaviour	How did you feel after?
7 June.	Found out I didn't get job interview.	Miserable, very low, feeling ashamed.	Reach out – tell someone how I am feeling. Call my sister.	Felt a little better. Glad to have spoken to her and feel like she understood me.

Building Upwards

From here you have the key building blocks to work your way out of depression. Starting small, you can introduce new values-based actions into your life and gradually expand outwards and build upwards to develop a life that is expansive, has room to move and is not completely dominated by the experience of depression. Becoming more *Active* means a willingness to develop the skills to be more *Open* to the thoughts and feelings that come with depression – to become more mindfully *Aware* of them, less on autopilot, so that these experiences guide your behaviour less and less and you get to choose how you live your life in the way that you want to.

6 From Vigilance to Values: Living More Effectively with Anxiety and Worry

Our anxiety does not empty tomorrow of its sorrows, but only empties today of its strengths.

Charles H. Spurgeon

Worrying is like a rocking chair, it gives you something to do, but it gets you nowhere.

Glenn Turner

Have you ever got caught up with worrying to the point where it has made it difficult to decide what to do? Have you had trouble doing things because you have felt too afraid? We will help you to understand how anxiety works to create problems in people's lives, and how you might use the *Open*, *Aware* and *Active* skills to find a way out of the trap that anxiety puts you in.

We will describe the ACT approach to the most common way that people have problems with anxiety – where worry has taken over your life and is leading you to avoid doing things that you care about.

What Is Anxiety?

When you are under stress, worried or afraid you could be experiencing 'anxiety'. Fear and anxiety are normal and common emotions for most human beings. People can describe feeling uptight, nervous, tense, irritable or 'wound up'. Your mind might jump from worry to worry, focusing on whether something awful will happen, and anticipating danger. You may avoid doing things that you would normally like to do, pace around and find it hard to relax, get flustered, and be irritable or snap at others more easily.

While fear and anxiety may feel very similar, they are actually two different states. While fear is the defensive response we have when a threat is present, anxiety occurs **in anticipation of** something threatening or scary happening. Fear, innate and learned, is present across animal species. Innate human fears include fears of heights and certain animals (snakes, insects, mice). However, we have the capacity to become fearful of almost anything through learning (culture and history).

Anxiety is evolutionarily beneficial: it provides the physical and psychological changes that enabled our ancestors to survive and reproduce (ultimately resulting in our being here!). Remember the story of The Bear and the Blueberry Bush, that we described in the *Open* chapter? It could be said that we are descendants of the creatures that chose to 'skip lunch, rather than possibly be lunch'. Paying attention to fear and acting cautiously worked for our ancestors' survival.

Although many humans now live in environments with fewer physical dangers and less conflict between each other, it can be thought that our nervous systems have not caught up with these improvements. We continue to experience fear, anxiety and worry even if we live in environments that are friendly and supportive, and provide us with all our material needs.

Our nervous systems are wired in such a way that we respond physiologically to danger: what has been called the 'flight or fight' response. Fear is processed in our brains from sensory information (our eyes, ears, etc.) reaching the sensory thalamus and very quickly the amygdala; information is also relayed to the cortex, which is needed for awareness, context and perspective. The combination of these two pathways determines whether we have a fearful response to what we perceive.

The 'flight or fight' response is a way for our bodies to prepare for either running away or fighting for survival. It prepares us to either avoid potential danger, or to escape from a threatening situation if we are already in it. This is a particularly useful skill when it comes to steering clear of awkward situations involving bears, tigers, snakes or any other variety of dangerous beast. But anxiety is a useful tool for the modern human in many other situations. Anxiety may help us to prepare thoroughly for an exam or interview, be more careful when walking down a dark alley or backstreet, or make sure that we are careful about what we say in tricky social situations. For most of us, the experience of anxiety is a common, perhaps even daily, occurrence.

However, there are times when anxiety becomes an unhelpful response, such as when it is out of proportion to a stressful situation, when it persists beyond the stressful event that triggered it, or when there appears to be no apparent reason for feeling anxious (such as can happen sometimes with panic attacks). Some people become consumed by the struggle with their anxious feelings and thoughts, and anxiety ends up taking over their lives.

If these struggles persist (from a medical point of view) a person may meet the diagnostic criteria for an *anxiety disorder*. These are a range of disorders where anxiety is considered the main symptom, and where the ability to carry on effectively is significantly impaired because of it.

How Common Are Anxiety Disorders?

Anxiety disorders are the most common of all mental-health problems. It is estimated that one in six people, in any given year, will experience anxiety or depression, to the degree that this causes problems with their everyday functioning. Problems with anxiety often involve interconnected symptoms and disorders: the most frequent form is a mixture of depression and anxiety.

Mental-health professionals tend to categorise problems, and anxiety is no exception! As a result, there are many different labels for different anxiety problems. The most common ways that anxiety shows up for people are worrying excessively (generalised anxiety disorder), or a fear of being judged by others (social anxiety). People may worry excessively about their health (health anxiety); have crippling fears (phobias) about animals, blood and injury, or vomit; and worry about perceived flaws in their appearance (body dysmorphic disorder). Other anxiety disorders include panic disorder, agoraphobia, post-traumatic stress disorder and obsessive–compulsive disorder.

What Is the Experience of Anxiety Made up Of?

When most people talk about anxiety they mean the feeling. But the experience of anxiety is made up of many different parts: a combination of emotions and bodily sensations, thinking and behaviour.

Emotions

We experience emotions as sensations in our bodies. When we are fearful and anxious there are physiological changes that can be experienced as unpleasant. These are caused by the brain sending messages through the nervous system to make the heart, lungs and muscles in the body work harder. In addition, stress hormones (adrenalin, for example) are released into the bloodstream to prepare the body for the 'fight or flight' response. This can mean that along with feeling fearful, we can have physical symptoms, such as nausea, a fast heart rate, a thumping heart (or palpitations), shaking or having tremors, sweating, dry mouth, chest pain, headaches and fast breathing.

These physical changes can have positive benefits in stressful situations. It can be an advantage if, when faced with a dangerous or threatening situation, the body responds by increasing the heartbeat because this also increases the blood supply to the muscles (which helps us to run away or fight); causes sweating (which can cool us down); and increases breathing (which can ensure that oxygen is delivered to the muscles quickly, preparing us for a rapid response).

For some problems with anxiety, disgust is also present. Disgust can play a role in certain phobias, such as blood–injection–injury phobia, obsessive–compulsive disorder (particularly where fear of contamination is a concern) and, sometimes, with post-traumatic stress disorder. Disgust is an emotional response of revulsion for something that is considered offensive or unpleasant. It is thought that disgust evolved as an infection-avoidance response: keeping us away from foods, body products, certain animals, death and decay. Disgust may motivate humans to keep themselves and their environments clean and free from disease. However, unlike the feeling of fear, disgust is associated with a decreased heart rate.

Thinking

Other major contributors to problems with anxiety are certain thinking styles and habits in terms of how and where we focus our attention.

When we feel anxious, the physiological changes in our bodies also influence our ability to pay attention to what is happening around us. When we are in a state of high anxiety the scope of our attention narrows, so that we are less likely to notice things happening in the periphery of our vision. People who struggle with anxiety may also experience selective attention, noticing and focusing more on potential threats than other more neutral information. This tendency can mean that uncertain situations are viewed by the person as threatening.

A *pessimistic thinking style* – getting hooked by thoughts that the worst is going to happen – can be a thinking style that lends itself to experiencing anxiety. While many people with pessimistic outlooks describe this as a 'realistic' way of seeing the world, it is likely that in many situations overly pessimistic thinking overestimates the chance of disaster. Being caught up by these thoughts can lead people to avoid engaging, to limit their investment in new directions, and to not persist or adjust when they experience difficulties, creating a self-fulfilling prophecy.

Thinking that focuses on all the things that could go wrong in the future is called *worry*. On the surface, worry also typically looks like it is a useful thing to do: by considering all the potential catastrophes that could occur, there may be something that you can do to avoid any catastrophe from happening. However, the process of worry typically involves both the overestimation of disaster and all the thoughts that loop around, going over the same issues, which results in more anxiety. This increases the likelihood of worrying further.

Some people also struggle with 'worrying about worrying':

fearing that they are doing harm to themselves by worrying so much (worrying that they are going crazy), finding the seemingly uncontrollable thoughts alarming, or becoming concerned about the physical symptoms they experience (such as a rapid heart rate or breathlessness).

Sometimes people can believe that worrying is a protective way of thinking – that being on the lookout for danger can help to recognise and avoid it. Unfortunately, being constantly vigilant for danger can lead to lots of false alarms, running the risk of seeing potential danger in safe situations. The extra time spent worrying about things that have little or no likelihood of happening is all-consuming, and worrying increases the amount of anxiety you experience, creating a vicious cycle.

Going back over the mistakes of the past, getting caught up in wondering how things could have been different, is a thinking process called *rumination* (this is also discussed in Chapter 5: *Depression*). The tricky thing about rumination is that – as with worry – it can also look as if it is a useful thing to do. If you could work out why things went wrong, perhaps then you can fix problems that may arise in the future, or at least help yourself to feel better about the things that went wrong. The clue about whether rumination is helpful is to notice the repetitive and unforgiving nature of it. Notice how certain thoughts and themes may loop round and round, and that typically when you ruminate there is not a sense of relief, instead, it feels as though things are stuck or even getting worse. It is also common that people ruminate about situations of hurt, failure and embarrassment. Engaging with rumination keeps these disappointments fresh and alive, making the past an experience in the present. We are not suggesting that you can easily 'turn off' this process: rumination is a frequent experience for many of us. Instead, we are going to encourage you to step back from engaging with rumination: to notice those times when you are falling into a hole, digging for answers, trying to find someone to blame, and playing over 'what ifs' and regrets (see later in this chapter).

You can notice that both worry and rumination take us away from the present moment: either by anticipating a catastrophic future, or by being stuck in a painful past. As our actions only occur in the present, focusing too much on the past or the future can also make us feel as if we are helpless and unable to change things. As we discussed before in Chapter 3 (*Aware*), being disconnected from the present moment can mean that we are out of touch with the possibilities of the here and now (being able to take advantage of the opportunities available to us, learning from experience and finding flexible ways to handle things). We'll discuss this more below when we talk about the *Aware* skills you can use when struggling with anxiety.

Perfectionism is another problematic thinking style. This normally shows up as setting excessively high standards and striving for flawlessness, to a degree that proves to be unworkable in the long-term. This can be accompanied by many self-critical thoughts and concerns about the judgement of others. When you get caught up in perfectionism you can be driven to achieve an unattainable ideal, and then worry about mistakes as a sign of a personal defect. People who struggle with perfectionism tend to measure their self-worth by productivity and accomplishment, punishing themselves for perceived failures. They fear imperfection, and feel that other people will only like them if they are perfect. For many people caught by this type of perfectionism, there can be a great deal of anxiety about potential failure and being 'caught out' as less than perfect. People who struggle with perfectionism also tend to ruminate over past events and mistakes, and be afraid of taking chances in case there is a risk of failure.

Sometimes associated with perfectionism is a *preoccupation with order and control* (such as strong desire for routines and things being predictable in the world around you). This can take the form of needing things to be planned very precisely, being overly cautious, and a dislike of spontaneous or unpredictable situations. People who get caught up with this can find it difficult to adjust as things change, find it hard to relax, and have a sense that they do not have enough time to carry out their plans, or that more effort is needed so that they can get things 'right'. For some people these are unwanted preoccupations, while for others this may be experienced as a desirable way to live.

The challenge, as we have suggested earlier, is when these thoughts and associated urges interfere with important life directions by appearing as something to struggle with, or be guided by. Either way of responding to this thinking could lead to you becoming rigid, less flexible, and to have trouble learning from your own experience. Hence the ACT proverb: 'If you always do what you've always done, you'll always get what you've always got.'

Behaviour

As we described above, fear and anxiety prepare us to avoid and escape from the situations that are dangerous (or we perceive them to be). We look for ways to avoid the things that we fear, and to escape from situations where we are in contact with them (as soon as possible!). The relief that we feel can strengthen using this way of coping when we feel anxious.

We can use escape and avoidance in a myriad of ways:

- Planning our lives to ensure that we don't experience what we fear (even if that means being out of contact with the things we care about).

- Seeking reassurance from the people around us about our worries.

- Checking and re-checking things until we feel confident that something won't go wrong.

- Using alcohol and substances to feel differently, reduce arousal, or become numb.

- Distracting ourselves.

- Trying to hide the outward signs of anxiety from other people.

- Limiting the contact with what we fear (e.g. averting our eyes, keeping some distance from it)

- Putting demands upon others so that we ensure that we don't come in contact with what we fear.

- Limiting our opportunities by deciding certain choices and direction 'are not for us' because we are afraid of them.

- Coming up with 'reasonable' excuses when others ask us why we won't do something that we fear.

- And many, many more . . .

One of the effects of excessive use of avoidance is that it can limit the possibility of learning how to handle the feelings of fear and anxiety when they do occur. A frequent challenge when using a great deal of avoidance is that you may not be able to learn from experience: discovering that the situation you worried about did not happen, or if it did, was not as bad as you thought, or if it was as bad as you thought, that you could cope with the situation better than you thought.

So, the different ways in which we escape and avoid may, as an unintended consequence, actually maintain the problem. This is particularly the case for people who struggle with anxiety, who may make choices that ironically increase the centrality of fear in their lives. For example, the person with social anxiety who never goes out of the house: by continually avoiding the thing that triggers their anxiety, they actually create more time for rumination and worry, making the anxiety even more powerful. Life can become a daily struggle against feeling afraid, and may result in a long-term problem: without the opportunity and space to relax, reflect and soothe, there is less chance for moments of pleasure and purpose. We can see this in the case of Tim:

Tim's Story

If you recall from the Introduction, Tim was feeling pretty stuck: worrying had taken over his life. He was also unhappy with the way he had been coping with all of these fears: spending heaps of extra time at work to avoid mistakes, not having much of a social life, drinking too much to take the edge off his anxiety. He sought therapy after getting to a point where he felt as if his life was being dominated by worry.

In the first session with his therapist Tim described the following symptoms of anxiety: excessive worry, avoidance, poor sleep, feeling fearful and being on edge. He also said he had some physical symptoms such as a nauseous feeling in his stomach and breathlessness. He worried that these were physical signs that he was going to lose control. These experiences were occurring frequently and intensely enough to create problems for Tim. He described other concerns too, such as persisting sadness, fatigue, lack of enjoyment, guilt and self-criticism. It may be that Tim was experiencing the symptoms of depression too, which emerged in his struggle with his anxiety (and probably made it harder for him to find a way through the quagmire he was in).

Why Do We Experience Anxiety?

It is understandable to wonder about **why** you feel anxious. Anxiety, in its various forms, is a multifaceted experience, and there are a number of causes that have been suggested. We will briefly outline some of these causes: our genetics, early experiences and life events, personality traits and thinking styles.

Genetics

Some people are more genetically prone to anxiety disorders than others. It is well known that anxiety disorders run in families, with the vulnerability to developing problems appearing to be passed down from parents to children, particularly for panic disorder and obsessive–compulsive disorder. It is thought that there are genes that work together to increase the risk for anxiety disorders, and that the contribution of these genetic causes is moderately strong (30–40% of the risk). It is likely that the interaction between genetic vulnerability and environmental factors is involved in developing an anxiety disorder.

Early Experiences and Life Events

Events in our childhood can increase our vulnerability to struggling with anxiety. In families, we learn how to respond to fear from watching others: if we have had a relative who was overly anxious we may also relate to our fears in a similar way.

Traumatic events in childhood increase the risk of problems with anxiety: this seems to be particularly true for children who have been abused or exploited, neglected, or have experienced the loss of a parent. Exposure to chronic stress as a child is likely to be a risk factor too. Traumatic events have the potential to alter the neural and endocrine systems involved in the response to stress: as a result some people are more sensitive to the effects of stress.

It is also known that stressful life events when we are younger, such as health problems, family discord, and exposure to traumatic events, can increase our sensitivity to experiencing anxiety (in essence, learning to be afraid of being anxious). This can mean that we are more vulnerable to anxiety disorders, due to focusing on bodily sensations when fearful and thinking that they are dangerous or catastrophic.

Anxiety can be the result of feeling as though we can't cope with the demands that have been placed upon us. Frequently, anxiety develops following a series of stressful life events. These life events don't necessarily have to be unpleasant to cause stress: a change that causes a readjustment, such as having a new baby or moving house, can be stressful. This is especially the case if someone has many different pressures at the same time. The demands of these life events can feel overwhelming, particularly for people who have limited support from friends or family.

Personality Traits

There are two broad personality traits that appear to be related to a higher risk of anxiety problems: high *neuroticism* and low *extraversion*. Neuroticism is the tendency to cope poorly with stress and experience negative emotions. People who are higher in this trait tend to feel anxious, sad, angry, self-conscious and experience vulnerability more often than those low in neuroticism. Extraversion relates to the quantity and intensity of social interactions and positive emotions: people high in this trait tend to be active, assertive, warm, excitement-seeking, and emotionally bright, compared to those who are more introverted. It is more likely that people who have anxiety disorders are also more introverted.

Other personality traits can be related to a greater risk of anxiety disorders. This is particularly the case for people avoiding social situations due to being extremely sensitive to rejection and feelings of inadequacy; and similarly for those who are extremely psychologically dependent upon others, feeling helpless and unable to cope on their own.

Thinking Styles

As described above, there are several thinking styles that may make it more likely that someone will experience problems with anxiety: getting caught up with thoughts that the worst possible thing is likely to happen; being constantly on guard in case something bad happens; and believing that there is value in thinking of all the awful things that could happen. All of these thinking styles may lead to a general increased level of arousal and anxious thinking! As we described earlier, it is likely that having thoughts about potential threats is quite adaptive for us as a species, although some of us have more than our fair share of these thoughts, along with experiences that have taught us to act overcautiously.

Putting It All Together

As we described earlier, it is possible that a combination of these factors influences the level of anxiety that people experience, and their vulnerability to struggling with anxiety. Fortunately, we are more than just a combination of our heritage and history. There are things that you can do that will reduce your struggle with anxiety, and help give you a greater connection with the things you care about.

More on this in a little while, first, let's consider Tim's situation:

Tim – Early Experiences

Tim grew up in the suburbs, the only child of parents who ran a small business. He described a happy childhood, feeling loved and supported by his parents. He described his father as a quiet man, who did not show much emotion, and his mother as more open and affectionate. Tim recalls his parents being cautious regarding his welfare: concerned that he did not play contact sports at school, and expressing worries that he might hurt himself when he did things like climb trees.

Tim has a key memory from when he was eleven years old when he sat an examination for a scholarship at a prestigious boarding school. If he had won this scholarship it would have meant moving away from his parents, and living in a city several hours away. It would have also opened up opportunities for him that weren't available at his local high school. Tim had been doing well in school, and frequently been the top of his class. His family made the trip to the city and he sat the examination at the school. Tim remembers that, while the examination was challenging, there were some questions that he felt were much easier than the others: he finished feeling confident that he would do well, and be awarded the scholarship.

A month later Tim received a letter about the examination result: he had not been awarded the scholarship. Tim recalled that when he had received this news he was devastated, and it felt as if the world had caved in on him. He had a strong sense of being a failure and being a disappointment to his parents. The thing that stood out to him was that he had made a big mistake with the questions on the exam paper by being too confident. Tim remembers that his father had also said to him that it was a pity he had not been more careful in the exam. He believed that his future was ruined, as this mistake could never be fixed.

He also described feeling much more anxious and doubtful about his abilities from this point.

Tim describes that there have been times in his life since this point when he had felt more worried about making mistakes, and could get into a pattern of being extra-cautious and rechecking his work. He describes that this happened when he was in secondary school, particularly leading up to his final exams. He describes learning that 'a simple mistake can cost you dearly', and 'worrying helps you stay careful, noticing what could go wrong'. He said that he learned to cope at these times by focusing on his work, checking over it before handing it in or sharing it with anyone. He also would dive into his worries in case there was something useful to find there, although the looping nature of worrying over and over again did distress him, as well as take up a lot of time. Tim learned to withdraw from others and his responsibilities towards them when he became stressed like this. This had caused some problems with his relationships in the past, as he would not share his worries and problems, despite their obvious impact on him. Similarly he had learned to delay decision-making – 'analysis paralysis' as he described it – by worrying about possible calamities. This would frustrate his partner and lead to arguments, which would worry him further.

As we can see from Tim's story, there were some early experiences that may have contributed to his tendency to have worrying thoughts, to find these threatening, and to respond by checking, delaying decisions and engaging in avoidance. You could think of these as a set of 'Life Rules' that Tim had learned to play by when he was stressed with demands to perform at school and work. Tim was so caught up in his thoughts and feelings that he didn't really have any choice about how he was living. Therapy was helping him to gain a different perspective on some of the unhelpful thoughts that were driving him so that he could begin to make conscious choices again – either continue to 'play by the rules' or focus on his values and the things that really mattered to him in life.

The Dig for Answers . . . or Acting in the Present?

While Tim's life experience can provide some clues about the rules he has learned to live by this insight does not necessarily provide him with the freedom to act differently.

As we discussed in Chapter 2 (*Open*) our minds are great problem-solvers. For many of us, life is such a puzzle, our minds like to deal with 'why things happen'. We can expend a great deal of time and energy digging into the past, trying to find all the reasons why we feel and act the way we do. We have been describing the difference between the quest to 'look for answers' versus looking at the things that *maintain the problem* (in this case, anxiety).

As described in Chapter 5 (*Depression*), when there is a quaint mountain village that is going to be crushed by a runaway boulder, is it more useful to consider what caused the boulder to roll down the valley, or to engage with what you could do to save the village? By noticing the tendency for our minds to look for answers we can become more attuned to when this tendency is useful . . . and when gently noticing what our minds are doing ('there it goes again, trying to find answers!', 'good mind, working it all out') and re-connecting with the present moment is the more effective move.

As this book is about helping you, we are more interested in how the experience of anxiety has an impact on your life. Does fear, worry and avoidance stop you doing stuff that is important to you? Do these problems get in the way of you leading a life that is vital and rich with experience?

Our goal is to help you to make the switch from living a life that is ruled by what you are afraid of to a life that is about consciously taking steps in your personal valued directions.

It is from here and now that you can practice becoming flexible and head in the directions that you hold dear.

Even if fear is part of the experience of doing this.

Anxiety – a Psychologically Flexible Approach

We are inviting you to consider how the experience of fear and anxiety can become a problem. In the ACT approach, life-limiting struggles with our experiences can happen when we are not *Open*, *Aware* and *Active*. In the Introduction, we considered Tim's problems in terms of these skills, and we encourage you to try this approach with your own experiences.

The next section will explore how you can use the *Open*, *Aware*, and *Active* skills to help you to engage in valued actions and limit how much anxiety is controlling your life. We will use Tim's example to highlight how the *Open*, *Aware* and *Active* approach could help someone to live a life with purpose and meaning, in the face of worry and anxiety.

Open – Closed

The struggle with anxiety and worry can be seen as being **closed** to these experiences. In a way this makes sense: who would **want** to feel frightened and fearful thinking about all the terrible things that could happen? So we can be **unwilling** to expose ourselves to situations that might involve anxiety.

However, if we are unwilling and closed to experiencing anxiety, then many opportunities also become closed to us: taking a risk with feeling vulnerable in a new relationship, applying for a new job, or anything else that might involve uncertainty.

The Struggle with Anxiety Is the Problem!

When we become caught up with anxiety, we can act as though we have a switch to turn it off. As we discussed in

Chapter 2 (*Open*), trying to control our emotions is hard work, and it usually means that we end up resorting to some life-limiting ways in order not to feel anxious.

The alternative we describe here is using *Open* skills to **choose** to experience the emotions, thoughts, sensations and urges that we have when we are anxious. By turning up our *Openness Dial*, opening up and making room for our experiences we may have more options available about what we then **do**.

Tim – the Life-Constricting Effects of a Struggle with Anxiety

In discussing his problems with his therapist, Tim was able to take stock of the **impact** of the choices and actions he had taken to try to keep anxiety at bay. In fact, there were negative experiences that he was having (loneliness, fatigue, lethargy, difficulty concentrating) that were probably affected by the way that he coped. Tim shared that he felt trapped – by his sense of responsibility toward work, not having enough hours in the day to have a life and being cautious in general. He shared that he saw his problem of worrying as 'silly' – as no catastrophe had ever happened. This did not stop him worrying though!

Tim had also noticed that instead of his worrying reducing over time, instead, it had become a larger and larger part of his life. It also seemed that Tim was caught in a cycle of rumination too: when he wasn't worrying his mind was going over 'why' he had these problems! At these times he would feel guilty and ashamed about worrying and procrastinating. It was as if he had fallen into a deep hole, and was spending all of his energy trying to dig his way out, but was actually only making the hole deeper. (In fact, this is one of the metaphors that Tim's therapist offered to him about how this problem seemed to work.)

Tim was like a **Man in a Hole** (a classic ACT metaphor). He did not know it, but life can sometimes involve falling into a deep hole, and finding your way out can be tricky! In Tim's hands was a shovel (his problem-solving mind – remember, back to Chapter 2 (*Open*)), and he was applying this tool to the problem he was in. This meant digging a deeper hole (by worrying, ruminating, procrastinating, and trying not to feel discomfort)! Life was becoming about living in a deeper and deeper hole, rather than about purpose and vitality. There were times when Tim tried to convince himself that he liked living in a hole, although his feelings suggested otherwise. He was doing the thing that seemed familiar and using the tool that was in his hands, digging. The therapist suggested that one of the first things to focus on was to try to stop digging further. By letting go of the shovel (being in his head worrying and ruminating), Tim may have a chance to discover some other ways of getting out of the hole. Tim reflected that this was going to feel uncomfortable, as he was pretty familiar with digging but not much else for the past two years.

From this perspective, Tim and his therapist could look at what the cost of struggling with his anxiety and worry had been to him. With his therapist Tim explored both the short- and long-term effects of living a life according to the rules of *worry*. Tim reflected that there were areas of his life that he had neglected because of his problems. He described how relationships were important to him, and that he found purpose by connecting to people in both his private life as well as in the work environment. While he was a dedicated worker (too dedicated!), he felt that there was a wall between him and other people in his workplace. He was unable to show that he was unsure or stressed in case he would be blamed for being irresponsible. This meant that he spent his time making sure he looked competent and well-informed about all the aspects of his job. He described that while his manager was support- ive and fair and did not reprimand others when things went wrong, Tim could not let himself show vulnerability.

Tim also noticed that aside from the work dimension of his life, there was little else. He stated that this was not the life that he would choose, but rather seemed to be the life that he was in (like being in a hole). Tim described wanting to spend time with his flatmates, to do things for enjoyment, and to exercise and be more healthy in his choices. He stated that if he had more time he would go on holiday, see his family, and be less serious as a person. It seemed that anxiety was taking up a lot of room in his life. And like a person stuck in a hole, more digging was causing the walls of the hole to crumble, dirt falling on top of him . . .

EXERCISE: Noticing Your Own Unwillingness

In your struggle with anxiety what have you noticed about your life – have the efforts to control and stop your unwanted experiences allowed you to be free of fear? Or have they ended up making it worse?

We would like you to take some time to think about your anxiety. Think back over the past few weeks to moments where you have experienced strong fear and anxiety. Consider what happened before this emotion: what was the triggering event? Then, what happened after? Did you find yourself engaging in unhelpful avoidance that took you away from what is important to you? Or did you use your *Open*, *Aware* and *Active* skills to stay on track with your values? It would help to reflect on several situations where you experienced fear, anxiety or worry.

What was the situation?

What were your Responses (emotions, thoughts, sensations, urges)? How willing were you to experience fear and anxiety (0 – not at all, up to 10 – completely willing)?

What did you do? Did this move you away from your Values (Avoidance) or towards your Values?

It's highly probable that the reason that you are reading this book is because you haven't found a way to have a flourishing, value-driven life by stopping yourself feeling anxious. It is likely that you have fallen into a hole like Tim, and then by trying to get away from feeling the way that you do when you are scared, you've been digging in various ways to escape and avoid.

Unfortunately, our very human tendencies to go for short-term comfort and to seek relief from feeling fearful, can sometimes mean that the hole we are digging becomes a prison for us. Ironically, when we try hard to avoid feeling scared, it can be the case that anxiety ends up being even more prominent in our lives, and the world comes to seem even more scary and threatening. The more we work hard against feeling anxious, remaining vigilant about threats, the more sensitive we may be to experiences that signal the potential to feel anxious. The small, narrow space of the hole is what is left when we are unwilling to feel anxiety and have dedicated our energy to avoiding discomfort. In this space we have no room for lives that feel purposeful, rich or meaningful.

EXERCISE: What Parts of Your Life Have Been Made Smaller Because of Anxiety?

We are interested in exploring the various ways that your life has been influenced by the struggle with anxiety. In this exercise please reflect on the areas of your life, and how they currently are due to the struggle. Reflect on each life area in turn before then going on to describe how you would like it to be.

When you describe how you would like it to be, write as though there were no barriers, as if you were able to effortlessly act like the person you really want to be.

Life Domain	How it is, because of the struggle with anxiety	How I would like it to be, based on my valued directions
Intimate relationship		
My health		
Work		
Leisure time		
Family relationships		
Friendships		

We are going to suggest something here that may not fit all that well with this motivation to be comfortable. Could it be that many of the most important and meaningful things in life involve vulnerability, fear and discomfort? It could be that feeling scared at least some of the time is the **price of admission** to having a rich, full and vital life.

Thinking: Watching the Alarms Go Off

In this section we will turn the spotlight on the types of stories that you receive from the thoughts, images, memories and urges that your mind creates when you are anxious. Taking these stories seriously, and basing your life upon them, can play a big role in how *Open* you are to having these thoughts as simply experiences.

Here are some examples of the thoughts and stories people with anxiety have described:

Story: Something terrible is happening:

- What if I lose my job?

- What if I have an accident?

- What if I develop a serious illness?

- What if I make a mistake?

Story: I am unable to cope:

- I'm weak.

- My emotions could overwhelm me/I'll have a panic attack.

- My worry is uncontrollable (I'm going crazy).

- I'm vulnerable.

Story: I am being judged critically by other people:

- I'm different/I don't fit in.

- What if people notice that I am shaking/sweating? People will think that I am abnormal.

- I don't know what to say. People will think that I am stupid.

- People won't like me.

- Think about the last time that you were anxious: what thoughts, images, etc. were running through your mind?

_____

_____

_____

_____

You should also notice the qualities of these thoughts: shrill and insistent, loud, getting your attention and narrowing your focus. They are hard to ignore.

The common thread across these thoughts is the story about the situation you are in and your ability to be there. It is like having a large alarm system:

This is a dangerous situation, you are vulnerable, and the best thing you can do is get away from here as soon as possible.

In one way we can appreciate having such a system, which only really tries to keep us safe. The only problem is that the same story is sent out, whether or not the situation is mortally dangerous, and regardless of what the 'best thing' might be for you. The answer is always to run away, and quickly!

As we described earlier in the *Open* chapter, the problem may not be so much that you have these types of thoughts, as **how much you get caught up by them**. Following these thoughts closely, and responding to every alarm, can result in our being unwilling to experience anxiety, and playing it safe (which can lead to living a very narrow life).

Aware – Threat Detection!

While there is a tendency for humans to be on autopilot, when we struggle with anxiety there is another mode that we can be in: threat detection. It is as if we are switched on to a system where every possible danger, threat and potential problem is coming up as an alert.

Instead of being *Aware*, we live a life of **vigilance**, watching for threats and danger, hardly open to the moment at all (because something awful might happen to us). The moment becomes about ensuring that we are safe and that nothing goes wrong. Our nervous system responds in a way consistent with this, providing the physiological changes to prepare us to fight or flee, and narrowing our attention to those things that may be potential threats.

Therefore, we end up disconnecting with what is around us. When we are so worried and anxious it is hard to have creative thoughts, appreciate the moment, or indeed notice and attend to anything else, as the present is tinged with danger, or the possibility that something awful will happen. Our lack of appreciation is due to our being 'in crisis mode', like in a Hollywood alien-invasion movie, when the US military calls to go to DEFCON 5!

As you may have experienced, along with the cost of your life being 'on alert', the effect of being vigilant all the time is exhausting.

You = Fear?

By using your *Open* and *Aware* skills you may notice that, when it comes to doing things that involve fear, your mind is accomplished at coming up with all sorts of reasons **not** to do them. And that's all right – in fact, we could thank our threat-detection systems for being so effective in getting these stories to us! As we have discussed before, there may be a difference between receiving the story of fear – after all you are hooked up to your nervous system – and **acting upon fear**. By being more *Aware* of how this works, you may have more choices and options about how to respond.

A particularly cunning thing that our story-telling minds can do is to generate reasons for avoidance that have to do with our **identity**. These types of stories can feel much more fundamental, as though they tell us something true and persisting about ourselves. Notice also what happens to your identity, as you struggle with anxiety and worry:

- You become the 'fearful, worried person'.
- Fear becomes your guide, rather than your values.
- You are the person who does not take chances.
- You = Anxiety.

This is clearly illustrated with Tim's story. Early in therapy Tim would find it challenging to consider doing things that may involve contact with his fear and worry, as his mind would start telling him that he was 'not the sort of person who takes risks'. His mind would also bring up all sorts of reasons why he shouldn't change things in his life: things could get worse!

So, there can be stories about yourself that are *self-defeating* or encourage playing it safe, even if this costs you dearly. The thing that we can notice about our minds is that because they want us to be comfortable and safe, they may overestimate the dangers to us. So, we are going to encourage you to notice your mind *and* also notice what you want your life to be about. For many of us, these two things do not necessarily fit together. And they don't need to! See if you can create some space for your mind to struggle with that.

What story has your mind come up with about your fear, anxiety or worry? How are you being defined by it?

_____

_____

_____

_____

_____

If your fear were not a barrier, if the story about 'your being anxious' were like a road sign that you could whizz past, as if you were travelling in a car on the highway, then what would you want your life to be about?

Tim: Reasons to Worry

Tim also reported that he had lots of reasons to worry. His therapist carefully asked him about these reasons: Tim said that he needed to keep his job, that doing a good job was important to him, and that he couldn't appear to be not in control. He described some advantages of worrying: that it meant that he had good attention to detail, that he was more likely to detect problems and fix them, and that he was more conscientious than others.

He also shared the belief that worrying did lead to solutions, even if it took a long time to get there.

Tim's therapist suggested that perhaps he was living life according to a set of rules, about how important worrying was to being successful. Carefully, they sketched out how these rules might work (like the rules to the Game of Life):

1. Tim must reduce the chance of something bad happening to zero.

2. If something bad happens, then it is a *catastrophe*.

3. Tim is responsible for making sure that nothing bad happens. If it does, then Tim is a failure, irresponsible and a fraud.

4. You can think your way out of every Problem. The Answer is out there.

Tim found it helpful to hear from the therapist that what he was doing was understandable and perhaps a logical thing, although this was not working in the way that he hoped. His therapist asked for whose benefit he was living by these rules? For Tim? Or for Anxiety? His therapist invited Tim to consider his worry and anxiety as experiences to be observed and to consciously decide whether to engage with them (trying to control them, or making choices based on them) on the basis *of whether or not they were helpful or unhelpful in moving him towards his values.*

Working with Worry and Rumination: *Aware* and *Open* skills

As we talked about earlier, worry is entirely normal. It becomes a problem when it takes over your life, leading you to spend greater amounts of time anticipating future disasters and catastrophes, and limiting your ability to **make the most of your life as you are living it now**. We know through studies of people who worry excessively that they tend to:

- Over-estimate the chances of something happening.

- Under-estimate their own resources and coping.

- Be hyper-vigilant to threats and dangers.

Worry, it seems, can make your threat-detection system much more sensitive and prone to setting off false alarms. Being connected to such a system creates more anxiety and stuff to be worried about. It may also be the case that people who worry also worry about their worrying: being scared that all the worrying is a sign that they have lost control of their minds, that it will do them permanent harm, or that they will be stuck like this forever.

We are going to encourage you to use mindfulness skills to notice when worry appears (to be *Aware*), and to make room for it (to be *Open*). This will help you to notice the **effects** of worry, and have more options about what you want to do when invited by your mind to engage in worrying.

Mindfulness Practice: Watching Your Worries, Rather than Being Caught up by Them

We described earlier how regularly practising mindfulness as a key *Aware* skill can be useful. By developing flexible contact with the present moment you are also likely to have more options in terms of your choices and actions. You can cultivate this contact by connecting with your breathing, and consciously attending to the various experiences available to you through your senses and the various things your mind does with these (judgements, predictions, memories, fantasies, etc.). This can also be where practising defusion techniques is useful (Chapter 2: *Open*).

Choosing to be **here and now** is not likely to be something that comes easily. In fact, for most of us, it takes a deliberate effort to disengage autopilot or to gently 'just notice' our Alarm system. There is a good chance that your mind is going to come up with all sorts of reasons why this is a *bad* idea! We encourage you to appreciate all the various ways that the process of being *Aware* will be made difficult: in fact, this is a good sign that you are taking steps forward!

Again, notice whether your mind is trying to keep score about whether you 'succeed' or 'fail' at being mindful. This will be particularly relevant when you notice excuses and reasons not to practise being mindful, or self-critical thoughts about how well you are achieving mindfulness, or making progress with your problems. These are also opportunities to notice how judgemental minds can be, and where or when this is useful . . . and when it isn't.

Remember that with the approach we are describing in this book we are not proposing that you aim to attain a Zen, blissed-out state where you never worry again . . . your connection to your nervous system will guarantee that you will continue to be bombarded with stories about potential threats and dangers. After all, it is just doing the job that evolution and experience has built it for!

Today, we invite you to make a commitment to practising noticing and mindfulness.

EXERCISE: Watching the Clouds in the Sky

We are going to ask you to do an exercise involving imagining that your experiences are clouds in the sky, and that you are just watching them. It is probably best to begin this exercise by reading the instructions so that you get some idea of what to do. Then close your eyes (or whatever helps you imagine) and start the exercise by practising awareness of your breathing.

First, take a couple of gentle breaths, and as you do so, connect with the experience of your breathing, in this moment. Notice the posture that your body is in, the way that it feels. Get present with whatever you are noticing right now, and if you are able, make room for your experiences.

Connect again with your breath. Notice the sound and feel of your own breathing.

Now, we invite you to imagine you are lying on a grassy hill on a warm spring day.

Imagine feeling the ground beneath you, the smell of the grass, and the sounds of nearby trees blowing in the wind.

Now, imagine you are looking up at the sky while lying on this hill, watching clouds pass across the sky. And as you do so, become aware of your thoughts and feelings.

Each time a thought pops into your mind, imagine that it is written on one of those clouds. If you think in images, place these on a cloud and let them float by.

Your task is to stay watching the sky and allow the clouds to keep moving by. Don't try to change what shows up on the clouds in any way. If the clouds disappear or you go somewhere else mentally, or you find that you are in a cloud, just stop and notice this happening and gently bring yourself back to lying on the grassy hill, watching the sky and clouds.

If you notice having any thoughts or feelings about doing this exercise, place these on clouds as well. If your thoughts stop, just watch the sky and the clouds. Sooner or later your thoughts will start up again.

Finally, bring your attention back to your breathing. Notice again the steady rhythm of your breathing that is with you all the time. Then, bring your awareness back to where you are. Gently open your eyes and notice what you can see. Just focus on the present moment, here and now.

You can write your reflections about the Clouds exercise here:

_____

_____

_____

_____

_____

The Four-Day Flexible Contact with Worry
(Expressive Writing Exercise)

We are going to encourage you to take part in a writing exercise as part of developing greater *Open* and *Aware* skills towards worrying. This exercise will involve you writing about a worry that you have, over four days, for fifteen minutes each day. The key with this exercise is to stick with writing for the fifteen-minute period, noticing any thoughts, images and sensations associated with this worry, and urges to think of other things or to act upon the worry.

Writing About Worry Instructions (adapted from Markowitz, 2007):[8]

Find a blank sheet of paper and a pen. Sit in a comfortable spot for writing.

Identify a key worry that you have – this could be the most frequent or distressing worry that you have struggled with lately. Write this worry at the top of the sheet of paper. And then follow these instructions:

> For the next fifteen minutes, we would like you to write about this worry. In your writing, we want you to really let go and explore your very deepest emotions and thoughts. You might tie the worry you write about to other parts of your life. For example, how is it related to your childhood, your

---

8 Markowitz, L., 'Written Emotional Disclosure about Potential Problems' (Unpublished doctoral thesis, University of Waterloo, Canada, 2007)

parents, people you love, who you are, and who you want to be? In addition, you may choose to write about what might happen or what the consequences might be if the situation you are worried about were to occur. Or you might write about what factors might make the situation more (or less) likely to occur. Whatever you choose to write, however, it is critical that you really delve into your deepest emotions and thoughts.

If you feel you have fully expressed your feelings about this potential problem before the fifteen minutes is up and have nothing left to write about, you may write about a different worry. Again, please be sure that you really delve into your deepest emotions and thoughts.

Ready? Start writing!

After Day Four of the writing exercise, reflect about what you noticed:

What was it like to write about your worries, connecting with your deepest emotions and thoughts?

What did you notice changed about your experience of worry? What remained the same?

You can write your reflections here:

_____

_____

_____

_____

_____

Other Perspectives

Think back to the Team of Advisers that we introduced in Chapter 3 (*Aware*) – do you notice that you spend your time listening to the most cautious one?

• Are there perspectives that you are less in contact with?

• Rather than dismissing these, would there be value in checking them out too?

Spend a few minutes getting in contact with these other Advisers – what would they say about the situations you worry about?

Adviser 1 [   ] would say:

"_____"

Adviser 2 [   ] would say:

"_____"

Adviser 3 [   ] would say:

"_____"

**EXERCISE: Watching the Worst Disaster Movie
in the World!**

Imagine that the thoughts and images that you experience when you are anxious could be observed,
like watching a cheesy disaster movie on TV. And
this one is the granddaddy of all disaster movies –
a skyscraper is on fire, with a tidal wave carrying a
passenger liner heading towards it; the tidal wave
has been caused by a giant meteor that has also hit a
nuclear power plant, and the chain reaction has given
birth to a giant monster that will devour the world!
And all the time there are aliens in their spaceship
preparing to invade the planet . . . of course, if there
is any sort of planet left, after the zombies have taken
over!

What would it be like to watch a movie like this? (OK, we're not holding our breath to pitch the idea to Hollywood.)

We are going to guess that when you get caught up with your anxiety, it is like you are a character in this disaster movie, and feel you are in mortal jeopardy! Terrible catastrophes are happening, and you are powerless to stop them.

Now, what if you could watch your experiences of anxiety like watching this movie?

Imagine that instead of these thoughts and images being inside you, you could instead see them flashing up on the TV, like scenes from this disaster movie. Each worrying thought appears on the screen. Each image of a catastrophe happening in your life is up on the screen. And, instead of being in the movie, you are taking a different position, that of just watching it.

We're going to invite you to notice a few things, and then see what happens as you flexibly engage with this exercise.

When you are anxious, how close are you sitting to the screen? How engrossed are you in the disaster movie that your life seems to be? Does it seem as if you have forgotten that you are watching a movie and instead are caught up in it?

Imagine that you have a little more distance between you and the TV screen, as if you are sitting further a way. What would this be like? Experiment with watching from an even further distance. What is your experience of the movie now?

Imagine that you could turn down the sound of the TV, and just watch the images. What would that be like?

Now, turn the sound back up, and play around with the picture making the movie lighter or darker, increasing the contrast, etc. What does this feel like?

Imagine that the movie is playing on a giant screen in a cinema. What do you notice about that experience?

Now picture the movie playing on a small tablet, which is lying flat on a coffee table. You are sitting on a sofa, having a sip of your favourite drink. You can see that the tablet is showing the movie out of the corner of your eye. The sound is at an audible level, so you know that it is playing. You are enjoying the drink while the movie plays in the background. What is that experience like?

While we are imagining watching our anxious experiences let's introduce some other perspectives:

- Imagine that you are a studio executive, watching the first cut of this movie, before it is audience-tested. What would be your opinion? Do you think that it will recover the cost of production? How do you think it would need to be marketed to get an audience?

- Imagine that you are a movie critic and you can comment on how well made the disaster movie is, whether the script is well-written, and how good are the special effects and the acting. What would be your review?

- Finally, let the disaster movie and the screen dissolve in your mind. Get in touch with the present moment – notice the sights and sounds around you, what sensations you are having in your body, and how you are breathing.

Reflect on the process of doing this exercise. What did you notice?

_____

_____

_____

_____

_____

_____

_____

_____

Breaking the Worry Rules – What If This Sounds Wrong to You?

We'd like to draw your attention to another clever trick that our minds play on us – we call it the Responsibility Trap. Some people's minds tell them that worry is the **responsible** thing to do. By anticipating all the things that can go wrong (so say their minds), they can find ways to reduce the risks. Despite plenty of evidence to the contrary, the Responsibility Trap can convince us that we need to hang on to worry to be effective.

But don't take our word for whether worry is the wrong or right thing to do! In this book we are interested in helping you to live effectively, rather than telling you what and how much you should be feeling. Anticipating the future and working out how to make the most of it is one of the skills that has led humans to be the dominant species on the planet.

So, trust your own experience of the effectiveness of worrying. The questions we would ask you to consider are:

- Does my worrying, although seeming like the right thing to do, limit my life in any way?

- What thoughts and images about myself would be proved to be wrong if I acted on my values, rather than my worry?

- Do I hold on to worry as the thing to do because I am unwilling to feel uncomfortable?

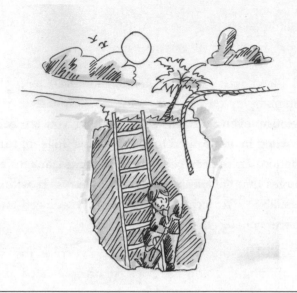

The Present Moment . . . Getting Out of the Rumination Hole

We are going to invite you to do an experiencing exercise. This will focus on one of the things that you ruminate about. In this exercise we are going to ask you to get in contact with the present moment and, from that perspective, notice the focus of your rumination as an **experience**. It may help to imagine that the thing that you ruminate about is like a hole in the ground, some distance away from you. We are going to guide you to take some steps closer to it, and then ask you to notice when you get caught up in the rumination (falling down the hole), and using your *Aware* skills try to step back to the edge of the hole . . . just with curiosity looking at the rumination.

Before we begin, first identify a situation or problem that you regularly ruminate about.

Briefly give this rumination a name: _____

_____

Notice, even with this step, whether you are being invited by your mind to 'fall into' the 'hole' of rumination. There may be feelings, thoughts, images and urges that have appeared that you struggle with, or usually take over. If this has happened, we invite you to gently notice these experiences. To go further, we invite you to be thankful for this happening, as this is a clue that you have chosen a great target for this exercise!

In any case, the next step is to use your *Aware* and *Open* skills to connect with this present moment. Noticing this moment that you're breathing, the posture of your body and the way it feels, and the sounds in the room. Spend a few moments just noticing your experiences as they arise in the present.

Now we will take another step closer. From the position of being in the here and now we invite you to step closer to the rumination, and notice any pull or urge for the present to disappear, and for you to be in the hole, back in the past. If you find yourself in the hole, then notice where you are, and get in touch with the present moment, through your breath or noticing the experience of your body as it is now.

Take enough steps to get close to your rumination, close enough for there to be an urge to fall into the hole. Notice the urge to get caught up by what has happened in the past: finding reasons, someone to blame or regrets, etc. Notice whatever is happening now, as part of your experience of observing the rumination.

Now from this position close to the hole, see if you can notice what it is like to be in contact with your rumination as an experience:

... Notice the images that come into your mind ... and gently allow them to be there.

... Notice the feelings that show up, and where in your body you feel them ... give them permission to be part of your experience right now.

... Notice the way that your body feels while ruminating ... from a kind and loving perspective to yourself ... open up to these feelings as experiences in this moment.

... Notice judgements about yourself and others ... willingly allow your mind to work, while you just notice this, as if you were looking into a hole to see what is down there ...

... Notice urges to blame, turn away or problem-solve ... as if they are inviting you to go back into the past (back down the hole) ... gently notice those tendencies too ... your mind likes to solve things ... notice how many times your mind has gone over the rumination ... and notice your experience of how useful this has been to you ...

And again, when you fall into the hole, or find yourself caught up by the past ... notice your breath and your body to be present. Find yourself standing back at the edge of the hole, just watching what is happening.

Finally, notice the present moment again, breathe into being here now, just watching your mind and your body, from a position of being a gentle, compassionate explorer. Do what you wish to notice the difference in experience between being connected to the present, and falling into the hole of the past, in rumination.

Take some moments to reflect on what you have experienced during this exercise:

_____

_____

_____

_____

_____

_____

_____

What Did Tim Do?

Tim worked with his therapist on strengthening his present moment contact by practising an Awareness of the Breath exercise (from Chapter 3: *Aware*). He practised both in the session and several times a week at home. His therapist also suggested other ways that he could practise noticing through his senses (such as stopping to notice colours, sounds, tastes, touch and smell) and while doing daily activities, such as walking to work and drinking a cup of coffee.

Through this practice, Tim noticed that a lot of the time he was either in autopilot mode – going through the motions in his life or, more often, caught up with worrying, which also took him away from being here and now. It seemed like a lot of his life was spent anticipating a future where disasters happened! Tim reflected that practising Awareness of the Breath helped him to notice when he got caught up in worry, and that there was an alternative – just being in the moment. Tim also noticed that because he spent so much time anticipating future catastrophes most of his energy was engaged in finding ways to escape from the anxiety that these fantasies generated. This left very little room for him just to be in the present moment, and to do things that might build the kind of life that he wanted for himself.

Tim practised further exercises to develop a flexible stance toward his worries and ruminations. In

the sessions with the therapist Tim practised noticing his worries as if they were clouds in the sky, and
the occasions where the clouds would disappear
and he would be hooked into worrying. Tim also
developed a more *Aware* approach to his ruminating, by imagining standing on the edge of the
hole his rumination tries to pull him into. Finally,
he noticed the effects of 'Breaking the Worry Rules'
and the stories that his mind came up with.

Active – Avoidance and Escape

Fear and anxiety are important in your emotional life.
Receiving the message that situations could be threatening,
and your nervous system preparing your body to handle
danger, has probably helped you many, many times. For
you to be reading this chapter, it is probable that there are
times in your life when this ability has not helped you in the
way it should have. The alarm system goes off, your body
prepares for 'flight or fight', your mind fills with worrying
thoughts and potential dangers: this is very hard to ignore,
or to simply switch off when there is a false alarm.

So, you can be left with trying to manage as best you
can – which may mean avoiding scenarios where you get
too anxious, and seeking relief by escaping from scary
moments. All the while your life is being held hostage to
crippling fear and worry, with the only options of escape
and avoidance leading to an existence with less vitality,
purpose and meaning. As one of our clients once said about

his struggling with anxiety, 'Basically, I'm just a life-support system for a panic attack!' You end up not being in the driver's seat of your life, instead you are a passenger, as your fear decides where you go, what you do, and with whom. It ends up being a cycle of:

- Taking short-term, feel-good actions.

- Leading to avoidance (or behaviour related to avoidance).

- And avoidance becoming a bigger and bigger problem.

Please don't misunderstand – there is no problem with avoidance as long as it doesn't cost you anything, and it may even be part of living effectively. We are not talking about becoming a masochist (seeking out pain for its own sake) or saying that you *must* face your fears (again, notice the rules creeping in here, making something that is supposed to be flexible into something that sounds like a command). Sometimes acting on our values may mean avoiding or escaping: choosing not to put ourselves in situations where we may be tempted to engage in unhealthy habits; deciding to end an abusive relationship; or giving up on a life choice that has not been working. We are, after all, the descendants of those who were skilled at threat detection and did the things to survive long enough to have offspring: it may be in our heritage to use these tendencies to do things that enhance our lives.

The problem with managing your life solely by escape and avoidance is that it is hard to move in a forward direction: it is as if you are looking around and watching for what might go wrong or hurt you. This could be like the scenario described earlier in Chapter 5 (*Depression*): imagine being chased by a zombie horde while you are driving a car to get away, and keeping your eyes on the rear-view mirror. While detecting danger and making sure that the zombies don't get any closer to you by continually checking the rear-view mirror . . . you also are not free to respond in the directions you would choose.

We are going to suggest an alternative: flexible contact with the things that you fear through practising the *Open* and *Aware* skills:

1. your willingness **to have anxious experiences as simply experiences** increases, and,
2. you will have greater awareness of the stories that your mind creates that invite avoidance and escape.

You will never need to like or approve of the experiences you have. You may not need to work out 'why' they are there either. You could experiment with dropping the struggle in feeling afraid, and see if this creates more space in your life for the things you care about.

Living a Broad-Horizon Life

This book is about living a more full and meaningful life, and, as you may have worked out by now, this will mean **being in contact** with all sorts of feelings and thoughts. All humans are faced with this choice, every day: do I make room for what is happening inside me right now, or do I try to control or stop these experiences? Faced with this choice, we can sometimes not notice what it costs us to struggle, until it is too late. We have encouraged you to look at your own experience of having this choice, and whether life becomes too small and narrow when you do too much avoiding and escaping. Throughout this book you have been presented with an alternative: to be *Open* to your experiences, *Aware* of what your mind is doing (when it tells stories about your life and who you are), and *Active* in choosing purpose and committing to doing what matters.

Living this way means letting go of digging a deeper hole in an effort to escape. It also means not settling for living in a narrow, cramped hole, trying to convince yourself that this is what you wanted anyway! Living this way means climbing out of the hole, being open to what you feel, noticing what your mind is saying, and exploring where you are: a life of uncharted territory and broad horizons. In exploring this life with your choices and actions, there are guaranteed to be unforeseen moments both scary *and* hugely meaningful. Living this way involves the willingness to risk having experiences such as:

- Feeling vulnerable.

- Feeling disappointed when you make a mistake.

- Feeling out of control sometimes.

- Not being sure if you will succeed.

- Being rejected by people.

Each time you choose to be open to these experiences, you increase the chance that your life will be broader, more meaningful. You also increase the possibility of learning new things (charting the territory).

Each time you try to close yourself to having these experiences, you are back in the hole, digging away. Controlling and stopping anxiety also means limiting your horizons. How much more is there to learn from living in the hole?

So, as a next step, we are inviting you to deliberately choose to have your fear as an experience, while not acting to avoid or escape it. This is a process called *exposure* (yes, don't psychologists come up with lovely names for things!). Exposure is one of the most effective things you can do to reduce the control that fear and anxiety has over your life.

Practising exposure provides the opportunity to engage in meaningful actions *and* strengthens your flexibility skills (making space for anxiety; noticing the stories that your mind comes up with; connecting with your values). It involves taking a risk – something your mind may not like!

We know from decades of research that exposure works best when:

1. You have long, continuous practice with the things you fear, rather than doing very short bursts of contact (which is likely to maintain anxiety as a problem, and could be, in essence, what you are doing at the moment).

2. Whatever task you are attempting is approached 'as if' you weren't afraid. We don't mean denying how you feel inside – rather, to *act* as though anxiety weren't a problem, so that you can maximise your contact. For example, if you are afraid of heights, taking your time when crossing a bridge, noticing the sounds, colours, smells, the way each step feels as your body moves, etc. (Similar to how we described in Chapter 3 (*Aware*) and on mindfully connecting with your experiences, both wanted and unwanted.)

3. You practise regularly. This means that there are going to be good times and bad times, as progressing is not usually a straight line. Regular practice is like regular exercise: it will strengthen the flexibility 'muscles' of your skills.

The flexibility skills described in this book can enhance the process of exposure:

1. Linking your practice to a valued direction will provide more purpose to being in contact with your fear. You are not doing this 'to be less afraid', instead you are doing it to broaden your life, and be more free to do the things that are important to you.

2. Practising willingness towards these unwanted experiences (bodily sensations, emotions) can help to create space for them. The energy that you used to control these experiences can instead be turned towards doing the things that matter to you.

3. Being in mindful contact with the thoughts, images, sensations and urges that usually act as barriers while doing exposure can strengthen your flexible response to these experiences. It is likely that these experiences are going to be there anyway when you do something you usually feel scared of, but you are becoming more skilled in noticing them and sticking to doing what you planned.

4. Shifting perspective – such as using the imagery we have introduced (e.g. observing the weather, watching a movie), or listening to the various members of the team of advisers, or looking at this like your hero would – will at the same time allow you to observe the constant stream of your experiences, while also being an observer of these experiences. The space these perspectives create may allow more freedom to choose based on your values.

The work you have been doing in this book will enable you to take this next step.

EXERCISE: Broadening Your Life

How Big Is Your Comfort Zone?

We are going to invite you to reflect on what currently is *in your comfort zone*, and *what isn't*.

Your comfort zone is made up of the areas of your

life and choices you make where you feel at ease (or at least less anxious). It could be that after living with anxiety for long time, and being guided by escaping and avoiding these feelings and sensations, your comfort zone is now quite small. It may also be that the comfort zone is not a rock-solid set of things that guarantee that you feel calm and relaxed. This is particularly the case if you have a tendency to experience panic attacks, worry excessively, or have anticipatory anxiety.

Through flexible contact, we are going to work on how to **broaden** your life, so that you can take steps outside of your comfort zone, and have more activities, people, places and things that you are engaged with.

Draw a circle on a piece of paper. Inside the circle, put the activities, things, places and people who would be in your comfort zone.

Now reflect on how things are at the moment: what is outside your comfort zone?

On the piece of paper, outside of the circle, list the activities, things, places, and people who are outside your comfort zone. See if you can place them close up or further away, depending on how anxious you feel about them.

Now notice what is on the **edge** of your comfort zone – perhaps with just a push, or being you on a good day, you could stretch to be in contact with them.

These things may be the focus of the first steps in doing exposure work.

You can think of the edge of your comfort zone as a little like an elastic band. When you stretch an elastic band beyond where it normally rests, it comes back to a size that is slightly larger than before. Your comfort zone works in the same way. When you stretch out beyond what feels comfortable you increase the size just a little. The more you practise this, the more room you will have in your comfort zone. What felt too frightening before, now sits within your comfort zone.

Living Life Beyond the Comfort Zone (Exposure Log)

The next step is to plan the steps you will take to broaden your life. The Exposure Log below will allow you do this. We would like you to **list the various situations (activities, things, places and people) where anxiety is a problem** at the moment. We're going call each of these a 'Step'.

For each step, we would like you to **rate your anxiety**, from 0 (not at all) to 100 (the most scared you could be). Then **identify what valued direction this step is about** (it could be about more than one direction): describe that direction in 1–3 words, if you can (e.g. 'being loving', 'striving', 'seeking connection', 'making a contribution', 'caring').

Then, describe **how you want to act** if you took this step in a way consistent with your values. Imagine what this would look like to someone watching you (i.e. the things you would do). Now, get in contact with **the experiences** you may have that will **invite you to struggle** (feelings, thoughts, sensations, urges). Also describe **the things that your mind may come up with to encourage struggle**.

Finally, describe how willing you are to have these experiences and take the step (do exposure). Rate your willingness from 0 (not willing) to 100 (completely willing). Also consider which number would this need to be for you to take the step.

Do this for each of the steps that you had listed in the previous Comfort Zone exercise.

Once you have a good sized list (six or more steps), then we invite you to choose a step with your highest Willingness rating. This will be the next step you take.

Choose to take the step. Use your *Open*, *Aware* and *Active* skills to: 1. make space for your experiences, 2. notice your mind, and 3. connect with your valued direction. As you engage with taking the step, notice if you become Unwilling: while noticing any urges to escape or avoid, use your skills to broaden your contact with your experiences, and hold your thoughts lightly. See if you can even bring a sense of curiosity to these experiences. Connect again with the chosen purposeful direction that this step is about for you.

Finally, after you have taken the step use the final column to reflect upon the process of doing this. We would suggest that you notice that by practising willingness you are broadening your life, whatever happened with taking this particular step. So, now reflect – what did you notice? If you were do to the step again, what skills would you use?

Tim – *Active* Steps

In the session with his therapist Tim identified one of the valued directions that he wanted to act on more regularly: behaving as a loving person. Now that he had made some progress with limiting the amount of time that he spent worrying, Tim reported that he had more freedom to go in the directions that mattered to him.

He described that he would like to act as a better friend: being more available, reliable and supportive to the people he cares about. He also identified that he would like to take steps that would increase the chance of his meeting someone and having an intimate relationship.

The challenge was that this also involved feeling anxious. He had been off the dating scene for months, and remembered the sense of rejection and hurt that he had from his last relationship.

Tim's steps are described in his Exposure Log below. He took his first step – organising a night out with his friends – and reflected upon doing this.

Step outside of comfort zone (activities, things, places, and people)	Anxiety (0–100)	Valued direction (that this step is about)	How do I want to act with this step? (If I acted on my values)	Experiences to struggle with – Feelings – Thoughts – Sensations – Urges	Mind tricks/ stories about these experiences	My willingness to have experiences and take the step	What did you notice when you took the step?

Step outside of comfort zone (activities, things, places, and people)	Anxiety (0–100)	Valued direction (that this step is about)	How do I want to act with this step? (If I acted on my values)	Experiences to struggle with – Feelings – Thoughts – Sensations – Urges	Mind tricks/ stories about these experiences	My willingness to have experiences and take the step	What did you notice when you took the step?
Organise night out with old friends Matt and Andy	50	Acting as a loving person	To go to the pub, connect with my friends – listen, share stories. Notice worries and ignore urge to go home and work	Worry (about work) Anxiety Urge to leave early	Story that if I worry then I must act on it Story that I am boring Focus on the future rather than right now	70	I called my friends and they were keen to go to the pub. A proper catch-up, I shared a bit about how I'd been struggling (was worried about doing that). Andy was great about it, very supportive; not sure what Matt thought

Sign up for Internet dating	60	Acting as a loving person	To log on to the website, put my details up, and be open to my worries and anxieties while doing this	Worry, Anxiety, Thinking I'm unloveable, Urge to cancel online dating account	Story: failure at relationships, Taking rejection as sign I'm flawed	50	Sign up for Internet dating
Go on a date	80	Acting as a loving person	Connect with the person on the date by listening, being present, and sharing about myself	Anxiety, Sweating, tense, Self-conscious, Worry	Story: failure at relationships, Focus on my performance, taking me out of being present	30	Go on a date
							We made a plan to meet again in a couple of weeks

The Process of Broadening Your Life

Taking Steps to broaden your life is probably going to involve persistence. By this we mean that it will involve doing something every day on your Exposure Log (or more if you can) to go in your chosen life directions, and practising flexible contact with your experiences. There will be something to learn from each time that you do this.

We would recommend persevering with doing exposure of a step until you find it takes less effort to be willing. Once you are finding this easy then move onto the next step.

A few tips:

- There are going to be both good and bad times. Your feelings and thoughts are likely to be more intense and difficult on some occasions.

- It is all right to get caught up with struggling. Noticing that you have been struggling strengthens your *Aware* skills.

- Persistence is not a feeling inside. Instead 'persistence' is doing what you planned, even if your feelings change. Some days it may be just about moving your body to take the step, rather than feeling like you want to do it.

- You are likely to become more aware of the various ways that you avoid, as you go along. You can then play with letting go of these coping strategies and see what happens.

- Be kind and compassionate with yourself. Doing things we fear is **hard**. Increasing your contact with these emotions and thoughts might feel a bit odd because you are doing something different with anxiety.

- Share with significant others about the commitment you are making to broadening your life. Their support will help you to stick to this.

From here you have the key building blocks to broaden your life from the narrow one that struggling with anxiety has created for you. Starting with the step you are most willing to take, you can introduce new values-based actions into your life and gradually broaden outwards to develop a life that is expansive, with room to move and not completely dominated by the experience of anxiety. Becoming more *Active* means a willingness to develop the skills to be more *Open* to anxious thoughts and feelings – to become more *Aware* of them, and less caught up with threat detection and finding ways to escape and avoid. Being *Open* and *Aware* gives you more room to move, so you get to choose how you ACTivate your life in the way that you want to.

7 Cooling the Anger Process

For every minute you remain angry, you give up
sixty seconds of peace of mind.

Ralph Waldo Emmerson

Anybody can become angry – that is easy, but to
be angry with the right person and to the right
degree and at the right time and for the right
purpose, and in the right way – that is not within
everybody's power and is not easy.

Aristotle

We want to start off by making it very clear that anger is
not 'a bad thing'. There isn't a human being on earth who
does not experience the feeling of anger from time to time.
It is a normal – even necessary – part of the full spectrum
of human emotions. It's not unusual for people to find
themselves struggling with minds that tell them that they
are wrong to be experiencing anger, and that there must
be something faulty with them for having such feelings.
As we've come to see, **it is this struggle that is often more
draining than the emotion itself**.

However, we know that for some people anger can become

consuming. More importantly, some find that the consequences of their anger – the behaviours that it drives – become so destructive that it is necessary to find a way of managing it in order to stop it from damaging their lives and the lives of those around them.

Why Do We Get Angry?

When you look around and consider all the harm that has been done in the course of history because of anger, we may ask why it is that we have developed to be able to experience this emotion at all? From an evolutionary perspective, for anger to have persisted as part of the human condition, it must serve some kind of purpose.

Charles Darwin suggested that the only traits that would be passed from generation to generation, which would develop and thrive while others faded away, were those that had 'survival value'. These were the traits that gave a species some kind of advantage in the battle to stay alive in a world of scarce resources. From this perspective we can begin to see how anger may be useful. It is an entirely appropriate emotional response to situations that pose a real threat or danger. Just as one of our ancient ancestors who stumbled across a member of a hostile tribe stealing food from her camp would naturally respond with anger, it makes sense that certain risky situations should provoke a similar response in us today. While it is rare that most of us (in the prosperous West at least) will face genuinely life-threatening situations with any kind of regularity these days, it is still possible to see anger functioning in this way today. From an ACT perspective, **the feeling of anger can actually be very useful as a source of information**. We spoke in Chapter 4 (*Active*) of the vital importance of values as a guide for the actions that will bring us a sense of fulfillment and meaning in life. These values are by their nature personal and precious to us – when we feel as if they are being denied, bypassed or attacked, we will inevitably experience some kind of reaction. Sometimes this reaction will be in the form of anger.

Think about the last time you felt really angry. Allow the memory to build and for all the thoughts and feelings that you were experiencing to grow as they did in that moment. Now pause and take a few deep breaths. From the perspective of your Observing Self just notice what thoughts and feelings are present, resisting the urge to evaluate or judge them. Now ask yourself: which of my values felt as if it was being threatened in this moment? Which of my values was my anger trying to defend? Was it a value around fairness? Was it a value around freedom? Was it a value around connection?

From this perspective there is interesting information in our anger, which we can use to help us make conscious choices and take effective valued action. However, some of us end up responding to anger thoughts and feelings in a particularly rigid and unhelpful way – we either struggle against them or switch into autopilot and follow where they want to lead us. In this way, **perfectly normal anger can become problematic**. We can become isolated from the people and things that are most important to us, and we can end up doing tremendous harm to ourselves and others.

In this chapter we will spend some time talking about what problematic anger is and how it works from an ACT perspective. How – when we aren't fully *Open, Aware* and *Active* – does anger turn toxic? Then we'll explain how, by practising your *Open, Aware* and *Active* skills, anyone can begin to live with anger without becoming its victim.

An ACT Approach to Problematic Anger

Part of the reason that anger can be so difficult to respond to effectively is that it is such a 'hot' and powerful experience. People for whom it has become problematic often say that they are suddenly engulfed by a barrage of internal experiences that quickly and – it seems to them – inevitably leads to some kind of anger behaviour. It can be useful to slow this process down a little, and become curious about what is really going on in these moments. Each anger episode will involve one or more of the following – the less effectively you respond to each part of this process, the more likely it is that the others will shortly follow:

Trigger Event

This could be something that happens in the outside world – something somebody does or says, or something that happens – or it could even be something internal, one of the random thoughts that our minds offer up over the course of the day that gets us hooked. It is possible that the trigger event could be something that is important to attend to and deal with – maybe something that is a genuine threat to ourselves – so it is worth being curious about what the trigger really is. However, it's tricky to see a situation clearly if we start getting caught up in anger thoughts.

Anger Thoughts

These kinds of thoughts often have a particular quality – **they tend to be judgemental, full of evaluations and quite black-and-white**: something is either right or wrong, OK or not OK. They often have a 'victim-y' quality – painting you as the victim and others as responsible for your situation. As a result there can be a lot of blaming as well. These are good examples of the 'sticky' thoughts that we talked about earlier. As we will discuss shortly, these types of thoughts are absolutely normal – but if we fuse with them too tightly we will usually end up experiencing anger feelings.

Anger Feelings

While there will be variations between different individuals in exactly how anger feels, how intense it is, and how quickly it takes hold, the quality is largely the same for most people: rapid heartbeat, breath coming fast and shallow from the chest, muscle tension, feeling hot and flushed, and maybe even physical trembling. Again, the truth is that these are 100% normal – it's the body's 'fight or flight' response gearing us up to deal with a threat. However, when we get caught up in these feelings they can be overwhelming and will often lead to anger urges.

Anger Urges

When we are riding the crest of a wave of anger it can feel like it's never going to end unless we **do something** about it. The feeling is so intense and unpleasant that the desire to get rid of it becomes extraordinarily powerful. When we buy into some of the thoughts that often accompany and fuel this process – thoughts like 'I can't take this', 'I feel like I'm going to explode' – we might find ourselves almost unconsciously searching our memories for ways we have successfully got rid of this uncomfortable feeling in the past, and we will end up resorting to an anger behaviour.

Anger Behaviours

The moment comes when we submit to the urge to act and allow the anger that has been building inside of us to come out. Sometimes this will be in the form of an explosion – shouting, door-slamming, even violence – but it may be expressed more subtly too – in hurtful words, name-calling, contemptuous silence, sulking or emotional withdrawal. Sometimes the anger behaviour may be more like an implosion, taking place entirely internally: we grit our teeth and swallow the feeling. Perhaps the feelings will start to subside and the thoughts will begin to reduce, but the hot anger has only been put on ice temporarily, ready to explode at a later date.

In the opening chapter we introduced you to Samantha, who referred herself for therapy after noticing that her anger was starting to have a negative impact both at work and in her personal life. Samantha is very familiar with the seemingly instant switch from trigger to anger behaviour. What she has struggled to do in the past though is to slow the process down and see it for what it is:

Samantha is having a rare night out with her best friend Leanne and over a bottle of wine they are comparing notes on their respective weeks at work. Samantha is talking about how frustrated she has been getting with her colleagues' incompetence recently: 'Honestly, I swear sometimes I feel like just walking out of there and not coming back!'

At this, Leanne chuckles and rolls her eyes. As quick as a flash Samantha's mind serves up the thought: 'She's laughing at me! She thinks I'm just moaning – this is all a joke to her!' This is a familiar thought for her – she has been told in the past that she 'moans' too much, and her mind throws the label 'moaner' at her multiple times a day. She feels her face redden and her ears start to ring. Her heart seems to catch in her chest and then start beating at double the rate it was before.

So powerfully she can almost feel it, Samantha is flooded by the urge to give Leanne a piece of her mind. More thoughts pile in, making her feel more and more angry, more and more justified, and making the urge even stronger: 'Call yourself a friend? We haven't all got rich husbands. What the hell do you know about anything?!'

'You know what Leanne, I don't sit there judging you when you moan on about your life, so I'd appreciate it if you didn't judge me!' explodes Samantha. 'I'm sick and tired of your crap. Enjoy your wine . . . !' With that she stands up abruptly, knocking the table and spilling both glasses of wine everywhere, and storms out.

Can you relate to anything from this scene? Do you recognise that rush from trigger to thought to feeling to urge to behaviour? Why not see if you can take a minute to reflect on the process, slow it down and get a different sense of what is going on in those moments.

EXERCISE: Breaking Down an Anger Episode

Think of a recent occasion on which you got really angry. As you have done before, take a moment to close your eyes and visualise the scene from start to finish, allowing it to come to life in your head. No need to strain to re-create it in perfect documentary detail – just let the memory formulate in its own way. Sit for a moment with the memory of what was going on inside of you at that time. When you feel ready, complete the Breaking Down an Anger Episode Worksheet as best you can.

BREAKING DOWN AN ANGER EPISODE WORKSHEET

What was the trigger? What happened – either outside you or inside of you – that seemed to start off the anger process?

What anger thoughts did you get fused with? As best you can, try to recall what your mind was telling you, and what thoughts were particularly 'sticky' for you.

What anger feelings arose for you? Try to describe the emotions you experienced and how they felt in your body as you experienced them.

What urges arose in you as you experienced these thoughts and feelings? What was 'anger' telling you to do? Make a note of all the things that you found yourself wanting to do or say, whether or not you actually followed through with them.

What did you actually end up doing? What was the actual outcome of the anger episode in terms of your behaviour?

A Closer Look at Anger Thoughts

We learned in Chapter 2 (*Open*) that the human mind has evolved in a particular way, primarily to keep us safe. As a result we have picked up thinking habits over the centuries that, while useful, can cause us problems if we are too inflexible in the way we respond to them. If we look a bit more closely, it's possible to see how a number of these habits can play a role in problematic anger.

If you recall, we explained that we have evolved to have minds that are fantastic storytellers: minds that crave clarity and coherence in an attempt to understand why the world is the way that it is and why people behave the way that they do. However, the world rarely provides us with clear answers to these questions, so our minds create stories to fill in the gaps.

What we also learned earlier is that our minds have evolved to be constantly on the lookout for threat – whether genuine physical threats that could put our well-being at risk, or social threats that might put our place in our 'tribe' in jeopardy. As a result we tend to see the world a little negatively – to perceive hostility and threat more readily than we might perceive goodwill and safety.

The combination of these two mind-habits can often be a recipe for anger. Perhaps somebody says or does something that we find confusing or hurtful – our minds will naturally start to write stories about why they might have behaved in the way that they did. If we buy into these stories, it can turn us into mind readers.

Angry Mind Reading

Our meaning-hungry minds will begin to speculate about what the other person must have been thinking when they did or said whatever it was that caused us pain. Our naturally threat-focused minds will then weigh in and start to cook up any number of negative stories about their intentions and motivations, often in the presence of little to no evidence.

Perhaps we see two colleagues laughing at the other side of the office and our minds create the story 'they're laughing at me because they think I'm bad at my job'. Or perhaps a partner or spouse is short with us on the phone and our minds create the story 'she is annoyed with me because I didn't do the washing-up last night'. In the example above, the actual behaviour that Samantha observed in her friend was a chuckle and a roll of the eyes, which her mind instinctively interpreted as being a sign of judgement and contempt – **which it may or may not have been!** It may just have easily have been an expression of sympathy because she might have had a memory about a similar experience she'd had herself, or she may have been thinking about something completely different!

Again, there is nothing wrong or unusual with this kind of negative mind reading – this is how minds work, and they will throw up countless thoughts of all different types throughout the day. But for some people, these are exactly the kind of sticky thoughts that they become fused with. From that place of fusion we start to lose sight of the different options that might be available to us and the likelihood that we will end up acting out on the anger thoughts is far greater.

EXERCISE: Mind Reading

Think about a different occasion in which you found yourself getting very angry – an occasion where the trigger event was something that somebody else either did or said. As you did before, take some time to close your eyes and re-live the experience as best you can.

When you are ready, open your eyes and complete the Mind-Reading Worksheet:

MIND-READING WORKSHEET

In purely objective terms, what did the other person do or say? (Stick simply to the facts of what happened or what was said, resisting any urge to add your interpretation of what it 'meant' even now or at the time, directly or indirectly.)

What did you assume was the other person's intention by doing or saying what they did? What did you think that they were thinking?

What are some other possible alternatives of what their intentions may have been or what they may have been thinking? Be creative, and really try to think of as many alternatives as possible!

Remember, the aim here is by no means to try to work out what the 'truth' is about another person's intentions or meanings. If anything it is to emphasise that, no matter how hard we try, this is something that we can never know. Mind reading rarely leads to anything other than misunderstanding. Actively putting yourself in someone else's shoes and trying to imagine what they **might be thinking and feeling** and what their needs might be in a spirit of openness and curiosity can be very useful, but we will come to that later.

We also learned in Chapter 2 (*Open*) that our minds have evolved to form evaluations – to identify people, places, and things as either good or bad, safe or not safe. When we are faced with a big snarling bear and a beautiful blueberry bush, this habit is extremely useful. However, when we take the mind's tendency to evaluate too seriously we can end up thinking in black and white – making broad generalisations about people and situations that prevent us from responding effectively. For one thing it can lead us towards unhelpful judgements.

Judgement and Hot Labelling

The evaluative tendency of the human mind – while sometimes useful – can also be very destructive. It can lead us to create hard, uncompromising judgements. If somebody treats us in a way that we find offhand, the judgemental mind will conclude, 'He is rude'. If somebody doesn't return a text message as promptly as we like, the judgemental mind will conclude, 'She is thoughtless'. Often the mind will begin to escalate this process by using the amazing tool of language to amplify these *labels*. 'He is rude' *becomes* 'He is an arrogant jerk'. 'She is thoughtless' *becomes* 'She is a self-obsessed moron'. The impact is that the heat gets turned up even higher on our anger. We call this *Hot Labelling* and it tends to keep us stuck in black-and-white thinking, turns up the heat on our judgements, and usually makes it harder to act on our values.

Of course, the process of judging and labelling is not only directed outwards. Holding on tightly to harsh self-judgements will often lead to us turning this hot labelling in on ourselves. This can fuel inward-focused anger that has the potential to be extremely harmful. We all have moments where we think 'I'm an idiot' or 'I'm incompetent' or worse. But some of us fuse so closely with those judgements and labels – whether about ourselves or others – and take them so seriously that we are far more likely to end up acting out on the anger that they might provoke.

Samantha was someone who often found her mind formulating some powerful hot labels at certain times.

It was a chaotic morning at the GP surgery. It was only 9.30 a.m. but already three of the doctors' appointments were running late. An older woman who had been waiting for fifteen minutes approached the desk to ask how long it would be before she could be seen. Samantha smiled as politely as she could and said, 'It shouldn't be more than another ten minutes,' but in her mind she was screaming, 'It will take as long as it takes you impatient old bag!'

No sooner had the patient sat down that the phone rang. Samantha answered and said hello. 'Oh, so you've decided to start picking up the phone there, have you?' came the sarcastic response. Immediately Samantha thought to herself 'Oh get stuffed, you grumpy pig.' Even after the call ended, she found herself ruminating on how rude the previous patient had been. 'What a rude, arrogant, ignorant idiot!' she said to herself, her heart starting to beat faster, and a pressure building at her temples. Eventually she found herself feeling so agitated that she had to go and calm down in the bathroom, leaving the reception unattended for ten minutes, and earning herself a reprimand from the practice manager.

How about you? Do you notice that your mind starts to judge and condemn and label people when you are in the throes of anger? Many people find that there are certain hot labels that their minds generate with more frequency than others, and that these are a very good predictor of some kind of anger behaviour when they emerge.

Make a note in the space below of the hot labels that your mind tends to create when you are feeling really angry. (It may feel uncomfortable and strange to do this – the stuff that our minds tell us when we are really angry is rarely the kind of stuff that we would wish to say out loud to others when we are at our best. **But, the more familiar you are with the way your mind works, the more choice you have about your actions**. Be as honest as you can.)

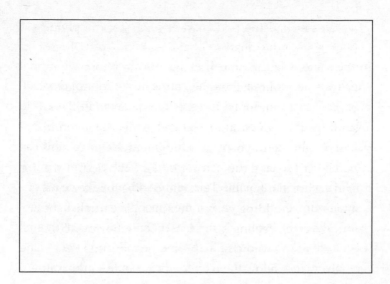

We've already established that most of us tend to respond to thoughts in two habitual ways: we either switch into autopilot and follow them wherever they might lead us; or – especially when they are thoughts we don't like – we struggle against them and try to control, challenge, or get rid of them. Just following anger thoughts automatically is a fast track to unhelpful anger behaviour. And what we know is that we don't have as much control over our thoughts as we might wish, so when we try to challenge or push away anger thoughts a common consequence is that we get that rebound effect – the harder we try to get rid of them the more they seem to bounce back into our consciousness. This might seem like a catch-22 situation. But the good news is that there is another way of managing anger thoughts so that they have less of an impact on us and our behaviour. We will talk more about that later in the chapter.

Understanding Anger Feelings

In the same way that, much as we may want to, we cannot effectively control our thoughts, nor can we control our feelings. We have developed to respond to events in the world around us at an emotional level and while this often brings pain it also brings great joy and fulfilment. However, this can often be hard to accept when we find ourselves firmly in the grip of a particularly painful emotion. And, while there may be a small number of exceptions, **most** people experience anger feelings as being extremely unpleasant and unwanted (though it is worth acknowledging that some people find anger – and the power it can allow them over other people – intoxicating).

As a result, our minds will naturally evaluate anger feelings as they arise, telling us 'I can't stand feeling like this', 'I shouldn't feel this way', 'What's wrong with me?' and probably worse besides. **It is by this process that the perfectly normal and necessary 'clean pain' of anger feelings becomes the 'dirty pain' of toxic anger** – it swells and grows in our minds and fans the flames of the anger by labelling it 'bad' and sets us struggling against it. Pretty soon the dimensions of the original emotion are so much greater that the desire to discharge the feeling will start to become very powerful and anger urges will follow.

While acknowledging that for most of us anger will never be a comfortable or pleasant feeling, perhaps it is possible to be willing to experience anger as being an inevitable part of a life that is lived to the full. Again, we will return to this later, and discuss some specific ways of approaching anger feelings without getting hooked by them.

However, to manage anger feelings more effectively, we need to recognise them when they occur. While this might sound really obvious, we know that many of us find it tricky to identify exactly what is going on inside us at an emotional level. People who struggle with anger often have a particularly hard time connecting with what is happening for them emotionally. **The truth is that anger is rarely an emotion that exists in isolation**. If you look beneath the surface there are usually other emotions there – hurt, shame, guilt, embarrassment, disappointment, you name it. If we can't accurately identify these when they are present we are much more likely to struggle with them or respond to them on automatic pilot, and they are far more likely to develop into full-blown anger.

Samantha had simply come to see herself as an angry person, and drawn the conclusion that something was wrong with how her emotions worked. It seemed that in difficult moments anger was the only emotion that was available to her. But when she spent somw time talking with her therapist about the day that she fell out with her friend Leanne, it became clear that there was actually a lot more going on than just anger:

> *Therapist*: So, when Leanne rolled her eyes and laughed, what was going on for you, how did you feel?

> *Samantha*: Well, I just felt absolutely furious straightaway.

T: And what else was going on?

S: What do you mean? I just said, I got really angry . . .

T: Well, you also said earlier that your mind was telling you that she thought you were moaning and that she thought that the situation you were describing was just a big joke to her. Without getting into whether or not that's actually what she *was* thinking, what was it about the idea that she thought you were moaning that was so hard for you to be with?

S: Well, it's embarrassing. The idea of me sitting there, going on and on and her just seeing me as this boring moaner is humiliating.

T: OK, so there were perhaps some feelings of embarrassment, even humiliation going on. Say more about what it was like to think you are being laughed at.

S: Well, yeah it's humiliating. Especially because it's your friend . . .

T: What's the significance of that, the fact that it's your friend?

S: Well, you want your friends to support you and to understand when you're struggling. When they don't do that it feels horrible – sort of like a betrayal. I've had it happen to me in the past and it's not nice.

T: So, part of you was feeling betrayed in that moment too?

S: Yeah, I think I did.

The thing with anger is that it is not really a particularly sophisticated emotion. As we said, it evolved to keep us alive and, because of the physiological process that starts to take place in our bodies when we get angry, we are only naturally equipped to respond in one of two ways: fight or flight. Neither of these is a particularly appropriate reaction for the situations that most of us face in life these days that might trigger anger. However, if you look below the bubbling surface of the anger, there is usually a lot more stuff there – emotions that perhaps we can respond to more creatively, which we might be able to draw information from so that we can get a sense of what we need in that moment. Samantha felt embarrassed, humiliated and betrayed. Perhaps, if she had been more aware of that stuff at the time she would have been able to respond differently.

The great thing about the human body is that it supplies us with feedback all the time. When anger feelings are growing inside us our bodies will try to let us know – remember feelings are really just physical sensations in the body. But again, **people who struggle with anger tend not to pay much attention to this bio-feedback**. They are so wrapped up in what their minds are telling them – usually stories about injustice, unfairness and hostility – that they don't notice their heart rates increasing, their muscles tensing, their jaws clenching, or any of the other telltale signs of anger. To deal more effectively with anger we need to practise getting out of our minds and starting to connect more with the here-and-now, including what is going on inside our bodies. In the Breaking Down an Anger Episode Exercise earlier we asked you to pay attention to the sensations in your body. The more attuned you become to these sensations the earlier you will be able to notice what is happening, and consider how you will want to respond – perhaps by practising some of the *Open*, *Aware* and *Active* skills we have introduced so far. We'll give you some examples later.

Stuck in the Thinking Self

Think back to Chapter 3 (*Aware*), and the idea that each of us is more than just our thoughts, feelings, memories, urges and sensations. We have the unique ability not only to experience life but also to **notice** that we are experiencing it, not just to think and feel but to be **aware** that we are thinking and feeling. We have these two parts to ourselves: the Thinking Self, which is the constant stream of words, images, judgements, evaluations and sensations that our mind produces every hour of the day; and the Observing Self, the part of us that notices and observes all that mind-stuff.

While anger is an entirely natural and instantaneous response to certain situations in life, it is the Thinking Self that can sometimes intervene to keep the fire of anger burning longer than is helpful.

Again, it is worth stressing that this this doesn't make the Thinking Self a bad thing – it is an absolutely vital part of human consciousness. However, we know that getting stuck in the Thinking Self takes away our ability to be creative and flexibly exercise choice about how we respond to the world around us and the mind-stuff that it triggers. People who struggle with anger often find that anger thoughts and feelings hook them so powerfully they lose their ability to connect with their Observing Self. **Unable to notice their thoughts and feelings for what they are – words in the mind, sensations under the skin – they respond to them in the same old ways they always have**.

We also talked in the same chapter about the value of perspective-taking: the ability to shift from the default position from which we normally view life, and look at things a little differently. But, unfortunately, when we lose touch with our Observing Selves we invariably lose the ability to be flexible in our perspective-taking. For one thing, we end up unable to take the perspective of anybody else and, when we are in an anger situation that involves another person, that is a good predictor of conflict. When we get stuck in our own perspective it is impossible to perceive with any clarity or creativity what might be going on for somebody else, what their needs might be, what they might be experiencing or what their intentions might be. All we are left with is a mind that is writing all sorts of negative stories about the other person and fuelling the fires of anger feelings.

Stuck in our own perspectives, writing stories about the other person, and with an ancient part of our mind feeling truly threatened, it no longer matters what the anger or conflict is actually about – often it ends up becoming a matter of **win or lose**. In our anger we become fixated on 'winning' the argument or confrontation, regardless of what the consequences might be for us or anyone else. This win-or-lose mentality is driven entirely by the thoughts and feelings raging within us, while our values become sidelined – in our urgency to win we lose sight of what is important to us.

There is a wonderful TED[9] talk by a successful American entrepreneur called Ric Elias. He was a passenger on the plane that hit headlines all over the world in 2009 when it lost both engines while flying out of New York City, forcing it to crash land on the Hudson River. In his talk he shares the experience of being on a plane that is going down, and of facing the seeming inevitability of his own death. Among other things he talks about how he reflected in the moments before the crash on 'all the time I wasted on things that did not matter with people that matter.' Thanks to the quick thinking of the pilot the plane landed safely, and Ric's life and the lives of the other passengers on board were saved. Ric talks about how he has changed since his brush with death, and one of the most profound differences in how he now approaches life: 'I no longer try to be right, I choose to be happy.' Not that he is happy all the time (like the rest of us, Ric's actual emotions are largely outside of his control), but he now aspires in each moment to make conscious

9   TED is a non-profit organisation which holds conferences and hosts speakers all over the world. Videos of hundreds of talks are available at www.ted.com.

choices in service of the things that **really** matter to him, and spend less time and energy trying to 'win' and be 'right' all the time.

The remainder of this chapter is going to be devoted to helping you do the same – to commit to following your valued directions, being the person you want to be, and disengaging from the mind's dance of anger.

So, What Can I Do to Manage My Anger More Effectively?

As with any other unwanted private experience, such as anxiety or depression, a common and natural question for those who seek help is 'how can I get rid of this feeling?' People who struggle with anger want to know what they need to do to stop feeling angry, or to feel less angry less often. But (as as you are probably getting a sense of by now), attempting to change or control our thoughts and feelings can be difficult in the long-term, and invariably results in our lives becoming smaller and less fulfilling. The aim of an ACT approach to anger is to develop the ability to feel angry **and also** be able to take action that is consistent with our values, meaning that we can live lives that are rich, fun and meaningful.

As we noted earlier, it can often feel as if anger outbursts 'just happen' – that there is a sudden flurry of internal experiences that quickly and inevitably leads to anger behaviour. But when you had the opportunity to slow down the process earlier, hopefully you were able to distinguish not only specific anger triggers but also the anger thoughts, feelings and urges that preceded the actual anger behaviour. So, clearly the process is not automatic. Nor is it inevitable.

As we said right at the beginning of the book – **you already have the skills!** It is just a case of using them more consciously and consistently. We're quite sure that there are hundreds, probably thousands, of occasions on which you have felt very angry indeed, but have not acted on that anger. Probably these occasions are so frequent that you don't even notice, with your mind instead focusing on all the occasions that you **have** acted angrily or aggressively.

Given that anger thoughts and feelings tend to feel very hot and present themselves very quickly, finding ways to just slow down a little in these moments is essential. We spoke earlier about the types of thoughts that tend to be associated with anger behaviour and aggression: they tend to be quite harsh, judgemental and evaluative and they often lead to the unhelpful mind-habits of hot labelling and mind reading. When we start going down these roads it is vital to pause and get some distance from thoughts that are liable to hook us – in other words, to practise some of the defusion skills we learned in Chapter 2 (*Open*).

Defusion

The more you practise these skills day by day the more easily you will be able to call on them when you need them. However, sometimes, even with the best intentions, you will find yourself getting hooked. It is important to have a plan for how to deal with these moments. Earlier on you had the opportunity to break down an anger episode – to get a clearer sense of some of the things that can trigger your anger, as well as the thoughts, feelings and urges that tend to precede anger behaviours. While it is different for everyone, many people find that it is actually the feelings of anger that they notice first – the heart racing, the breathing speeding up, and so on. If that is the case for you, that can be a useful prompt to start the process of getting **curious** about your thoughts and perhaps practising a little defusion.

Take a single deep breath and ask yourself:

* Just what is my mind saying in this moment?

* Is what my mind is saying an accurate reflection of what is going on around me?

* Is what my mind is saying helpful? Do I feel open and vital? Or do I feel closed and constricted?

* Are there other perspectives on this situation my mind is discounting?

* What's most important in this situation? Getting the job done or being right?

Checking in with some of this stuff can allow you to see a bit more clearly what is actually going on. If you realise that you truly are at risk of getting hooked then follow up with a few of the defusion skills that we discussed in Chapter 2 (*Open*) that have worked best for you in the past:

- **Thanking your mind**: Just notice what your mind is telling you and offer it your thanks for doing such a great job at helping you to avoid being harmed or eaten!

  'She's making fun of you!' Thanks mind, I appreciate your input!

  'If I have to wait for this bus for a second longer I'm going to scream!' Thanks for looking out for me, mind!

  'No one appreciates me – why the hell do I bother?' Thanks mind, that's an interesting perspective!

- **Funny voices**: Repeat the thought to yourself in the voice of a famous person or character.

- **Singing your thoughts**: Sing the thought to a popular tune of your choice.

Remember that these techniques are not intended to make light of or invalidate these thoughts. The aim is to help you to experiment with some different ways of being with mind-stuff that you don't like, in service of being a bit more flexible and creating space to make choices based on your values.

Maybe even try a different defusion skill? How about this next one – it's particularly useful in those moments where you are getting wrapped up in a self-judgement, or when your anger is directed towards yourself.

EXERCISE: I'm Having the Thought That . . .

This technique involves just slightly shifting a thought that you are getting fused with. It involves three simple steps:

1. Take the negative self-evaluation and say it to yourself in a sentence beginning 'I am . . . ', for instance, 'I am out of control' or 'I am useless'.

2. Now repeat the thought again, but this time precede it with the words 'I am having the thought that': 'I am having the thought that I am out of control' or 'I am having the thought that I am useless'.

3. Now repeat the thought again, preceding it with 'I notice that . . . ': 'I notice that I am having the thought that I am out of control'; 'I notice that I am having the thought that I am useless'.

Why not try it out for yourself? Bring to mind a negative, judgemental thought about yourself or others that often seems to either trigger or increase your anger, placing it into a sentence beginning 'I am . . . '.

Now spend thirty seconds really allowing yourself to get wrapped up in that thought, buying into it and believing it as much as you can. Really treat it as if it were the truth. Notice how it feels.

Now, add the words 'I am having the thought that . . . ' and spend thirty seconds focusing your awareness on that thought.

Finally, add the words 'I notice that . . . ' and spend thirty seconds focusing your awareness on that thought.

What did you notice about the difference in quality between those thoughts? Many people notice a sense of distance from the original negative self-judgement when they add 'I notice that I am having the thought that . . . '. The thought doesn't go away, but maybe it feels a bit less prominent, a bit less intense, and perhaps you may feel a bit less inclined to take it seriously. Try it out!

These defusion skills are really useful to experiment with when you notice your mind starting to get into those old familiar patterns: when you start judging others or judging yourself; when you start intensifying those judgements by adding hot labels; when you find yourself wondering what somebody meant by something they did or said, and start mind reading; or when your mind starts creating any of those stories that you know play a big role in getting you, or keeping you, angry.

Opening Up to Anger

As we've established, problematic anger is more than just a 'feeling' – it is a complex interaction of feelings, thoughts, urges and – when we fail to manage it effectively – behaviours. However, it is the feeling of anger – the powerful churn and tide of emotions – that many of us find most uncomfortable and unwanted, and that we can end up struggling against. Experimenting with some different ways to be with anger and the emotions that usually come along with it can be the difference between **responding on autopilot** and **consistently taking action that is in line with your values**.

If you remember, in Chapter 2 (*Open*) we talked about how we often tend to react to unwanted emotions as we would respond to loud music that we hate on the radio – by reaching straight for the volume control and trying to turn it down. Unfortunately, we can find ourselves struggling with a volume control that seems to be stuck on full. The secret is the Openness Dial at the back of the radio – if we can set that to high then the volume can move freely. It may be high, it may be low, but at least it is now free to move in its own time.

As it is such an unpleasant feeling (at least for most people), we tend to walk around with our Openness Dials permanently set on low for anger. Now, while we don't expect you ever to like feeling angry, we would strongly propose that developing the ability to at least be willing and open to experiencing the feeling is crucial to living a fulfilling life. In the same chapter you had the opportunity to practise an exercise that was designed to help you open up to your feelings and to get a slightly different perspective on them – simply as sensations within the body. Go back to the Opening Up to Emotions Exercise and repeat it, specifically using anger as the emotion to practise with.

How was it? Did you notice your Openness Dial slipping up or down during the exercise? Don't worry if it wasn't always at full volume. Know that the more that you practise acceptance, the easier it will be to comfortably accommodate even the most powerful surges of anger when they show up.

EXERCISE: Breathing Into the Anger

There will always be times when we will be caught unawares, when we will suddenly find ourselves in the midst of a hot flare of anger for which we feel completely unprepared. The natural instinct in these moments is just to go with the feeling. Having a plan to manage hot and powerful anger when it shows up is incredibly useful. Next time you find yourself in a situation like this try the following five-step approach:

Step One: Notice that you are breathing.

Step Two: Notice the feeling of anger within you and acknowledge it to yourself: 'Here is a feeling of anger'.

Step Three: Connect with your breathing and, as you do so, deliberately open up and make space for the feeling. Breathe into and around the feeling. As you do so imagine a space opening up around it.

Step Four: From the position of your breath and this feeling, broaden your awareness as if you were expanding the spotlight. Open up your awareness, to take in everything else you can feel within you, and then everything else you can see, hear, taste, touch and smell.

Step Five: Reflect on your values; think about the kind of person you most want to be, the kind of person you are at your best. From this perspective, how do you choose to behave? What do you choose to do next?

It is important to make clear at this point that the aim of this exercise is **not** to get rid of the feeling. If that is your aim then you will end up struggling with it and getting hooked. This is about simply making space for a feeling, which happens to be present in the moment. When you make space for feelings they are that bit less likely to overwhelm you, and you then have more room in which to make conscious, values-based decisions on how you want to behave and what you want to do next.

Beyond Anger Feelings

As we said earlier, anger is an emotion that rarely exists in isolation. However, it is such a powerful one that it can often drown out some of the subtler, quieter emotions that might also be there. In fact, some people find that they actually become quite familiar with anger over time. While a few even enjoy the feeling and the power it seems to give them, there are others who find that it is more comfortable than some of the other, less familiar emotions – emotions like embarrassment, shame or guilt.

Getting in touch with some of these other emotions, being willing to be with them, and seeing what they have to say can be an important step in learning to manage anger more effectively, as well as in finding the skills to deal with situations that might trigger anger.

If you recall, earlier in this chapter we caught up with Samantha in a session with her therapist, discussing the argument she had had with her friend Leanne, which ended with her lashing out verbally and storming out.

What had initially seemed to her like 'just another' occasion in which her anger had got the better of her actually turned out to be more than that: as well as anger there was also embarrassment and a feeling of betrayal. How do you imagine being able to get in touch with these other emotions – and being willing to experience them – at the time might have given Samantha a few more choices in how to respond?

EXERCISE: More Than Just Angry

Already in this chapter you have spent some time reflecting on and visualising previous occasions on which you have found yourself feeling very angry. We are going to ask you to do so again – feel free to call to mind an incident that you have thought about before or something different.

As before, spend a few moments calling the situation to mind. Imagine looking out from your own eyes, remembering what the situation was like. Where were you? What time of day was it? Who was there with you? Just spend a few moments really getting absorbed in the situation.

As best you can, try to get in touch with what else you were feeling in that moment **other than anger**. What was it about the situation that you found so difficult to be with? What was it about the situation that triggered your anger? Why do you think that bothered you so much?

Make a note in the space below of anything else that
you notice.

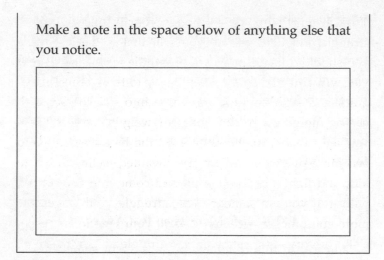

Just because the emotions that tend to get overwhelmed by
anger are often quieter and more subtle doesn't necessarily
mean that they are any more pleasant or easy to be with.
Indeed, for some people, anger becomes the go-to emotion
because it is actually **more desirable** than the alternatives like shame, embarrassment, despair or hopelessness.
Looking back at the other emotions that you noticed were
also there in the situation you reflected on above, are there
any that you know you find it particularly difficult to be
with? Which ones do you tend to avoid at all costs, or find
yourself struggling with when they do show up?

As perverse as it may sound, it is these emotions – the ones
that we hate and would do anything to avoid or get rid
of – that we most need to learn to accept and make room
for. Inevitably, our risk-averse minds will tell us to do the
opposite: to reject them and to escape as fast as possible.
But it's a little like what you need to do if you find yourself

stuck in quicksand – even though your instinct will be to struggle and fight to free yourself, that is the last thing you should do. **The more you fight, the faster and deeper you will sink**. The only reliable way to free yourself from quicksand is to lie back and come into full contact with it. The more you spread out your weight, the less likely you are to sink. In the same way, the best way to avoid becoming overwhelmed by an unwanted feeling is not to kick and fight, but to open up and come into full contact with it. If you are someone who struggles with anger, the more you practise acceptance of all your emotions – especially the ones that you find most unpleasant – the more likely you will be to respond effectively in the presence of your anger.

We showed you above how to use the Breathing Into the Anger technique to help you manage hot, powerful anger when it shows up, without either struggling against it or switching onto autopilot. This technique works with **all** emotions, not just anger. Why not practise using the technique with an emotion that you know you really hate and that often shows up during anger episodes? Perhaps return to the space above where you listed other emotions that showed up during a previous anger exercise and use that to practise with. Select one that you know you cannot bear – that you know or sense you might use anger to mask. As you have done before, vividly call to mind an occasion on which this emotion was present, even if only fleetingly. Allow yourself to linger on it, even allowing the emotion to build to a level that feels uncomfortable. Then follow the Breathing Into the Anger process exactly as you did before, remembering that the aim is *not to get rid of the feeling*, but simply to make space for it.

What was that like? What was different between how you normally respond to the emotion you chose and how you responded to it just now? Some people find that the emotion seems to recede or decline in intensity. Others find that it remains but seems to soften somewhat. Some people even find that it seems to grow. What almost all find, however, is that in consciously choosing to open up to the emotion it is less likely to escalate and morph into anger. Please do experiment with this technique as you go forward.

What Do You Need?

Another great thing about consciously engaging with the other emotions that are activated (but perhaps drowned out) when your anger has been triggered is that it provides you with information. As we said at the beginning of this chapter, **we often respond with anger when we feel like our values are under attack**, or when there is some kind of need that is not being met.

On one occasion Samantha was speaking to her therapist about an argument she had had with her husband, Colin, when she 'totally lost control'. The argument was about domestic chores – Colin's failure to help out around the house is a frequent trigger for her anger. Samantha described a day when she was at work, but Colin was at home. She explained that she returned home at 6 p.m. to find him asleep on the sofa, with the kitchen in a mess and an unwashed load of laundry in the machine. Samantha said that she 'completely flew off the handle' and 'called him every name under the sun', and even ended up smashing a vase on the floor. She said that she can't remember ever being as angry as this before and that she really scared herself, because she genuinely felt like lashing out and hurting him. Colin refused to talk to her for several days after the incident, and Samantha says that it took her a long time to regain his trust.

Therapist: Wow, I can see how that was a scary experience for you. You seem sad even talking about it now.

Samantha: It *was* scary. I guess what is frightening is not knowing where all this anger comes from . . . it's like a monster inside me.

T: Yup, I understand that desire to figure out why and where it comes from. And, in fact, it would be interesting to spend some time reflecting on what it was that triggered your anger. You said it was that Colin had been at home all day and hadn't done anything around the house. And you've said that you feel like he doesn't help out enough.

S: Yeah, that is true, but I can't honestly sit here and say that the way I reacted was in proportion to the problem . . . I mean, he's a great husband. I know loads of men who are terrible around the house. He deserves better . . .

T: OK, and maybe it's true that he doesn't deserve to be on the receiving end of your anger. But the impression I get is that, if you strip away the anger, and all the guilt that you feel about the way you express it, there is something going on here.

S: What do you mean?

T: What I mean is that your feeling that you need more help around the house is kind of being lost in the mix here. Because the way that you express that need is through anger, the need itself is not being addressed.

S: OK.

T: I mean, to what degree do you feel it is legitimate to ask for more support at home?

S: Well, I mean, objectively it is legitimate. The fact is that I do feel like I am on my own sometimes and that he doesn't care.

T: And I know from what you've told me already is that for you, teamwork and respect in a relationship are important values. I wonder if letting Colin know how you're feeling about this could be a step in the direction of these values?

EXERCISE: Standing Up for Your Values

We'd like to ask you to try out another practice. Return in your mind to the scenario you explored earlier, when you made a note of the emotions that you were experiencing beyond just anger. Revisit that incident exactly as you did before. Then, when you are ready, complete the Standing Up for Your Values Worksheet.

STANDING UP FOR YOUR VALUES WORKSHEET

What was the legitimate need that you were expressing ineffectively through anger? (Perhaps if someone was short with you in a meeting the legitimate need might be 'I need to feel like I am being listened to'.)

Next – like at the start of the chapter – make a note of the values that your anger was defending; the values that felt as if they were coming under attack.

Now, armed with this information, and bearing in mind the kind of person you want to be and the impact you want to have on others, speculate about some other ways that you could have responded in this situation: ways that might get your needs met whilst avoiding anger behaviours.

It may well be that your mind is saying, 'Well this is all very nice but there is a big difference between writing down how I'd like to act and actually following through in practice.' That's OK – that's just your mind trying to keep you safe, because change can feel risky. Trust us when we say that the more you practise all the exercises in this chapter the easier it will be. You could even consider repeating the exercise above with situations that you know often result in you acting on your anger, and rehearsing your response.

Another Perspective on Anger

At the beginning of this chapter we talked about how the level of anger is increased significantly by the Thinking Self, and how people who struggle with anger tend to get so hooked by the thoughts and feelings associated with it that they lose touch with their Observing Selves. In doing so, they sacrifice their ability to be flexible in their perspective-taking, making it far more likely that we will end up responding to anger on autopilot.

We also talked about our tendency to indulge in a spot of amateur mindreading when we are really caught up in anger, creating stories about what someone *really* meant when they said or did something that hurt or confused us: stories that are often based on little to no evidence! We gave you a brief exercise to get you started on noticing some of the assumptions that you were making on an occasion in the

past when something that another person said or did was
the trigger for anger. Well, that was only the first part! We'd
like you to revisit that exercise now and take it on a step.

EXERCISE: Mind Reading Revisited

Go back to the Mind Reading Worksheet and remind
yourself of the specific incident: what happened,
how you felt, what you assumed the other person's
intention was. Now recall how you responded.
How did you display your anger? What did you do?
What did you say?

Now we would like to invite you to imagine that the
other person in that situation is sitting opposite you.
Take a moment to fully visualise them and connect
with their humanity. Consider them as a person just
like you – vulnerable, imperfect, and trying their best
in a world that often seems confusing and scary. Like
you, this person has had moments of being afraid and
uncertain. Like you they have experienced moments
of joy. Try to remember when they may have felt
these. Sit for a moment and just connect with them.

Notice your own breath: the rise and fall of your chest
as you breathe in and out. Allow the breath of the person sitting opposite you to come into line with your
own. And when you are ready, imagine that you are
sitting in their seat, seeing the world through their eyes.

From this perspective of **the other person**, recall the
incident: what happened, what was said, what it felt

like, what it was like to have anger directed towards you. Allow yourself to imagine the scene unfolding through their eyes.

Reconnect with your breathing and now visualise yourself sitting opposite, eyes closed. When you are ready move across so that you are sitting in your own chair again, back in **your own** perspective. Take a moment to reflect on your experience of seeing the world through another person's eyes. Notice any judgements or evaluations that show up – about the exercise, the other person or yourself. Notice any feelings that emerge – curiosity, shame, indifference or anything else. Make space for all of them – whatever shows up is just part of the experience. When you are ready return to the here and now.

Now, as best you can, answer the questions in the Mind Reading Revisited Worksheet, below:

MIND READING REVISITED WORKSHEET

> What did you notice about what the other person was thinking and feeling when you experienced the episode from their perspective?

What did you notice about what it was like to be the target of anger when you were in the other person's perspective?

From what you learned in the other person's perspective, how do you feel they would wish to be treated?

From what you learned in the other person's perspective – and based on what you know of your own values and chosen life direction – how would you choose to act if you were to be in this situation again?

There is something very powerful about just allowing yourself, even if only briefly, to connect with the essential humanity of another individual and step into their shoes for a moment. In stepping out of your own perspective and trying out another one a little bit more information becomes available to you, and with that information usually comes a little bit of choice as well.

When you get stuck in just one perspective you lose your choice about how to respond to the world, even the choice to act in service of your happiness. On the other hand, when you approach your internal world with a quality of curiosity and flexibility, it is possible to access the limitless perspectives that are available within **you**. As President of the 'United States of You', you can choose which of your cabinet of advisers to call upon depending on the situation you find yourself in. However, when you adopt a stance that is rigid and inflexible, you lose this choice and it is usually the cabinet member who shouts loudest and longest who takes charge. Few of them are louder than the Secretary for Anger – as we know, anger thoughts tend to be harsh, judgemental and black and white. Unless we are mindful about how we respond to such thoughts we are likely to respond from a place of anger.

A perspective that often goes missing for those who habitually struggle with anger is that of compassion: compassion towards others – who despite having perhaps hurt us are always just human beings like us, trying to do their best – and compassion towards ourselves. **In the same way that being stuck in a perspective makes it impossible to see clearly what others' needs might be, disconnecting from a**

sense of self-compassion means that we become unable to see clearly what our own needs are. As a result it becomes impossible to communicate our needs to others, and the cycle of anger in conflict is likely to continue.

Moreover, when we lack self-compassion we are likely to respond to our own human fallibility in a way that is harsh and punitive, rather than open and understanding. We will beat ourselves up for feeling angry, we will roundly criticise ourselves for falling victim to our emotions again. In abandoning self-compassion and embracing self-criticism we can tell ourselves that we are 'taking responsibility' (and truly taking responsibility for our feelings and actions is certainly very important), but much of the time all we are doing is making it harder for ourselves to actually get back on track with acting on our values and living lives that are consistent with what really matters.

Developing a compassionate perspective on your own suffering is going to be vital if you want to manage your anger more effectively. Continuing to condemn yourself and treat yourself harshly in moments of pain is a sure-fire way of keeping the cycle of anger rolling. If you notice that your mind spends a lot of time beating you up for feeling sad, disappointed, betrayed, upset or any other painful emotion, why not try practising one of the self-compassion exercises Chapter 3 (*Aware*), such as 'Extending Compassion Towards the Child Within'.

By practising self-compassion you **are** taking responsibility for your anger. You are acting in a way that will make it less likely that you act on anger in the future. Practising self-compassion – even when your mind is telling you something entirely different – is absolutely vital to breaking the cycle of anger.

Surfing Your Anger Urges

When something triggers our anger a powerful message is broadcast from an ancient part of the brain: a primal threat-response designed to over power anything that the rational part of the brain might have to say. The message is clear: **do something now or your life is at stake!** We call this an urge.

The call to action is strong, as is the instinct to respond to it mindlessly and automatically. But (as some therapists like to say) how is that working out for you? Each time we respond automatically and experience the sudden drop in the intensity of the urge we are reinforcing the behavioural pathway that identifies this as being the 'right' thing to do.

But remember what we talked about in Chapter 2 (*Open*): urges will inevitably pass in their own time, whether or not we actively do something to relieve them. Like waves on the ocean, they will reach their apex and then start to break and fall. Most people who identify their anger and its consequences as something they would like to change have tried at some point to resist their anger urges – usually by struggling heroically with them. Maybe you have tried counting to ten, or digging your nails into your palms, or clenching your fists as tightly as you can. Sometimes this may even have worked. But you will probably recall how much energy it took out of you. You will probably also recall plenty of occasions on which you have fought with all your might but found yourself overcome by an urge that feels just too powerful (probably with a resolve that was weakened by a mind generating lots of stories why you should just let go and let it out).

The bottom line is that struggling against anger is a losing battle. **More effective is to practise surfing the urge of anger**: bringing a quality of openness and curiosity, and observing it like a curious scientist or a space alien that has never experienced an urge before; noticing where in your body you feel the urge most prominently, and where you barely feel it at all; and noticing its natural ebb and flow as it increases, decreases or just stays as it is.

Your mind may well be telling you 'well that's easy to say but hard to do'. And your mind may well be right. Certainly the more you practise mindfully observing your urges, the easier it becomes to respond to them effectively. Why not try a little experiment?

EXERCISE: Surfing the Urge to Eat a Sweet

A little like with the 'awareness of eating a sweet' exercise, this is another that can easily be done with a raisin or a segment of orange if you prefer. But as we may have mentioned, we quite like sweets, so would suggest finding a hard sweet or even a chocolate.

The aim of this experiment is simply to notice what you are experiencing as you hold the sweet in your mouth: noticing the thoughts that your mind is offering up, noticing the feelings and sensations in your mouth and elsewhere in your body, and also noticing the urges that follow in their wake, allowing them to come and go without acting on them

Find a comfortable position, close your eyes and take a few deep breaths. Then, allowing your breathing to return to its normal rate and pattern, take the sweet and place it onto your tongue. Then just allow it to sit there.

Notice the sensation of the sweet on your tongue. See if you can trace the edges of it using only your tongue as a guide. Feel the weight of it.

Notice exactly where on your tongue it is sitting. Is it near the front or near the back? Notice any urge you might have to adjust its position. Just allow the urge to build if it is there, knowing that it will pass. Give it a score between 1 and 10 as to how powerful it is. Breathe into the urge and try to make room for it.

Notice your mouth starting to fill with saliva. Where do you feel it, where is it accumulating? What is your mind telling you? About the sweet, about the sensations in your mouth, about this exercise? Just notice those thoughts and allow them to come and go.

Notice any other urges that are there. Is there an urge to swallow? If so then just observe that urge with gentleness and curiosity. What is it like? How does it show up? Notice how the urge builds in intensity like a wave swelling on the ocean. Allow it to build. How powerful is it between 1 and 10? Just try to make room for the urge.

Give yourself permission to sit and observe the thoughts and feelings coming and going, the urges rising and falling, for as long as you want to.

And, when you feel like you want to, bite down into the sweet. But do so mindfully, bringing the whole of your awareness to the experience – the tastes, the textures, everything about it.

So how was that? What was it like sitting with the urge to swallow the saliva that was accumulating in your mouth? To bite into the delicious sweet that was sitting on your tongue? Did you notice the rise and fall of the urge? How sometimes it would stay at what feels like a high level of intensity for some time? Maybe at these moments your mind would have been pleading or bargaining with you to give in and bite down. And yet, for a time at least, you chose to do something different – just allowing the urge to be there, noticing the habitual pull to act and doing something different. Whether it is the urge to eat a sweet or the urge to lash out at someone or something that has triggered your anger (even yourself), it is always possible to do something different. Just noticing the experience with a sense of gentle curiosity can be the difference between exercising choice and acting on autopilot.

Expanding Rather than Contracting

When we discussed *Aware* skills earlier, we said that we wanted you to practise developing a quality of awareness that was conscious, curious and also **flexible**. We all have a tendency to be a bit rigid with how and where we focus our attention, and one of the times that we can be most rigid is in the midst of anger. Think about a time that you have been really, really angry. Where was your attention focused? What was the quality of that attention?

What many people find is that in these moments their awareness seems to become very intensely focused indeed. Sometimes focused inwardly – the shutters come down, the outside world falls away and they are left isolated with their racing thoughts, the various physical sensations of the anger rising within them. Others find their focus directed intensely outward – specifically towards the person or the thing that has triggered their anger. In either one of these cases, anger behaviour is rarely far behind.

Given that a very narrow focus is often a red light for aggressive or angry behavior, perhaps it would be useful to experiment with softening up and expanding our attention a little. Many of the awareness exercises we have asked you to practise so far have encouraged you to focus – whether it is on your breathing, on your thoughts, or on various different physical sensations. In this next exercise we want you to expand outwards – rather than have your awareness be narrow and focused like a spotlight, we want you to broaden it out, taking in everything that is around you and inside you.

EXERCISE: Expanding Your Awareness

This is an exercise you can do anywhere at any time. No matter where you are right now, you can practise it. While you are reading these instructions your attention is probably going to be focused very closely on the words on the page. When you have finished reading these instructions we would like you to put the book down, lift your head, and slowly expand your awareness outwards.

Gently open up to the various different aspects of your experience as they are right now: everything going on around you that you can perceive with your five senses – everything you can see, hear, feel, smell, taste; everything that is going on inside you – any thoughts that are appearing and then retreating in your mind; any feelings or sensations under your skin; anything else that is there. You don't need to focus in on any of them particularly – just let them be; allow them all to wash over you and just allow yourself to experience them.

When you feel ready, perhaps allow your attention to flit about a bit. Let it come to rest for a moment on one particular aspect of your experience – a sound you can hear, a sensation you can feel, a thought you are having. Then, in a moment, allow it to move on and focus on something else. And before your attention has time to get too comfortable there, allow it to move on again. Like a bee, buzzing from flower to flower, let your attention wander, drink in whatever is available where it lands, and then move on. Sometimes you may like the spot where your attention lands. Other times you may find it really unpleasant. Whether you find it pleasant or unpleasant, try to bring a quality of openness, curiosity and willingness to it. Allow it to be what it is, notice it, engage with it, and then move on.

When you feel ready, relax your focus once more and allow the whole of your experience into the frame again. Whatever is going on around you or within you, make space for it all by expanding your awareness. Notice whatever is there with gentle curiosity, knowing everything is as it should be.

What was that like? What did you notice as you expanded your awareness to take in everything at once? Some people immediately find it to be a calming experience, experiencing themselves as almost being at one with everything around and within them. Others can find it uncomfortable, overwhelmed by the volume of data and sensation. Whatever your experience was, it is fine. As always, there is no right or wrong. It is just useful to practise the skill of expanding your awareness outwards: first noticing when you are becoming so focused on something that you are losing the ability to make values-based choices about how you act; then consciously and purposefully allowing the spotlight of your attention to grow and expand; then just noticing how the world looks from this more expansive vantage point, and making a decision about how you want to be and behave in that moment.

When It All Goes Wrong

We spoke earlier about the importance of self-compassion in managing anger more effectively – making room for pain and extending the same quality of compassion to yourself as you would to somebody else who is suffering. But there is another moment when it is particularly important to go easy on and nurture yourself. That is the moment where you have tried your best – to defuse from the stories that your mind is telling you, to open up and accept uncomfortable feelings, to surf the urges driving you to lash out – and have acted out on your anger anyway. At times like this your mind is almost certainly going to go into self-judgement overdrive! As tempting as it might be to punish yourself, and buy into the thought that the only way to learn is to give yourself a hard time, self-compassion is vital. Not, of course, that we are proposing you just breezily forget about it and move on – rather that you take positive action to make up for whatever damage might have been caused, and to make it less likely that you will end up doing the same thing again in the future:

> **Apologise**: If anyone has been hurt or upset by your actions then consider apologising for your behaviour. Sometimes our minds will tell us stories to minimise the harm that we might have done and let us off the hook ('It wasn't really that bad ... She knew I didn't really mean it ... It's no worse than what he's said to me in the past'). Just notice these stories, unhook from them and check in with your values – how would you most want to behave when you have hurt or upset someone? How would you want someone who has hurt or upset you to respond?

> **Defuse**: As well as defusing from the stories that might let you off the hook and persuade you that it

is not necessary to apologise, you will also probably have to defuse from other stories too – stories about letting yourself down, about being a terrible person, about giving up, or worse. It is natural that your mind will throw these stories up. The best thing that you can do is to simply notice them, acknowledge them, and defuse from them in whatever way works best for you. Remember that you are learning a new skill, trying out some stuff that is going against the way that most of us habitually operate. Why not go easy on yourself while you're getting the hang of it?

Open Up: The feelings of disappointment, guilt, and self-blame that may follow anger behaviour can be pretty powerful, and can set us struggling against them. Notice the feelings for what they are – sensations in the body – and use the skills that you have learned to open up and come into full contact with them.

Forgive Yourself: Remember that you are only human. You are not the first person in the world to act out on anger and you won't be the last. Step into that perspective of self-compassion and practise forgiving yourself.

8 Moving from Self-Esteem to Self-Acceptance

> To be beautiful means to be yourself. You don't need to be accepted by others. You need to accept yourself.
>
> **Thich Nhat Hanh**

Do you ever find yourself looking at other people and thinking to yourself, 'Wow – now that person has it made. If only my life were like hers! Things would be so much better. But instead I'm stuck with being me. I'm not beautiful enough. I'm not successful enough. I'm just not *enough*!'

Modern celebrity culture has given us an endlessly renewing cast of characters to judge, analyse and compare ourselves to. Angelina Jolie has probably caused a considerable number of women (and men) to look at themselves and feel totally inadequate over the years. Wealthy, successful, married to Brad Pitt, and regularly named among the most beautiful women alive. It must be wonderful being Angelina Jolie! When this suggestion was made to her in an interview, her response was perhaps surprising: 'Oh, God, I struggle with low self-esteem all the time! I think everyone does. I have so much wrong with me, it's unbelievable!' If even Angelina Jolie looks at herself and sees a lot of flaws and imperfections, what hope do the rest of us have?

Do You Like Yourself?

Self-esteem is an interesting concept, and a widely misunderstood one. There was a time when the only people who talked of 'self-esteem' were psychologists, psychiatrists and other mental-health professionals or academics. Now, however, it is part of the popular vocabulary. Not only are people quite comfortable assessing their and other people's levels of self-esteem but also it is frequently seen as a sufficient explanation for why some people succeed and thrive in life, while others struggle and suffer. But what do we actually mean by 'self-esteem'? And does a lack of it really represent a barrier between you and a life that is satisfying and meaningful?

What Is Self-Esteem?

Put simply, self-esteem is just a term that we use to describe a set of opinions – **the opinions that each of us holds about ourselves**. While many people label themselves as having either 'high' or 'low' self-esteem the truth is that the quality of these opinions will change over time – from day to day, even from minute to minute.

However, most people find that there is a consistent overall pattern to the types of thoughts and feelings they have about themselves. Those who hold a predominantly positive opinion are said to have 'high self-esteem', while those whose opinion is predominantly negative are said to have 'low self-esteem'. Over the past few decades the belief that one's self-esteem is integral to the quality and success of one's life has become so widespread as to be viewed almost as common sense. People with high self-esteem, it is said, are likely to be more prosperous, more effective, to have better relationships and, to simply, be happier and more fulfilled. On the other hand, those with low self-esteem are destined for failure, a life of struggling and unhappiness. But there is a lot more to this picture than meets the eye.

For now, let's put to one side how accurate or otherwise these popular assumptions might be and consider that many people who have what we would call low self-esteem don't like the way things are and would like them to be different. Maybe it would be useful to ask why it is that some people seem to have *unhelpful* opinions about themselves, which stop them from moving forward in their lives. From an ACT perspective – thinking about being *Open*, *Aware* and *Active* – what exactly is the problem?

Everyone's a Critic

As we have established, our minds are programmed to judge, evaluate and criticise. The seemingly limitless success of gossip magazines and websites demonstrates that we humans are more than comfortable turning our evaluative gaze outwards and judging others. However, we are also naturally inclined to turn our judgements inwards too.

Has anyone ever said to you that you are your own worst critic? While all of us have minds that will naturally generate self-critical, evaluative thoughts – automatically comparing us to those around us and assessing whether our position in the 'tribe' is safe – some people find themselves fusing particularly tightly with these kinds of thoughts. They find themselves spending endless time and energy ruminating on the various ways in which they are just not good enough. **Each of us will have our own variation on the 'I'm not good enough' story.** What's yours?

- I'm not skinny enough.

- I'm not wealthy enough.

- I'm not assertive enough.

- I'm not attractive enough.

- I'm not funny enough.

In fact, we talked in Chapter 7 (*Anger*) about the tendency of the mind to super-charge these kinds of stories with language that significantly increases their power. We called it 'hot labelling'. Maybe your story sounds more like one of these:

- I'm disgusting and fat.

- I'm worthless.

- I'm a pathetic doormat.

- I'm hideous and unlovable.

Everybody will have these kinds of thoughts from time to time – if anything their presence is evidence that the self-preserving 'don't-get-killed machine' of the mind is working properly. But some people find themselves being constantly hooked by these stories and responding to them in ways that have a profound impact on their lives – either buying into them and switching into autopilot, or struggling desperately with them. They find themselves in an endless loop, comparing themselves to others, seeing how they measure up, and evaluating their worth as a person on the basis of their findings. This can be something of a difficult process. It may be that we sometimes compare ourselves to others and come out better: 'Hmm . . . I earn more than you'. And we get a nice little warm feeling inside of satisfaction and safety. However, the reverse is that our minds will always, **always**, find someone else to compare ourselves unfavourably to: 'Huh . . . I earn more than you, but my boss earns a lot more than me . . . ' and the warm feeling quickly disappears. When we play this game, we put ourselves in danger of getting wrapped up in constantly comparing ourselves to others (and doing things to make sure we compare favourably – or at least so that others don't see how we don't measure up), at the expense of getting in touch with what is personally important and meaningful to us in our lives.

For now, let's just spend a little time getting to know what your personal version of the 'I'm not good enough' story is. When your mind is really beating you up – really intent on letting you know that you are not as good as everybody else – what does it say to you? If we could hold a magic device against your head that could hear your thoughts in those moments, what would it pick up? Write down anything that comes up in the space below:

Just take a second and review what you have written down. Does anybody else in your life ever speak to you as harshly as this? We're guessing not. Most of us really are our own worst critics, walking around with minds that treat us far more harshly than we would allow others to treat us, or than we would ever dream of treating them.

Everyone's a Winner

Probably one of the most pervasive 'I'm not good enough' stories sounds something like this: 'I'm just a loser. Everyone else always succeeds and I'm the one being left behind. Everything I try I mess up. I'm going to go through life as a screw-up and a failure.' We look around and see a world of winners, constantly on the cusp of another triumph, while we languish in failure.

As you probably anticipated, this is yet another example of the mind's natural habits misfiring again. The evaluative mind tends to think in black and white – things are either 'safe' or 'unsafe', 'good' or 'bad'. In the same way, there is a tendency to round down the many nuances of any pursuit or endeavour to whether it was a 'success' or a 'failure' – to see those who have been successful as 'winners', while those who are not are 'losers'. Given that our minds tend to be a little negative and oversensitive to signs that we may not be doing well enough, is it any wonder that many of us sometimes look inwards and decide that we are 'losers'.

Maybe there are a blessed few on this earth who have never quietly called themselves a 'loser' or some variant on the theme, but you can bet that they are few and far between.

More common are those who experience some kind of disappointment, have relatively brief but very real moments of thinking of themselves as 'losers', and who find their minds moving on naturally. Indeed, most people find that their minds offer up a constantly changing set of judgements about themselves: one day telling them that they are excellent at their jobs, witty conversationalists, and really rather attractive, but the next day telling them that they are imminently about to be discovered as an incompetent imposter at work, are dreary company, and look like death warmed up. Some, however, find that the 'I'm not good enough' and 'loser' stories are so powerful for them – hook them so consistently and comprehensively – that they begin to treat them as **facts, rather than opinions**. They effectively confuse the entirely subjective judgements of their minds with real life.

The distinction between opinion and fact is an incredibly important one to draw attention to here. 'Arsenal is a London-based football team' is a fact. 'Arsenal is a really good football team' is an opinion. If we stop distinguishing between opinions and facts when it comes to thinking about ourselves, 'low self-esteem', and all of the uncomfortable stuff that accompanies it, will not be far behind.

Playing by a Different Set of Rules

One thing that we often notice about those who struggle with 'low self-esteem' is that they seem to be playing by a different set of rules than other people. To be more precise, they seem to be carrying around in their minds big, heavy rule books, full of rules about themselves, about other people, and about the world. If you grabbed that magic mind-listening device we mentioned earlier, and spent a few moments looking at the stuff that goes through the mind of someone with low self-esteem, you would quickly get a clear insight into the kinds of rules they are playing by.

In the first chapter we introduced you to Marcia. Marcia lives at home with her mother, who is unwell and needs a lot of care and support. While her friends see her as being confident and bubbly she struggles with self-critical thoughts and has a whole book of rules that she – unconsciously – is living her life by. Here are some examples:

- I must always be there for my mum.

- I should be more sociable.

- I shouldn't be single at this age.

- I must eat healthily all of the time.

- I should be happy like everyone else.

What do you notice about the language here? Notice all the 'shoulds' and 'shouldn'ts'; the 'musts' and 'mustn'ts'? All the non-negotiables that leave Marcia with almost no choice whatsoever about how she lives her life. There's no doubt that some rules can be useful. They provide certainty in an unpredictable world; they can give us a sense of clarity in our actions when we feel unsure of what to do. **But – crucially – they deprive us of our ability to make active, values-based choices about how we live our lives.** Rules are by their nature not responsive to the dynamic, fluid nature of life. Not only that, if we hold onto our rules too tightly, we can end up feeling hurt and disappointed when life's events – and especially when we ourselves – don't conform to them. Think about how much time you've spent telling yourself off or ruminating over having broken some kind of self-imposed rule (I must work out every day; I should read more; I must never shout at my kids).

We're not saying that it is wrong to have clear guidelines for how you want to be and the way you want to behave in life. In fact, we see it as essential – we call those guidelines 'values'. The difference between values and rules is that values are flexible and adaptable, while rules are rigid. Kelly Wilson, a professor of psychology and one of the originators of ACT, says of values: '**Hold them lightly, but pursue them vigorously**'. When we stop holding our values lightly they become rules: we lose some of our choice about how we pursue them and how we live our lives.

Earlier on you wrote down some of the stuff that your mind says to you when it is really trying to give you a hard time and remind you that you are not good enough. In the space below we'd like to invite you to make a note of some of the rules that you hold – about yourself, about other people, about the world – that you know have an impact on how you live your life.

```
┌─────────────────────────────────────────────┐
│                                             │
│                                             │
│                                             │
│                                             │
│                                             │
│                                             │
└─────────────────────────────────────────────┘
```

Self-Esteem and the Thinking Self

With its judgements, evaluations, rules, and never-ending supply of horrible difficult thoughts, you can probably tell that self-esteem (whether low or high) is entirely a creation of the Thinking Self. And while we will always respect the Thinking Self as an incredibly useful resource, we know that it can be a double-edged sword. For one thing, when we are stuck in our Thinking Selves we tend to become extremely rigid in the way that we think about who we are. The Thinking Self focuses on solving problems, and one of the areas where this ability is over-extended is it treats **You** as a 'PROBLEM TO BE SOLVED'.

In Chapter 3 (*Aware*) we talked about the idea of perspective-taking, and how each of us has multiple facets to our character, and a range of viewpoints that we can take on the world. But when we are stuck in our Thinking Selves we tend to default to just one of a few familiar perspectives. For the person with low self-esteem, this is likely to be a perspective that goes with those 'loser' and 'not good enough' stories. When we are in these perspectives our minds develop some interesting habits. We might find ourselves continually keeping score – keeping track of what is going on in our lives and the lives of those around us, and trying to work out who is doing the best, and who is currently 'winning' or 'losing'. We will compare ourselves to others and usually find ourselves wanting.

As you can imagine, Marcia spends a lot of time in a 'not good enough' perspective. She has a friend called Theresa whom she opens up to sometimes.

Theresa: Are you still doing the Internet dating?

Marcia: Oh, I've given up with all that. What's the point? It's too late for me now. Who's going to want some old maid living with her mum anyway?

Theresa: Don't say that! You're a catch!

Marcia: Well you're kind, but it's OK for you. You've got a husband. Everybody's got a partner except me. Who else do you know my age and still single?

Theresa: Lots of people! Jane is single. Marcus is single. My sister is single . . .

Marcia: But your sister has got her own place! She's down there in London living life to the full, with her exciting job.

Theresa: I know for a fact that it's a lot less glamorous than you're imagining. Anyway, you're great at your job.

Marcia: I'm OK, but I'm nothing special.

Theresa: Marcy, you were given a special award less than six months ago for that fundraising event.

Marcia: That was just a token! It was a team effort anyway. Plus, I may have the 'award', but Henry ended up getting promoted, didn't he?

Notice how Marcia's mind compulsively seeks out evidence that other people are doing better than her, and how she slips into autopilot, following those thoughts wherever they want to go. When she is in this familiar 'not good enough' perspective it acts as a filter, catching every scrap of proof that she is losing in the game of life and that others are winning, but missing everything else.

If Marcia were able to get in touch with her Observing Self she might be able to experience that there is more to her than this 'not good enough' perspective might suggest; that there are countless other perspectives from which she could approach the world. But for now – like many people who struggle with self-esteem – she feels stuck. We will talk later about what it might take for her – and you – to get unstuck.

Playing It Safe

Living as they do in worlds that are full of rules, and winners and losers, with minds that come stocked up with negative opinions about themselves, many people with low self-esteem find that they stop taking chances. They avoid situations where there is any chance that they might fail, be rejected, or look bad. Their minds are already Olympic-standard at ferreting out evidence that their version of the 'I'm not good enough' story is true – why would they take the risk of providing it with even more?

As a result, their lives get smaller. As we said in Chapter 4 (*Active*), pursuing almost anything that is of real value in life is going to take us out of comfort zones and will mean taking a risk. If you have a strong value around creativity, at some point you are going to have to put pen to paper or brush to canvas, with no guarantee of what the outcome is going to be. If you have a strong value around relationships, at some point you will have to pick up the phone, or say 'hello' to somebody, with no guarantee of how enthusiastically you will be greeted or how scintillating your conversation will be.

For some people, the thoughts and feelings that arise when they consider exposing themselves to situations that might challenge their self-esteem are so powerful and uncomfortable that they just steer clear of such situations altogether. They end up actively avoiding external life experiences rather than having the unwanted, internal experiences that are likely to accompany them. The upside is that they temporarily get away from uncomfortable thoughts or feel bad about themselves. The downside is that they are denied all of the stuff that makes their lives worthwhile; all the stuff that brings them joy and fulfilment and makes them feel like they are living the kind of lives that they would choose.

An alternative to complete withdrawal is 'playing it safe'. Playing it safe means making gestures towards following your values, but doing so in a cautious, tentative way – designed to minimise the pain if your step out of the comfort zone doesn't work out the way you wanted. The problem with this is that those who play it safe very rarely get what they want. What feels like caution to them often shows up as half-heartedness.

There are few experiences in life more nerve-wracking, and that feel as if they pose more of a threat to our self-esteem, than asking someone out on a date. Marcia is someone who has a very important value around love and connection. Almost more than anything, what she wants is to find a kind, affectionate, intelligent partner. About six months ago – and only after rigorous coaching by her friend Theresa – Marcia finally published a profile on an Internet dating website. Since then she had barely logged in, but a few weeks ago she received a message from a man called Pete who seemed nice, and they went on to exchange numerous emails. Marcia was very keen to meet up with Pete, but was extremely reluctant to actually say this to him. Every time she thought about it, her mind would say to her, 'What if he says no? What if he is so embarrassed and mortified that he never even emails again? Anyway, it's the man's job to ask the woman out, why should I even have to?'

Eventually, Theresa hassled Marcia into committing to sending Paul an email suggesting that they go to the theatre. However, when – after much procrastinating – she eventually sat down to write she couldn't bring herself to actually ask outright. Instead, she ended up hitting 'send' on the message below:

> Hi Pete!
>
> How has your week been so far? Not too stressful I hope.
>
> Mine has been pretty boring. I was talking to my friend who said that there is another one of those 'jukebox musicals' starting at the Royal Theatre. I can't remember if it's Take That or the Spice Girls

or what! It sounds silly to be honest. On the other hand, it could be pretty funny too, couldn't it?

Anyway, take care. Speak soon.

Marcy

Marcia spent the next two days agonisingly anticipating Pete's response, which seemed to take forever arriving. When it eventually did he agreed with her that the new trend for 'jukebox musicals' was funny and that they could indeed be entertaining, but that he preferred classics like *Oklahoma*! and *Cabaret*. He then completely changed the subject. Marcia was devastated. She was so mortified by what she saw as his rejection of her invitation that she couldn't bear the thought of writing back to him. Every time he emailed her she immediately sent it to the trash bin, and pretty soon he stopped messaging her altogether.

At first, Theresa was full of sympathy. But when she eventually read the email that Marcia sent she was incredulous: 'That's not asking someone out on a date! All you've done is tell him your opinion about a particular style of musical theatre!' By hedging her bets to protect her self-esteem, Marcia ended up communicating so indirectly that her meaning was hard to read. In the process she missed out on what could have been an exciting opportunity, and moved another step away from her values of love and connection.

Building Walls and Keeping Others at Arm's Length

Of course, not everybody responds to low self-esteem in the way that Marcia does. She responds to her uncomfortable and unwanted thoughts and feelings by slipping into auto-pilot – she avoids challenging situations, puts others first, and does all she can to avoid any attention being focused on her at all. Some people, however, choose to struggle. And when they struggle, their low self-esteem – paradoxically – often shows up as behaviour that can seem rude and arrogant, or perhaps cold and distant.

Think of moments in your own life where you may have found yourself lashing out at someone or 'cutting them down to size'. What was going on for you? Were they really 'asking for it', or was there something they had said or done (or was there just something about them) that hurt you or challenged your sense of who you are? People with low self-esteem have minds that are constantly telling them that they are not good enough. One great way of silencing that voice momentarily is to make someone else feel as if *they* are the one who is not good enough. If you do it skilfully enough you might even convince yourself – but only temporarily. As with all struggle-responses, it is just not sustainable in the long-term.

Similarly, do you know someone who, when you first met them, struck you as cold, aloof and unfriendly, but as time went on and you got to know them better, you realised that they were actually lovely, warm and kind? There may be any number of reasons why your first impression was the way that it was. But we have already established that the person with low self-esteem will do almost anything it takes to avoid exposing themselves to situations where they might be rejected or seen to 'fail'. One way of doing this would be to avoid contact with other human beings altogether. Given how difficult this is on a practical level (people are **everywhere!**), an alternative is to just keep others at arm's length, and stop them from seeing the 'real you'. Or to portray a hard, invulnerable image to give others the impression that you can't be hurt.

While the outside world sees someone who is tough and unapproachable, what is going on inside is actually very different. And just as surely as if someone who was hiding away entirely or allowing others to put their needs before their own, the person who responds to low self-esteem in this way will find themselves drifting further and further away from their values, and feeling more and more unsatisfied and unfulfilled.

EXERCISE – Playing It Safe

Take some time now to complete the following worksheet. We'd like you to think about all the different ways that you play it safe. How do you keep in your comfort zone? How do you protect and stop yourself from getting hurt? What do you do to stop others seeing the soft, vulnerable part of you?

PLAYING IT SAFE WORKSHEET

In what ways do you play it safe?	What thoughts and feelings does playing it safe protect you from?	How does playing it safe impact on you being *Active*?

How Did I Get Here?

Most people who find themselves struggling with something in life (whether it is with anger, anxiety, depression, low self-esteem or something else entirely) at some point ask themselves 'Why is it like this? How did I get here?' And while we don't feel that being able to answer the question 'why?' is sufficient – or even necessary – to be able to start making positive changes, it can be useful to look back a little. There is information there and we can use what we see to start to get a sense of what some of the habits – of thinking and behaviour – might have been that contributed to the situation as it is now.

When Marcia stopped to reflect on this a little, she started to get a sense of how circumstances in her life had made it much more likely that she would find herself struggling with low self-esteem.

As a child, Marcia's natural inclination was to be 'good' and 'helpful'. Her family and teachers appreciated these qualities in her and gave her lots of affirmation and praise every time she was 'good'. On the other hand, on the few occasions that she was 'naughty' she was reprimanded. She has a particularly strong memory of a teacher telling her 'Marcia, I expected better of you'.

Marcia's mother was frequently unwell and, because her father died when she was young, she found herself taking care of her mother a lot. While her mother never tried to stop her from seeing her friends or doing the things that she enjoyed, Marcia sensed that she was disappointed and hurt when she did. She recalls how her mother would sigh deeply and become tearful when Marcia talked about having weekend plans. This would make Marcia feel dreadfully guilty, and she soon came to associate looking after her own needs with feeling bad.

As Marcia grew up the values that she naturally held around kindness and being of service to others hardened into strict and inflexible rules, her mind telling her that she must always make herself available when others need her, and that it was selfish and wrong to do what she wanted to do. Because she didn't seem unhappy, friends and colleagues saw Marcia as caring and 'easy-going', and became accustomed to not giving too much thought to her needs, feeling comfortable that she would 'go with the flow'. Every now and then she would find herself feeling annoyed or angry, but when she did she would struggle bitterly with the feeling, her mind telling her how selfish she was to expect others to behave the way she wanted them to, and how pathetic she was for getting upset.

She ultimately found herself at a point where her habit was to consider herself as less important, less competent, just less than other people in general. But, given some of the experiences she has had in life, isn't it at least understandable how this came to be the case? It's neither her fault nor the fault of the people around her. Marcia simply followed her values as a child (one thing children are great at doing is following their values), and circumstances were such that her mind grabbed onto some of them and turned them into tough, rigid rules about how she should be and how she should live. The more she followed these rules, the harder it became for her to do anything different, the worse she would feel if she tried. And somewhere down the line she started to feel stuck, and decided to do something about it.

All of us will have a similar story. Any unhelpful habit or behaviour, anything that we struggle with in life, will have started as the expression of something quite natural, and then developed into something that just isn't working for us anymore. And here is the good news: **the answer isn't to somehow eradicate the 'problem'; it is simply to take something normal and healthy that has become unworkable and learn to approach it in a way that is workable.** Let us explain . . .

Is Low Self-Esteem Workable?

While no one would dispute that low self-esteem and the thoughts, feelings, memories and sensations that come with it are unpleasant, a more important question is this: is it workable? By which we mean: is it possible to have a mind that offers up a stream of negative opinions and stories about the self *and* still live a life that is rich and fulfilling?

And the answer to this question is a resounding **yes** – but **only** if we learn to respond effectively to the mind-stuff that we associate with low self-esteem. However, because many of us fail to manage this effectively, we end up falling into habits that drive us away from the lives that we want. From the perspective of being *Active*, we do less and less of the stuff that matters and become increasingly isolated from our values.

If we respond to the opinions, stories and rules of low self-esteem on autopilot, what most people find is that their lives become smaller. If our minds are constantly keeping score of who is winning and losing, we feel reluctant to put ourselves in situations where we may 'lose' so we avoid them or play it safe. If we are constantly comparing our own worth to that of others, we will avoid instances in which our worth might be judged or tested. We will stay within our comfort zones and inevitably drift further and further from our values.

The point we are making here is that if you are reading this and feeling like your low self-esteem is having a negative impact on your life, our intention for you is **not** that you try to develop high self-esteem. Our intention for you is that you learn to manage your mind-stuff more effectively and commit to doing what matters to you in life, regardless of whether your opinions about yourself are positive or negative. We would even go so far as to propose that the idea that high self-esteem is a passport to a life of success and fulfilment is a myth. Have you ever met somebody who seems to have cast-iron confidence in all situations, and exudes the energy of someone who is fully convinced of their own intrinsic worth and even superiority? What kind of impact did they make on you? Imagine if somebody absolutely bought into the story 'I am a fantastic person, and everything I ever do is a success'. How useful do you think this would be in helping them to form valuable relationships, to develop and grow, to learn from their mistakes?

Fusing and buying into any stories about the self is risky, regardless of whether those stories are positive or negative. The most reliable way of moving towards fulfilment in life – to consistently and committedly following your values – is to do what matters irrespective of whether your self-esteem is high, low or medium. We aim to show you some skills and practices that can help you do just that.

It will be important to keep in mind that the three skills we've talked about in this book, *Open*, *Aware* and *Active*, will all apply to effectively tackling self-esteem issues. All of them work together to help you unlock a stuck situation and get moving again. Keep this in mind as we go over each of the skills below.

An *Active* Starting Point – What Matters to *You*?

An Invitation – Pause

Our invitation to you is to take some time to simply pause. To stop in the middle of your life. A life that is no doubt filled with all sorts of activities, roles, people, routines and things. Just for a second, take a moment to step outside of all of this to ask yourself: what is it all about?

In Chapter 4 (*Active*), we spent time going through a variety of different ways to help you to contact personally what a life of meaning, purpose and vitality would look like for you. Well, we'd like to revisit this question with you now, both because it's an incredibly important question, and also an incredibly difficult one. Let's return to Marcia to get a sense of what we mean here:

Marcia vividly recalled how one day, whilst browsing books in her local second-hand bookstore, she came across a small, slim book, entitled, Man's Search for

Meaning *by Viktor Frankl. She picked it up, remember-*
ing how an old friend had once suggested she read it.
She took it home that night and read the story of the
author, who was both a psychiatrist and Nazi concen-
tration camp survivor. She was captivated by the idea
that an individual could even think about meaning and
purpose under the conditions that existed in the camps.
As she read, she thought about herself and what for her
represented meaning and purpose, realising, with a deep
sense of sadness, that she had never really stopped to
think about this question. Her life had been focused on
either following a set of internal rules to make sure that
others around her were happy, or constantly denigrating
what she did have in her life as she relentlessly compared
herself to those around her. At its heart, her sense of low
self-esteem had revolved around a set of behaviours that
worked to keep her safe. She began to wonder what her
life would look like if she were to choose more freely how
she spent her time, what she did and who with.

EXERCISE: Imagine if No One Cared
What You Did

In this exercise, we would like you to use the power
of your imagination as we invite you to transport
yourself to an alternate universe. In this alternate
universe, everything is exactly the same in just about
every respect, except for one. In this universe, no one
cares at all what you do. It doesn't matter what you
do, no one is going to get upset with you, get angry

with you, praise you or give you any feedback whatsoever. You are completely free to do whatever you
want. Take some time to fill in the spaces below:

What would you do next?

What would you do in your work?

What would you do for fun?

What would you do or say with your friends and family?

How would you spend your time?

Ok, so we know this is an artificial situation; however, we
think there is some value in pausing for a moment and
separating out all the things you do in life **for other people**.
When you're racing around in life, focused on keeping others happy, and playing it safe to avoid criticism it can be
easy to find yourself in a situation where your whole life is
run without consideration to **the things that matter to you**.

As you begin to entertain such ideas, no doubt there will
immediately be a ton of mind-stuff that comes along for

the ride. Remember that this is completely normal and part of the process that takes place when you begin to consider what is really important to you. Figure 3 is a useful reminder of this process. It's only when you start to step outside of your comfort zone, where things feel safe and cosy, that the real magic can start to happen. This will mean opening up to all sorts of experiences that may be outside of your control. You may have feelings that perhaps you would rather not have, such as anxiety or worry, as you begin to take some risks. You may notice an increase in thoughts or negative evaluations about yourself, like 'you can't do it' or 'you don't deserve that' or our personal favourite, 'you're just being selfish, thinking of what you want'. Rather than viewing these as signs to stop what you are doing, we'd like to suggest that these are in fact the very signs that you are making progress. The trick is to be able to recognise them as such, and lean into them rather than doing what you might normally do when running on autopilot, which is to avoid these experiences and situations that create them.

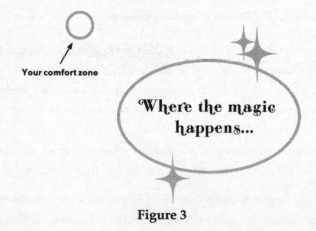

Your comfort zone

Where the magic happens...

Figure 3

Opening Up

You've now got the sense that effectively tackling low self-esteem is not simply about replacing it with high self-esteem. We're more interested in helping you to work more effectively with the thoughts, feelings and behaviours that go together to keep you stuck.

The problem with paying too much attention to your self-esteem is that thoughts and feelings end up guiding what you do in life and you completely lose focus on how you want to lead your life. Consider this metaphor of *Passengers on the Bus*:

Imagine you are the driver of a bus; your 'Bus of Life'. This bus represents your journey in life, the directions you take with your actions and behaviours. And as with any decent bus service, you have passengers on your bus. These represent all the stuff you experience under your skin – your constantly changing thoughts, feelings, moods, memories, worries, urges to do certain things, and so on.

Being a good bus driver, you dutifully pull into all the bus stops along your journey to allow passengers on and off the bus. Some of your passengers have been on your bus for a long time, just about since you started out on your journey. Some have only recently jumped on for the ride. What you notice is that some of the passengers constantly pipe up. Your minds, for example, will tend to give a sort of running commentary, like a constant chatter, about what's going on – where your bus is going, how you're doing as a driver, and so on. The more encouraging passengers are like the nice old ladies at the front of the bus who tell you what a great driver you are. But not all of your passengers are quite so nice. Some are like bullies, threatening you, telling you what you have to do, where you have to go. 'You've got to turn left', 'You've got to go right', and so on. Others criticise you, telling you that you're doing a terrible job or comparing you unfavourably to other bus drivers. These more unhelpful passengers can sometimes hold us back, and interfere with moving our bus in a direction that we really want to go in.

Understandably, you don't like these passengers as much and you'd much rather they kept quiet and left you alone. So you try to make a deal with them. You say to them, 'You sit in the back of the bus and scrunch down so that I can't see you very often, and I'll do what you say.' This works well in some respects. They become quieter and you don't have to deal with them anymore. However, the problem with this deal is that you end up doing whatever they ask in exchange for getting them out of your life. Pretty soon they don't even have to tell you, 'Turn left' – you know as soon as you get near a left turn that the passengers are going to cause a fuss if you even think about not doing what they want. In time you may get good enough that you can almost pretend to yourself that they're not on the bus at all. You just tell yourself that left is the direction you wanted to turn anyway.

Take a moment to reflect if any of this resonates with you. Do you have any passengers on your bus that you really find it hard to make room for? Do you find yourself responding nearly automatically to ensure they keep quiet? What is the cost of this for you in terms of your life?

If you are interested, there is a YouTube animation of this allegory, which you can view and download here:

http://tinyurl.com/PoBanimation

Part of the task here is to be able to notice those moments in your life that represent turns on your bus journey and carefully listen out for how the thoughts and feelings (passengers) get louder. When you're responding on autopilot, it's like you don't even have a chance to decide what you want to do; you've in fact already made a decision a long time ago by agreeing on a deal – 'I don't want to feel these feelings or have these thoughts so a right turn towards what I really want in life is not even an option'. By slowing this down and developing your *Aware* skills, you can begin to mindfully notice how this process works and the degree of habitual responding that can occur. Undoubtedly these passengers carry a lot of weight for you and probably have a lot of history too. Those passengers that have been on our buses for the longest often do. As you start to entertain the idea of taking risks and moving outside of your comfort zone, you will begin to get a feel for which thoughts and feelings act as key obstacles to moving forward in your life.

Such thoughts can have a real pull and can work to effectively move us off course. When on autopilot, it can be extremely easy to let these thoughts guide our actions. As soon as we notice this process at work, we begin to have many more options in terms of how we respond to these thoughts. Remember from Chapter 2 (*Open*), we talked about different ways to be able to step back from thoughts that are not helpful. These techniques help to build in some space and distance when our minds are busy judging, criticising or comparing. Here's a reminder:

- **Get good at noticing your thoughts.** Use your *Aware* skills to tune into your mind and listen in, particularly when you are about to take a step outside of your comfort zone. Keep in mind, these thoughts work for us; they are useful. At least in part. When we automatically buy into such thoughts they can serve to protect us from all sorts of uncomfortable and unpleasant emotions and feelings. They can stop us from doing things such as opening up to others and saying what we really think or feel, which can involve taking a risk. They can stop us from the feeling of discomfort that can come when we look after ourselves. They can prevent us from feeling anger that may come along with asserting ourselves. Who are the *Passengers* who are getting really loud? Which way do they want you to move your bus? Is this actually the way you want to go in?

- **Keep an eye out for thought fusion.** Some clues that you are fused with your thoughts could include:

  Your thoughts have a 'same old, same old' feel to them. You've heard this many times before.

  Your thoughts are very critical with lots of self judgements.

Your thoughts have a very 'black and white' feel to them.

Your thoughts involve lots of comparisons with others.

Your thoughts involve lots of negative predictions about the future.

- **Thank your mind.** Remember, your mind is working hard to keep you safe, stop you from getting hurt and protect you. It's helpful to remind yourself of this as you start taking steps outside of your comfort zone. Sometimes simply thanking your mind is a helpful way of reminding yourself that your mind is doing its job *and* you may not have to take what it says as a literal truth.

  'I can't ask for what I want.' Thanks, mind, it's not always easy asking for what I want *and* it's also important to me.

  'I'm not as good as anyone else.' Thanks, mind – that is one perspective on the situation.

  'I can't handle them being angry with me.' Thanks, mind – I appreciate you doing your best to keep me safe.

An important part of developing *Openness* is to recognise the ways in which we hold on tightly to thoughts may in fact protect us from feeling unwanted emotions. So, in order to truly have choice about which direction we go in our lives, we need to be prepared to be open to certain emotions.

A Leap of Faith

It all comes back to the idea of 'willingness'. Are you willing to gamble to win? Are you willing to take a leap of faith rather than just dip your toe in the water of life? Are you willing to keep taking those leaps of faith – and all the uncomfortable, scary thoughts and feelings that will inevitably accompany them – in order to get more of what you want out of life? Are you willing to take a risk, not knowing what the outcome might be?

If your answer to these questions at the moment is 'no', that's OK! Later on we will show you how to use some of the *Open* skills we showed you earlier on to manage the mind-stuff that will show up when taking a step into the unknown and putting your self-esteem on the line. But at this point we do want to stress what a powerful experience it can be to take a chance even when you don't know what the result will be, even in the face of fear and self-doubt. Do you remember the story about the unwelcome party guest in the *Open* chapter? The idea of just getting on and enjoying the party even though there is a loud, obnoxious idiot getting in everyone's faces? The idea of proving that you are bigger than your scariest thoughts and feelings, that you are more than just the sum the stuff that your mind churns out? The learning that will come from stepping out of your comfort zone is probably more valuable than anything else you will do or have as a result of that step.

A common story that keeps people stuck sounds something like this: 'I *would* apply for a new job/go to the party/tell my boss what I think of him *if only* I had more self-esteem'.

The logic of this story is that we can somehow learn to control our thoughts and feelings in such a way that one day we will suddenly realise that we have 'high self-esteem' and *then* we will march forward into our lives and do all the stuff we have always dreamed of. We would like to politely suggest that this is unlikely to be the case. What people inevitably find is that doing what matters in life does not depend on high self-esteem so much as being willing to be more guided by values and less guided by thoughts and feelings.

From Self-Esteem to Self-Acceptance: a Step Toward Kindness

In Chapter 3 (*Aware*) we talked about the important concept of self-compassion and this is particularly relevant when it comes to issues related to self-esteem. Kristen Neff, a researcher into self-compassion, identifies three important components to this concept.[10] The first is *kindness*: developing a stance of warmth and gentleness towards ourselves particularly at those points in which we fall short, suffer or feel less than adequate. This is in contrast to criticising ourselves or ignoring our pain all together. The second is *common humanity*: recognising that we are not alone in our struggles with difficult thoughts or memories and painful feelings. It can be sometimes too easy to think we are the only ones on the planet who aren't measuring up, being rejected or failing. The third is *mindfulness*. This refers to

10   Neff, K. *Self Compassion* (Hodder & Stoughton, 2011).

the ability to develop observing qualities to our experience, without becoming over identified with thoughts and emotions.

To enact these qualities does not necessarily require you to *feel* self-compassion towards yourself; simply that you behave in a self-compassionate way. Consider some of these questions:

- How can I demonstrate kindness towards myself?

- If I were to act in a more gentle way towards myself, what would I do? Who would I talk to and how would I do it?

- If I were to comfort myself, how could I embody this in a gesture?

- If someone else were in the situation I am in, how would I act towards them? Could I behave the same way to myself?

It's very likely that initially, developing self-compassion may feel a little unnatural, even strange. This is the same for developing any new habit or skill – it can take some time. Here's how Marcia started to use these ideas to break a very familiar routine:

Marcia was coming home after her first date with Pete. After some more prompting from Theresa, she had plucked up the courage to directly ask him out on a date. She'd been sick with anxiety waiting for his reply, expecting him to turn her down. She couldn't believe it when he had said yes. Although Marcia was initially tense and awkward, she had eventually relaxed and ended up enjoying their evening out. As she walked in the door, she realised that it was much later than she'd thought. Her mother was waiting up, clearly looking very anxious and agitated. She started to chastise Marcia for being home so late, saying she'd been so worried about her. Marcia immediately felt a sinking feeling in her stomach and had the thought, 'I can't believe I've been so selfish, what a terrible daughter.' Normally, this would send her into a spiral of self-criticism and endless apologies to her mother. However, this time, she recognised the pattern of thoughts and feelings as familiar and it gave her pause for thought. In this space, she remembered a small comment Theresa had made last week – 'Be gentle with yourself Marcia, anyone would find your mother hard work. I think you manage her really well, all things considered.' She took a deep breath and reminded herself that she was doing OK and maybe she wasn't completely responsible for how her mother felt all the time. She helped her mother to settle, but at the same time not apologising for being late, even though she felt a strong urge to do so. Later that evening as she went to bed, she noticed she felt a little bit proud of herself for responding differently to her mother.

A Word about Pleasing Others

Now don't misunderstand us: there is nothing wrong with wanting to please others. It's a good thing and an essential ingredient to harmonious and co-operative, friendships, relationships and communities. But sometimes, it can get a little out of control and you may end up making most (if not all) of your decisions to please others, to make sure they aren't upset or that they don't think badly of you. Most people who work very hard to please others are usually very well liked. They are reliable, dependable, and will always go the extra mile for others. These are great qualities and getting feedback from others about what a nice person you are feels good, right? Here are some types of thoughts that are pretty common for people with low self-esteem:

- It's just easier not to speak up.

- I wouldn't want to put anyone out.

- I don't like causing a fuss.

- I can't stand the thought of people being upset with me.

- I like making other people happy!

Sitting underneath this is a message that 'My needs are not as important as everyone else's'. When you are operating on autopilot, it can sometimes be easier to simply prioritise other people's needs so you don't have to deal with the uncomfortable thoughts and feelings that arise when you say what you want and need. As in the *Passengers on the*

Bus metaphor, sometimes it can end up that you may nearly convince yourself that what other people want is actually what you want anyway. Slowly, over time your whole identity becomes based on other people while your needs and values fade into the background.

Based on what we've discussed in this chapter so far, here are some practical tips to consider in helping you move from people-pleasing to doing what's important for you.

First of all, when in a situation where you are being asked to do something by someone else or you feel the urge to do something for others, see if you can:

1. PAUSE. Take a moment before agreeing to anything.

2. Use your *Aware* skills to check in with yourself. How are you feeling in that moment? What thoughts are going through your mind? What passengers are a little louder? What urges to action do you feel? If your thoughts seem largely like rules (I have to . . . I should . . . I must . . . I couldn't possibly . . .), this may suggest you are not acting on your values. Similarly if you are feeling strong feelings and corresponding urges to get rid of these feelings, this may suggest your values are not at the forefront, guiding your actions.

3. If you were to focus completely on **you**, what actions would you take? What would a step in a valued direction for you look like?

4. If you were to take that step in a valued direction, what feelings would you need to make a little room and space for? Also, what old, familiar passengers would you anticipate are going to try to convince you to 'play it safe'? Is there scope to notice these as passengers, with a valid but limited perspective, while also being firm that they aren't actually in charge of where your bus goes?

5. Finally, be gentle. It's actually OK to people-please. See if you can do your best not to beat yourself over the head if you have acted to please others and not considered your own values. Often, putting others' needs first can have a long history. You may have grown up in a family where it wasn't all right to express your needs or where putting others before yourself was heavily rewarded. So, sometimes it can take some time to develop a new habit and learn a new skill.

Assertiveness – Effectively Expressing Your Needs

Expressing your needs can mean a range of different things. At its heart it means letting someone else know what you are really thinking or feeling and what you want. This can be easy if you are letting them know something nice that they want as well. But it becomes more difficult when it is something they may not want to hear. This could include telling your boss you are too busy and can't take on another project right now. It could mean telling a friend that you are upset that they haven't called you and you'd like to be in touch more often. It may mean letting your partner know when they have behaved in a way that has annoyed or irritated you.

It could be the case that you may worry that if you do begin to say what you want, you may not be able to manage the feelings that go along with this. Or you may not have had practise at expressing your needs and wants in helpful or workable ways. In such instances it can be useful to have some practical strategies.

In Chapter 7 (*Anger*), we talked about the purpose of the emotion anger and how it can serve to let us know when something happens to us that we don't like or has crossed a personal boundary for us. In this way, it's an extremely useful tool, without which we would end up being walked all over or having no sense of what worked for us and what didn't. But the key is to be able to let other people know when they have done something that upsets or annoys in an effective way.

Essentially, what we are talking about is assertiveness, which is the appropriate expression of anger – assertiveness effectively sets boundaries. This can mean a range of things, such as letting others know when they have hurt our feelings, behaved in a disrespectful way or tried to take advantage of us. In such situations, we need to be able to communicate this effectively so that the other person knows how their behaviour has affected us, and hopefully so they won't do it again. The trick is also to communicate this in a way that is respectful to the other person (especially if the relationship is important to us).

Here are four tips to help assertively express your anger:

1. Use 'I' statements.

2. Describe how you were feeling in response to the other person's behaviour.

3. Describe what you think the other person was feeling.

4. State clearly what you would like the other person to do differently.

Using these steps will help you to clearly identify to the other person what you were feeling, and how this related to what they did. Using 'I' statements helps to take the blame out of the situation and focuses you on taking responsibility for your part in the interaction. Finally, describing how the other person was feeling can be vital to keeping the interaction cool. Most arguments occur when people think they aren't being understood. Although it can take some effort, taking the other person's perspective can help to ensure they do feel understood. Or at least they can see you are making an effort to get into their shoes. Let's see how Marcia tried this out the next day after coming home late from her date. Choosing her words carefully, Marcia said to her mother:

Last night I felt that very criticised when I came home later than expected. When you got angry with me, I felt sad and upset. I know you were anxious and worried about me and also about being on your own. Next time, I'd like it if you could be less critical of me.

Using Your *Aware* Skills

When on a sailing boat, any sailor will tell you that you need to always be watching for the wind, keeping track of its direction, strength and any changes. When you set your sail to catch this wind, the boat can surge forward, as the power of the wind is translated into the motion of the boat through the water. If you catch a strong gust of wind, this can be absolutely exhilarating, but at the same time can be scary too!

The same applies to taking steps outside of our comfort zone and moving towards what really, truly, deeply matters to us. It can be thrilling and, chances are, a little (or very) nerve-wracking at the same time. This is where it is vital to use your *Aware* skills. **Doing so will allow you to mindfully track the swirl of thoughts and emotions that will no doubt occur as you begin to take steps forward in your life.** Mindful awareness of these experiences will allow you to notice them. They are important and will give you good information about when you are moving forward. At the same time, they are not the only thing to be aware of. You need to keep track of the heading you are on and sometimes this means you will need to be aware of your thoughts and feelings but be able to simply allow them to be there without necessarily getting caught up in them.

The occupational psychologists Paul Flaxman, Frank Bond and Fredrik Livheim, refer to this process as *de-emphasising thoughts and feelings:*[11] allowing them to take a back seat while values become the more prominent guides to the course and therefore direction of our lives.

Bringing It All Together – Developing a More Flexible Sense of Self

To summarise what we have talked about in this chapter, problematic self-esteem is, at its heart, an issue with identity. Or more specifically, a rigid identity or story about yourself that is based around viewing yourself as in some way less than, or not as good as, other people. These stories develop for good reason. They usually (but not always) originate from our early life experiences and, although on the surface they may look painful or unhelpful, they do serve a purpose. Usually that purpose is to keep you safe – encouraging you to stay in your comfort zone so you don't get hurt. Let's give these stories full credit; they are doing a great job and in all likelihood have served you well over the years. So, we want to give them respect, but we also want to learn to hold them lightly and develop some flexibility around them.

11 Flaxman, P., Bond, F., & Livheim, F., *The Mindful and Effective Employee* (New Harbinger Publications, 2013)

Think about the example of what happened with Lance Armstrong, the former professional athlete and cyclist. The narrative that was built up around him was extremely powerful. He was someone who had survived very serious testicular cancer that had spread throughout his body (lungs, abdomen, brain) and made a miraculous comeback to win the Tour de France races. He also set up the charity Livestrong to provide support to survivors of cancer. This was such a powerful narrative that it made it very difficult for the media and his supporters to see the overwhelming evidence to say that Armstrong was using illicit performance-enhancing substances that eventually led to him being stripped of all his Tour de France titles and banned from competitive cycling. Even following his eventual highly publicised admission, some fans continued to believe the story that he had not been involved in illegal drugs.

The point we want to make here is that the stories that we hold about ourselves can be incredibly powerful and when we hold on to them too tightly, it can sometimes blind us to alternative perspectives available to us. As you start to develop your *Open*, *Aware* and *Active* skills, you will begin to open yourself up to a range of new experiences that will provide different ways of seeing yourself: different and perhaps surprising facets will emerge. We would encourage you to allow yourself to notice these changes and be curious about them. At the same time, see if you can hold whatever comes your way a little lightly. These new experiences need not define you either. They will be part of you; they will say something about you but will not be the whole story. In this way, you will be learning to take the perspective of the Observer Self more and more, so you are able to notice, to watch, to observe all aspects of your experience: holding them lightly, being neither too attached nor completely detached. This is the key to developing a flexible sense of self.

9 Keeping It Going

It's better to have something to remember than anything to regret.

Frank Zappa

The best way out is always through.

Robert Frost

We are what we repeatedly do. Excellence, then, is not an act but a habit.

Will Durant

Changing Your Life Is Hard Work

You will have hard-won, and rich, experience of this if you have been trying out what we've described in this book! Through the chapters we have explored the potential of using the skills of Acceptance and Commitment Therapy to enhance your life. We started with a general description of three skills, and then went into detail about how these skills can help you with problems such as depression, anxiety, anger and low self-esteem. We used the stories of Tim,

Dave, Samantha and Marcia to illustrate how these problems can involve the life-cost of struggling with unwanted experiences and being on autopilot, not noticing the process of our mind's storytelling.

We hope that we have shared with you that ACT is more than just dealing with problems: the same skills help us to flourish and engage deeply with what is important. Each of us (J,O., J.H. and E.M.), have experienced the benefits of doing ACT for ourselves: in writing this book we hope that these ideas have expanded your life too.

Finally, we hope that by this point your life has had more moments of vitality, meaning and purpose because you have practised three skills:

- **Being *Open*** to your emotions, feelings, sensations, thoughts and urges;

- **Being *Aware*** of and noticing the stuff that goes on inside you and around you in the world; and,

- **Being *Active*** through choosing and acting on your personal values, rather than being held hostage to your fear or rules about how you 'should' be.

In this final chapter we are going to discuss the process of **persisting flexibly.** We are going to touch on how you can handle moments of failure, urges to procrastinate, and some good ways to form habits that support your flexibility. All of this will help you to further ACTivate your life.

And, would you believe we are going to suggest that this process is also about practising being *Open*, *Aware* and *Active*?

ACTivating Your Life Is Like . . . Kayaking

For anyone who has never kayaked before, like any skill, it takes a fair amount of practice to become competent. How to balance yourself in your boat; how to get the right angle on your blades as you pull your paddle through the water; and how to steer yourself in the right direction. At first, most people tend to keep their head down and be focused on just one skill at a time without co-ordinating all the skills at once. However, with time and practise, they will become familiar and bring all the skills together at the same time to start really moving efficiently through the water. At this point, they begin to trust themselves and, knowing that they have learned a new set of skills, they begin to look up and around. They can then focus on a point in front of them to guide the direction of travel. Learning the skills of *Open*, *Aware* and *Active* is a little like this. As you get better and more co-ordinated, you will be able to trust yourself with these new skills, lift your head up and start moving your life in the direction you want to go in, with richness, fulfilment and fun.

How to Make ACTivating Yourself a Habit

Forming habits and having them stick is about **making changes to your lifestyle**.

A commonly held idea is that people who are successful in forming habits have strong **will power**. It would be great to say that we have the inside knowledge on how to have super will power . . . but this isn't the case.

In fact, it seems that the idea of 'will power' – the belief that it is this magical quality that we either have or don't have – can be one of the biggest obstacles to our creating new and helpful habits. This is because accepting an idea like that can set our Thinking Self to making comparisons ('I'm not as strong-willed as her'), judgements and predictions ('I'm lazy', 'I will probably fail, I have no will power'), and seeking answers about something that may be unhelpful anyway ('Why do I have no will power?')! All the busy work of our minds can invite us to pay attention to the 'I lack will power' story, rather than focus our energies on what may actually work.

The central irony is that in trying to control our behaviour, we have to acknowledge a fundamental lack of control over what are usually thought of as the core aspects of 'will power': emotions and thoughts.

So, It Isn't about Will Power

One of our heroes, the psychologist B. F. Skinner, put no stock in internal causes, such as will power, for how habits may be strengthened. Instead, his view was that the environment influenced behaviour, and through making changes to the world we live in, behaviour may be strengthened or weakened. And this was an approach Skinner used in his own life. He would remain curious about how his working environment could support him writing scientific papers and books, by experimenting with changes to his routine, using clocks and gadgets to focus his attention on writing, and various ways to measure his output and track his progress. As a result, his office did not look like something from *Ideal Home* . . . but it worked to produce a body of work by one of the most influential psychologists in history.

We are going to encourage you to approach forming habits in a similar way – by tinkering with changes to the world around you, and holding very lightly the stories your mind will undoubtedly have about your 'will power'.

There are several ideas here that should assist in doing this:

- Connecting the habit to a valued direction.

- Holding results of habit change lightly, while imagining the process of achieving the goal (the doing and feeling).

- Getting started by setting a small daily quota.

- Using existing habits to trigger the new one by creating a new link in the chain.

Let's unpack each of these points:

Your connection with your values is going to be a great ally in developing habits. As we have discussed, a view of the 'light on the hill' (see Chapter 4: *Active*) will help you to persist and learn from experience for those times when making changes involves discomfort.

One particularly awkward little mind trick can be to hold on too tightly to the **results** of the habit. We can get caught up in excessively fantasising our goal of 're-inventing' ourselves all at once, which may increase the gap between how you are now and what you hope you will be doing in the future. As you know from Chapter 3 (*Aware*), getting tangled in thoughts about the future can be at the cost of doing things in the present (this is probably why New Year's resolutions hardly ever last. Also, when you dive head first into a new habit without clearly defining your goals, it will start to weaken, and it will be very difficult to stay consistent.

It is better instead to **imagine the process of your getting to a very achievable goal**: *picturing the steps it will involve* and *the emotions you will be in contact with*. You can do this by using your *Aware* skills to get in contact with the present moment, before deliberately imagining taking each step toward the goal, and noticing what emotions and thoughts show up while doing this. Especially notice any urges to get caught up with your desire to achieve the goal and how wonderful the future will be, with gentleness. Let these just be there, and make room for them as part of the experience.

A similar mind trick can be the invitation from your mind to be intimidated about the level of change you are making:

finding it difficult to imagine how you will achieve what you are setting out to do. This is where **setting yourself a small quota every day** – the minimum amount you can do to make the goal a reality – can be helpful.

Quotas can make the task approachable. Find somewhere to begin and set yourself a quota, even if only a very small one, just to get you moving. For example, Samantha wanted to look after her health (valued direction) by exercising more (goal). She did this very rarely and had not been able to get into a regular routine. She set herself a quota of exercising for just five minutes every day by going for walk around her neighbourhood. For Samantha this got her moving (literally!), and actually resulted in her exercising for more than five minutes most days.

Samantha got past the 'analysis paralysis' phase to *actually doing something*. **We are far more likely to finish things if we can just get over the hump of starting.** This is a powerful point to remember: whatever way you find to get started, you increase the chance of taking steps toward your goal dramatically by just doing something.

Finally, **habits are more effectively triggered if they are 'another link in the chain' with existing habits and routines**. So, following up on an already existing habit (e.g. arriving home; eating lunch) with a 'new link in the chain' is a good way to start a habit. Samantha used her daily routine of arriving home from work to start her exercise: she would park the car and instead of walking into the house, deliberately walk to a nearby park for exercise. Samantha found that by doing this she also had the added benefit of 'decompressing' from a busy work day. As exercise was linked with arriving home from work, Samantha increased the odds that she would do this in the future.

Recommitment – Handling Frustration and Relapses

It is likely as you start to make changes, that you are going to come across frustrating moments and suffer relapses (such as doing things that you committed to stop or reduce). In fact, we expect that if you are working on being more *Open*, *Aware* and *Active*, it is almost guaranteed that these things will happen. Learning how to accept this process and what you do with it is a key stage in expanding your life.

Relapses and frustrating moments are tempting occasions for our minds to give us excuses to skip our commitments, or to trick us into thinking it's all right just to give up when we make a mess of things. These are the 'I can't be bothered' moments . . . said while holding up our hands and bemoaning our inability to change!

Our minds can come up with some amazingly compelling stories for why we can't flexibly persist with the changes we decided to make (including the 'I have no will-power' story from earlier). Our minds might also come up with the story that since you have had a relapse, you've ruined everything and so you may as well give up (for example, someone dieting being disappointed about eating a small slice of cake, and so follow up by eating ice cream, biscuits and chocolate). The reality is that most people who are trying to change problem behaviours will slip at least once.

So, what can you do instead? Well, being familiar with this book, you know that we are going to suggest a combination of *Open, Aware* and *Active* responses:

- To begin with, gently notice the invitation from your mind to criticise yourself for being weak, useless or pathetic (or whatever variation on a theme your mind is in the mood for). Notice any urges to give up your commitment. Where would this lead you? Is that direction the one you want for yourself over the long-term?

- Deliberately be kind and open with yourself. Be curious about what happened. For example, tell yourself, 'I made a mistake. What can I do differently next time? How can I learn from this?' It may be difficult to look at what happened – use your *Aware* skills to stay in the present moment, and be *Open* to the experiences you are having.

- Breathe, get present and notice. Increase your willingness to have urges or cravings as *experiences*. By deliberately choosing to be guided by your values and live a bigger life than your fear, this will put you in contact with situations where these urges will show up. In fact, this contact could be a sign that you are expanding your life.

- There may be a greater need for your *Open, Aware* and *Active* skills when you are stressed, have negative emotions, or are exposed to people, places or situations associated with your problem. See if you can anticipate these occasions and keep in mind that each time this happens it is actually another opportunity to practise your skills.

Handling Procrastination

A frequent challenge is *procrastination*. Typically we procrastinate when we are doing things that involve discomfort or anxiety. You could think of procrastination as a pattern of behaviour that takes us away from being *Open*, *Aware* and *Active* – procrastination is usually about **avoiding discomfort**. We make ourselves very busy with doing something else – anything that can seem less unpleasant or scary than the task we are avoiding (ever find the house suddenly becomes a lot cleaner when there is a deadline or something big to do?). Procrastination is successful . . . in the short-term, as it allows us to temporarily escape feelings of discomfort. In the long-term, well, you've probably experienced the disadvantages of procrastinating, perhaps even vowed you wouldn't do it again!

Noticing what we are avoiding by using our *Open* and *Aware* skills can be a useful first step here. What is making this choice or action so immense and scary that we have the urge to turn away from it? Can practising willingness to experience the discomfort allow you some flexibility to approach the task? Flexibility may involve openness to experience, connecting with the purpose behind the task, or approaching it in a different way (for example, breaking it into smaller bits or embracing the possibility of failure and doing it less than perfectly.).

An old psychology professor of ours would say repeatedly: 'To be shaped, you have to emit'. These words have been a reminder through the years that to become skilled at anything, you actually have to do something. Just thinking about doing it won't allow you to be shaped by experience and feedback. For example, as we discussed earlier, learning a musical instrument involves playing a lot of wrong notes! Rehearsing a situation in your mind may help to get you to the starting line, but to go further actually involves moving your hands and feet. Learning through experience is made harder if you won't welcome the feelings and thoughts that are an essential part of gaining experience!

How to Handle Failure . . . or Redefining Success

Fail often in order to succeed sooner.

David Kelly, Founder IDEO

A vital part of acting in a committed way is *how we handle failure* and things not turning out the way our minds predicted that they would. As you engage increasingly in the here-and-now, and take a greater number of actions guided by your values, it is likely that you will experience life more intensely. This includes moments of disappointment and failure.

David Kelly, a technology entrepreneur, talks about approaching situations of failure 'sooner': trying things out, putting yourself outside of your comfort zone, and being in touch with the effects of your choices and actions is a valuable way of learning. From this perspective, a vital part of living effectively is being in contact with the possibility of failure, and embracing it when it happens. Rather than avoiding failure, it appears that successful people actively seek it out. Studies of successful people consistently show that being effective in a chosen area involves *doing plenty of practice and work*, **as well as** doing things outside of your comfort zone. Starting a business, learning a challenging musical composition, developing unfamiliar skills, changing career, meeting someone new with the potential of a long-term relationship: all of these involve being out of your comfort zone. The possibility of failure (however you define it) is present in these situations.

The strength of choosing your values is that they are not cancelled out by experiences of failure, mistakes and wrong turns. In fact, it may be possible that these experiences are part of acting on a value. Striving to produce a creative work, such as a symphony or painting, is likely to involve even the most accomplished artist in many hours of trying out different things.

No doubt, it will hurt when you fail. And it may hurt very much. This is why we suggest that handling failure is about the *Open*, *Aware* and *Active* skills. Learning from failure, by staying flexible and connected with your valued directions, will involve willingness and gentle noticing. **Success**, from this perspective, is *working on something*. Notice that with this definition of success it is within your control, as your choices and actions are something that you decide. This includes the choice to embrace failure as part of the *experience* of a life 'lived on purpose'.

How To Practise These Skills Repeatedly as Your Life Expands

As you will have realised by now, we are suggesting that as you live a larger life, with your actions guided by your values, there will be many opportunities to practise the *Open* and *Aware* skills we have been describing in this book. It could be possible that at the edge of your comfort zone are the experiences that you have struggled with or got caught up by. In a way, when these experiences show up for you, it could be a clue that you are in a situation of growth.

Our experience has been like this: the skills of ACT are skills for living a richer, more meaningful life, and in practice, there is no finishing line for this. Instead, there are more opportunities to take a position of openness, awareness and action with what life gives you. So, similar to our description earlier in the book, the ACT approach is to start from the place where there is nothing wrong or broken in you. As humans we can struggle or get caught up in situations where there is the opportunity to act on values and expand our lives. This gives some useful clues when we are struggling, as we can notice the struggle and ask:

- Could this is be a moment of growth?

- Could I introduce purpose and connection to my valued direction into this moment?

- What will that involve choosing:

    In terms of acting on my values?

    In terms of willingness toward the experiences that I am already having?

    In terms of a perspective that will be part of my life expanding?

Revisiting Tim, Marcia and Samantha and Dave

In the Introduction you met four different characters, each of whom was struggling with different issues. Over the course of this book, you've followed their journeys. Now, one last time, we'd life to revisit Tim, Marcia and Samantha and Dave to see how things changed for them as they learned to become more *Open*, *Aware* and *Active*.

Tim

Tim said that the biggest difference he's noticed in his life since he started consciously trying to become active is that he now feels like he actually *has* a life! In hindsight he could see that he spent so much time and energy worrying that he was barely living at all.

As an example, he talked about a particular afternoon at work: it was 5.30 p.m. and his colleagues were leaving the office for the evening. 'Fancy coming for a curry, Tim?' asked his manager, 'A few of us are popping out for a bite to eat.'

Tim had an important presentation the next day, and he immediately noticed himself slipping into the 'catastrophe perspective' that he knew so well. From here it seemed obvious that unless he spent the evening refining and rehearsing his presentation it would surely be a disaster.

But now he was able to observe what was happening, and he decided to try on a different perspective. Stepping into the 'good enough' perspective, he checked in with his values. From here he could see that an important value around friendship and connection had been neglected for some time. So – despite his mind protesting – he closed his laptop. 'Yes, I could do with a curry! I'll grab my coat!'

Marcia

Marcia had made a lot of progress since she had begun the process. The biggest change for her was that she had decided to move out of her mother's place and live on her own. She found this to be one of the hardest things she had ever done. She had worried intensely for weeks in the lead up to telling her mother about her decision and felt strong feelings of guilt.

During the process she had kept her values in mind, particularly her desire to take care of herself, even though her mind sometimes very loudly yelled that she was being selfish. Her mother had expressed a lot of fear about living alone, which

Marcia found hard to manage. However, several weeks after moving she realised she had made the right decision. She experienced a greater sense of strength in herself and her identity. She also noticed that her relationship with her mother had begun to improve. Marcia was able to assert herself more effectively and not get hooked into always pleasing her mother.

As she began to look after herself more, Marcia decided to carry on with dating. She wasn't certain she actually wanted to be in a relationship but was enjoying meeting new people and having different experiences. She found she was much more often out of her comfort zone, but by being *Open* to her thoughts and feelings, she was able to be gentle with herself and she embarked on a new, exciting part of her life.

Samantha

Samantha stuck with her mindfulness practice, applying her *Open*, *Aware* and *Active* skills on a daily basis even when it seemed like the world was conspiring to put her to the test!

There were still occasions when she felt 'wound up' at work, and she still couldn't fathom some of the decisions made by management. But she also noticed that she got less hooked by judgemental thoughts and found it easier to put things into perspective.

She said that this was partly because she had come to realise that it was her relationship with Colin, her husband, and her children that mattered most – it was here that she felt most determined to make changes.

Samantha explained to her therapist that she now was much quicker to notice the signs – in her mind and in her body – when she was getting angry. Often just noticing was enough to slow the process down and put her into a space where she had more choice about how to respond.

And she could see the difference it was making in her life! The children were happier, and she noticed that she and Colin were closer than they had been in a long time. She had been making an effort to let him know when she was upset or hurt and she found he responded much better and listened more. They both began communicating in a way they had seemed unable to before. Like everyone they had their good days and bad days, but Samantha said she felt like things were moving in a good direction.

Dave

After being very reluctant to begin therapy, Dave had slowly realised that it was the best thing he could have done. He found the process hard work, but gradually, with the help of his therapist he had learned more about how his depression had trapped him. He slowly became more skilled at noticing his mind at work, particularly at times when he was really very low.

One of the toughest things he had to work on was being kinder to himself when he was feeling low. Over time he had opened up to his therapist about his experiences growing up and, with her encouragement, practised opening up to people around him. He spoke to his sister about what he was going through and was surprised that she seemed to understand and didn't judge or criticise him. At the same time, he also reconnected with an old university friend: she shared that she had previously experienced depression herself. As he opened up to her, he realised he wasn't quite as much on his own as he'd thought.

As Dave's depression began to lift he thought a lot more about his work and realised that he wanted to do something that was more meaningful. Although his previous job had been important to him he realised this was more about proving himself to others so he felt better about himself. Once he set all this aside, he noticed a deep sense of wanting to make a difference for other people. Based on this, he recently submitted an application for a position within a youth return-to-work charity and was offered an interview. On the day of the interview, he noticed himself feeling very tense and caught his mind saying, 'Why bother? You've got nothing to teach kids about work!' He took a breath, paused and said to himself, 'Thanks, mind – that's a familiar story. This is important to me, so I'm going to keep going.'

Now, How *Open*, *Aware* and *Active* Are You?

In this section, we'd like to invite you review how *Open*, *Aware* and *Active* you now are. We'd like you to fill in the worksheet below, answering the prompt questions, to help you get a sense of both where your skills now are and also the areas where you could make further progress.

OPEN, *AWARE* AND *ACTIVE* WORKSHEET

Briefly describe here the main problem(s) that you had in mind when you picked up this book. Keep this problem in mind as you answer the following questions:

Open

Generally, how open are you to internal experiences such as thoughts, feelings, emotions, memories and physical sensations?

- *Which are the internal experiences you struggle with particularly?*

- *Are there times when you're able to be open to uncomfortable internal experiences?*

Aware

How aware are you of your thoughts and feelings as they occur? How able are you at recognising and labelling them?

- *Do you find yourself often running on autopilot, wrapped up in thoughts?*

- *How easy do you find it to step out of yourself to take someone else's perspective?*

- *Do you find it difficult to go easy on yourself and be self-compassionate?*

Active

Do you have a clear direction forward in life? Do you know what is important to you? Or do you feel lost and confused about how you want your life to be going?

- *What are the moments when you feel most alive, vital and engaged?*

- *How good are you at setting a course in life, making goals and sticking with them – even when things get rough?*

Open, Aware and *Active* Chart

Once you've completed the *Open, Aware* and *Active* worksheet, use Figure 4 to map out where your strengths lie
and where you need to further develop your skills. Give
yourself a score on each of the three skills from 0 to 10.
Then place an 'X' on the corresponding line. Compare this
to Figure 1, which you completed on page 29, to see how
you've developed.

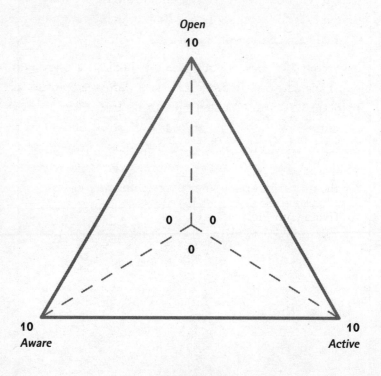

Figure 4

In filling out Figure 4 we return to where we began: asking you to take a step back, assess your life, and ask yourself how *Open*, *Aware* and *Active* are you? The whole aim of asking you to reflect on this and – over the course of this book – to develop skills in each of these areas, has been to help you to manage your thoughts and feelings more effectively **so that you can live a life that is rich, fulfilling and meaningful**. Because what is life if not for living?

As you will know well enough by now, life is not always easy. It will not always be pleasant or fun. But by fully stepping into it and opening yourself up to everything it has to offer you are guaranteed one thing – it will be an adventure!

Our request is that as you close this book you carry with you Helen Keller's words: 'Life is a daring adventure or nothing'. We firmly believe this to be true. Step into the adventure, be the author of your own story. Stay *Open* to what life has to offer. Be *Aware* of the amazing stuff going on inside and around you at every moment. Be *Active* in pursuing the things that really mean something to you.

ACTivate your life!

Index

Addis, Michael 202
adrenalin 263
agoraphobia 263
alcohol *see* drinking
Allen, Woody 124
amygdala 261
'analysis paralysis' 144, 277,
    442
anger 16–19, 63, 70, 89–90,
    96–7, 205, 330–88
  breaking down episodes
    337–9, 352, 357
  breathing into 362–3, 367
  causes of 331–2
  defusion skills 356–60,
    387–8
  expressing 430–2
  and hot labelling 345–6
  problematic 333, 360
  and responsibility 378
  and traffic 130–1
  triggers of 333–4, 356
anger behaviours 335, 356–7
anger feelings 334–5, 348–52,
    356
anger thoughts 334, 339–40,
    356
anger urges 335, 356, 379–80
anhedonia 124
Annie Hall 124
anti-depressants 200

anxiety 7–10, 70, 101, 259–329
  and avoidance 269–70, 314
  causes of 272–5
  and childhood 272–3, 275–7
  and mind tricks 288–90
  nature of 260–2
  and personality traits 274
  and responsibility 307
  and rules 294, 313
  struggle with 280–8
  and thinking styles 264–8,
    274–5
  and vigilance 291
anxiety disorders 262–3, 272
apologies 387
appetite, changes in 198, 210
Archer, Rob 31
Aristotle 330
Armstrong, Lance 434
assertiveness 429–32, 451
Australia 163
awareness, distinguished
    from thinking 77
Awareness of Breath 84–6,
    312

Bear and the Blueberry Bush,
    the 31–2, 42, 260, 344
behavioural activation 202
BIF: Beautiful, Interesting,
    Funny 128–9

body dysmorphic disorder 263

Bond, Frank 433

breathing 175, 247, 296, 298, 312, 374, 444
 into anger 362–3, 367
 see also Awareness of Breath; Three-Step Breathing Space

breathing rate, increased 263–4, 334, 357

broadening your life 319–29

Brown, Brené 207

Callahan, Steven 239–40

cartoon characters 55

'catastrophe perspective' 101–3, 450

celebrity culture 389

chest pain 263

Chifley, Ben 163

chocolate cake 73

Churchill, Winston 197

comfort zone, living beyond 319–22

committed action *see* purpose

common humanity 242

curiosity 78

cycling 65

dancing 49–50

Darwin, Charles 331

dating 400, 404–5, 451

de-emphasising thoughts and feelings 433

depression (and sadness) 21–3, 47, 70, 124, 196–258

 and avoidance 198, 206, 211, 223–4, 250

 causes of 199–203

 and choice 222–3

 and inactivity 209–13

 and mind tricks 227–34, 249–50

 physical symptoms of 198–9

 and purposeful activity 250–6

 and responsibility 231–2

 and self-compassion 235–9

 and shame 242–3

 triggers and responses 221–3

despair 197, 238, 366

disaster movies 303–6

disgust 264

Dittmar, Suzy 128

drinking 10, 14, 22–4, 58, 61, 73, 165, 199, 207, 251, 269, 271

drugs 58, 61, 165, 199, 207, 269

Durant, Will 436

Eating a Sweet 126–8, 247, 380–2

Elias, Ric 354

embarrassment 118, 266, 349, 363, 365–6

Emerson, Ralph Waldo 330

emotional radio 68–9

emotions 56–72
 acceptance of 63–4
 beyond anger 363–8

and depression 205, 207
getting to know 65–7
opening up to 70–2, 361
unwanted or difficult 60–1
see also urges
engagement 123
eudaimonia and *hedonia* 140–1
exercise 61, 79, 442–3
Expanding Your Awareness
        384–6
exposure 317, 328
Extending Compassion
        Towards the Child
        Within 119–20, 378

failure, handling 446–8
fear 260–1, 269, 279, 291–2,
        313, 317
see also anxiety
'fight or flight' response 261,
        263, 334
fitting in 149–51
Flaxman, Paul 433
flexible persistence 437, 443
flexibility 79, 98, 121, 123, 236,
        318, 383, 445
and sense of self 433–5
food 61, 123, 207
football 110
Frost, Robert 436
Fry, Stephen 196
funny voices, and anger 358

gardening 179–80
Getting Things Done 188
goals 143–9, 182–3, 186–9,
        441–2
SMART goals 186–7

Gretzky, Wayne 226

habits, forming 439–42
happiness, longing for 12–15
headaches 263
health 8–9, 137
health anxiety 263
heart rate 263–4, 334, 352, 357
hot labelling 345–6, 356
Hudson River crash landing
        354
human ancestors 35–6, 91,
        260, 331

Imagine if No One Cared
        What You Did 414–16
inactivity 209–13
Internet 61, 207
introversion 274

Jacobson, Neil 202
Jolie, Angelina 389–90
'jukebox musicals' 404–5

Kabat-Zinn, Jon 83
kayaking 438
Keller, Helen 6, 459
Kelly, David 446
kindness 424–5

language 34–5, 345
Life as a Work in Progress
        184–5
life directions *see* values
Life of Approach 191
lifestyle changes 439–43
Light on the Hill 163–4, 441
Livestrong charity 434

Livheim, Fredrik 433
loneliness 12, 22, 70, 142, 281

McArthur, Amy 176
man in a hole metaphor 282
Mandela, Nelson 159–60
Martell, Christopher 202
masochism 314
meditation 83
mind
    and anger 340–6, 358
    and anxiety 278–9, 288–90,
        292–3
    and depression 203–4, 209,
        211–12, 227–34, 249–50
    and drama 44–5, 123
    evaluative 395
    and identity 292
    and storytelling 37–8, 182,
        292, 340
    at work 53–4, 172
Mind Judgement Dial 191–3
mind reading 340–4, 356,
    373–5
mind tricks 227–34, 249–50,
    288–90
mindfulness, and self-esteem
    424–5
'mindy' 244
Mitchell, Gordon 176
muscles 190, 264, 334, 352
music 61, 241
musical instrument, learning
    a 143–4, 446

Neff, Kristen 424
neuroticism 274
neurotransmitters 202

New Year's resolutions 441
Noticing That You Are
        Noticing 92–3, 247
Noticing, Watching,
        Observing 94–5

Observing Self 91–5, 98, 102,
        108, 132, 154, 209, 332,
        352–3, 373
    and self-esteem 402, 435
obsessive–compulsive
        disorder 263–4, 272
Openness Dial 68–9, 281, 361

pain, 'clean' and 'dirty' 61–2,
        117–18, 130, 348
panic attacks 9, 262, 314, 320
panic disorder 263, 272
parenting, and depression
        200–1, 217–18
parties 58–60, 98–9, 120
Passengers on the Bus
        metaphor 417–20, 427–8
paying attention 76–80
Peak Moments 164–9, 171,
        184
Peanuts 204
penalty shots 39–40
perfectionism 201, 207, 267–8
persistence 185–6, 188, 328
    flexible 437, 443
perspective-taking 90, 99–117,
        121–2, 319, 332, 353, 400
    'catastrophe perspective'
        101–3, 450
    and values 153–4, 156–7
Philips, Emo 39
phobias 263–4

Pitt, Brad 389
'playing it safe' 403, 407–8
playing small 149
pleasing others 427–9
post-traumatic stress disorder 263–4
poverty 202
preoccupation with order and control 268
procrastination 198, 207, 282, 445
proud moments 33
public speaking 37–8
purpose
    committed action 182–4, 189–91
    and goals 145–8
Purpose Dial 191–3

QI 196
quotas 442

redundancy 21–2, 102, 109, 205–6, 220
relapses and frustration 443–4
relationships, and values 137–8, 314
responsibility 231–2, 307, 378
routines 212–13, 268
rules 151–3, 294, 313, 397, 402
rumination 198–9, 201, 207–8, 244–7, 266–8, 270, 282, 308–11, 313
running 14, 65
Ryff, Carol D. 140

sadness *see* depression
sailing 178, 432

Seinfeld, Jerry 188
self-awareness, and choice 82
self-compassion 117, 119–21, 189, 235–9, 329, 377–9, 386, 388
    developing 424–6
self-criticism 120, 235, 250, 267, 271, 296, 378
    and self-esteem 391–5
self-esteem 389–435
    and assertiveness 429–32
    and flexibility 433–5
    and rules 397–9, 402
    and self-acceptance 424–6
    and willingness 423–4
    and workability 411–12
self-forgiveness 388
self-indulgence 120
self-soothing 240–2
senses 209, 241
sex 61, 198, 207
shame 242–3, 251, 349, 366
singing 55, 358
Skinner, B. F. 440
sleeping 9, 198, 212, 214
social anxiety 262, 270
social deprivation 202
Socrates and the Road to Athens 99–100
Spurgeon, Charles H., 259
stress, and depression 200–2
stress hormones 263
success, definition of 447–8
sweating 263–4
swimming 65

Team of Advisers 111–17, 236–9, 302, 319, 377

television watching 23–4, 61, 73, 123, 199, 206–7, 214, 251
thalamus 261
theatre 109–10, 404–5
Thich Nhat Hanh 389
thinking, distinguished from awareness 77
Thinking Self 91–5, 104, 108, 126, 154, 209, 352–3, 373, 439
    and self-esteem 399–400
Thought Bingo 42–4, 94
thoughts 34–56
    anger thoughts 334, 339–40, 356
    and *Aware* skills 80–2
    and defusion 50–1, 132
    experimenting with 54–6
    and fusion 46–9, 123, 421–2
    and observer perspective 91–3
    positive 49–50
    and rebound effect 41
    as tools 38–9
    see also rumination
Three-Step Breathing Space 87–8, 96–7, 247
Tour de France 434
tremors 263
Turner, Glenn 259

Up 138
urges 73–4
    anger urges 335, 356, 379–80

values 136–95

acting on 175–95
and anger 368, 370–1
and avoidance 314
construction of 142, 153
and depression 208, 211, 221–5, 229, 235, 252, 258
and failure 447–8
feeling and doing 190–1
five-year perspective on 138–9
and goals 143–9, 182–3, 186–9
and guiding stars 163
metaphors 178–80
and personal choice 149–51, 170–2
and perspectives 153–4, 156–7
and pleasure 140–1
and purpose 182–4, 189–93
and recharging 177–8
and relationships 137–8
and ripple effect 176–7
and rules 151–3, 399
and self-esteem 402–3
trying out 161–2
video gaming 177
vigilance 35–6, 291
vitality 136–7

Watching the Clouds in the Sky 298–9, 313
will power 439–40, 443
Wilson, Kelly 399
worry *see* anxiety
worrying about worrying 265–6, 295
Writing about Worry 300–1

Your Best Friend 158
Your Eightieth Birthday
    154–6
Your Heroes and People You
    Admire 159–61, 319

Zappa, Frank 436
zombies 58, 211, 303, 315